Mud Pu

PROGRAMMI

AND PLANNING

IN EARLY CHILDHOOD
SETTINGS

PROGRAMMING AND PLANNING
IN EARLY CHILDHOOD
SETTINGS

Leonie Arthur
Bronwyn Beecher
Sue Dockett
Sue Farmer
Elizabeth Richards

University of Western Sydney
(Macarthur)

HARCOURT
BRACE

Sydney Fort Worth London Orlando Toronto

Harcourt Brace & Company, Australia
30–52 Smidmore Street, Marrickville, NSW 2204

Harcourt Brace & Company
24–28 Oval Road, London NW1 7DX

Harcourt Brace & Company
Orlando, Florida 32887

National Library of Australia Cataloguing-in-Publication data

Programming and planning in early childhood settings.

   Bibliography.
   Includes index.
   ISBN 0 7295 1262 2.

   1. Educational planning.   2. Early childhood education.
   I. Arthur, Leonie.

372.1

Printed in Australia by Star Printery

CONTENTS

Part 2 Processes of planning and programming

PREFACE

The 1980s was a period of growth in children's services, and in some areas, also a period of growth in the number of pre-service training courses for early childhood educators. In particular, two new courses were introduced in the Sydney region to train staff to work within the field of early childhood.

The authors of this book were involved in the early stages of one of these courses and, while able to draw upon their own experience in direct service provision, found little Australian reference material that considered the changing nature of children's services and the processes of planning and programming most appropriate to these. Much of the material presented in this book was developed to meet the needs of this course, and has since been discussed in a range of in-service and continuing education programs.

The purpose of this book, then, is to consider a range of perspectives and issues that relate to programming and planning for children in the early years in Australia.

The development of a new early childhood course provided an opportunity to consider the changing role of the early childhood educator. Within the last decade there have been significant changes both in the role of early childhood educators and in the types of services in which these educators are employed. There has been a substantial increase in the number of long day care centres since the early 1980s, and some of the changes that have resulted relate to working in such centres. For example, staff working in a long day care centre are working as part of a large team, and account needs to be taken of the diversity of their training and experience. Similarly, early childhood educators are also working with an increasing diversity of children and families. In addition, early childhood educators in long day care settings are often seen as managers as well as teachers, with an accompanying change in the professional expectations of the educator.

This book is directed both at students completing their training as early childhood educators and at those educators who are already directly involved in the field of early childhood.

One of the aims of the book is to present principles and issues for discussion that encourage early childhood educators to evaluate their current approaches to programming and planning for young children. This approach provides the opportunity to confirm, and affirm, those procedures that are developmentally appropriate and to suggest directions for future innovation and change in those areas that need to be strengthened. As a reflection of the possible uses of the approaches outlined in the book, a number of working examples have been developed by students and by educators working within the field. The use of these examples also illustrates the point that the book does not aim to provide a recipe approach, or a quick fix solution to programming and planning; rather it presents guidelines that can be adapted to suit individual situations and settings.

The book is divided into three sections. The first section presents an overview of the development of children's services and the changing nature of Australian society. The need to acknowledge and respect the diversity within Australia and to assist children, families and staff in developing positive self-identity and empathetic understanding of others is highlighted. An important focus is the need for effective communication between all families and staff in services and on developing strategies that aim to empower parents and families.

Section two draws together the actual processes of planning and programming, starting with the need for staff within settings to identify and reflect on their own philosophy relating to the development, operation and implementation of an early childhood program. The processes involved in analysing a variety of early childhood settings are then detailed, leading to the consideration of a range of approaches to the planning and the implementation of these. The particular approach supported in this section focuses on planning for the strengths, interests and needs of individual children within a range of early childhood contexts. Completing this section are discussions of the purposes and processes of evaluation and the effective utilisation of resources, both human and material, within settings.

The third and final section considers developmentally appropriate practice for young children. It stresses the importance of having a sound understanding of growth and development in relation to young children and being able to use this understanding to develop realistic, yet relevant and challenging, expectations for individual children. This section suggests that the basis of a developmentally appropriate program is a matching of the planning to the actual and identified strengths, needs and interests of children. In other words, it is a program that has been shaped to fit the child, and that continues to change as the individual child changes.

Throughout the book, the term early childhood setting has been used to refer to a range of early childhood environments, including long day care, neighbourhood children's centres, preschool, the early years of school, occasional child care, family day care, mobile services, out of hours school care, and the many other diverse settings that involve children under the age of eight years. While recognising that these settings are diverse and operate in very different ways, with different staff, families and children, and according to different demands and constraints, the principles and issues outlined in this book stress the importance of a focus on the individual children within each of these settings. In this way, the general approach may be similar, but will be adapted and applied within these settings in a variety of ways. For example, it is important for all early childhood educators to have, and to articulate, their own philosophy of how children learn. These philosophies will undoubtedly be different for many educators. However, the process of developing and reflecting on these philosophies may well be similar.

One of the great strenghts of those working within the field of early childhood has been their ability to adapt and modify approaches to suit the individual needs of particular children, families and settings. This book outlines a range of strategies that relate to programming and planning within early childhood settings in the confidence that early childhood educators will continue to assess these and adapt them to suit their own specific needs, strengths and interests.

PUBLISHER'S NOTE TO STUDENTS AND INSTRUCTORS

This textbook is a key component of your course. If you are the instructor of this course, you undoubtedly considered a number of texts carefully before choosing this as the one that would work best for your students and you. The authors and publishers spent considerable time and money to ensure its high quality, and we appreciate your recognition of this effort and accomplishment. Please note the copyright statement.

If you are a student, we are confident that this text will help you to meet the objectives of your course. It will also become a valuable addition to your personal library.

Since we want to hear what you think about this book, please be sure to send us the stamped reply form at the end of the text. Your input will help us to continue to publish high-quality books for your courses.

ACKNOWLEDGMENTS

There have been many early childhood educators, services and students whose help has been instrumental in developing and writing this book. In naming specific people, groups or services, we would inevitably omit some of those whose help has been invaluable and have therefore opted to express our appreciation generally.

We acknowledge the ideas and support that we have individually gained from working with different staff, families, children and organisations in a range of early childhood setting. The support has come from those we have worked with in settings, as well as from networking with a range of other early childhood educators.

Specific examples have been drawn from a range of individual settings and organisations throughout the book, and these have been acknowledged in the text.

In particular, it is important to acknowledge the input from a range of early childhood students, in both pre-service and postgraduate programs, at the University of Western Sydney, Macarthur. These students have provided many creative ideas as well as support, constructive criticism and commitment to the processes discussed in the book. Many of the examples used in the book are those developed by students and implemented by them during practical experiences. In these cases, individual students have been acknowledged for their contributions.

To all these people, and to all the others who have actually supported our endeavours we extend our thanks.

Part I
CHILDREN'S SERVICES AND AUSTRALIAN SOCIETY: AN OVERVIEW

INTRODUCTION

The first years of a child's life are the most important. This message comes from many sources — families, researchers, services for young children, and sometimes government bodies. This understanding was recently summarised by Duffie:

> The importance of the early years of the child is now internationally acknowledged as the time of most rapid learning and development. It is the responsibility of all early childhood educators to honour the importance of the early years by providing for the care and education of all children entering early childhood services. (Duffie 1991 p.10)

In recent years we have gained a much clearer understanding of the ways children grow, develop and learn. Children change dramatically during their early childhood years. They move from being totally dependent on the adults in their life, to being able to participate in a social group and be independent in their learning. During this short span of time, changes that take place from birth to the first years of school have been widely recognised by families, early childhood workers and researchers, as having powerful effects on the individual for the rest of her/his life.

The family of each child varies in their lifestyle and employment patterns, and consequently their needs for children's services. In addition,

1

over time each family's needs for care and education of their children may vary. For example, families may require occasional care whilst carrying out short-term appointments; long day care in centre-based or family day care, preschool, school whilst engaged in study, or full or part-time employment, and before and after school care, when a child goes to school. The choice of services that are currently available to each family is a result of the social, political and economic developments in society and in the early childhood field over the past century. The children's services currently provided throughout Australia vary from state to state but generally include long day care, preschool, family day care, out of school hours care, occasional care, mobile services, playgroups and schools.

The following chapters will set the context for planning and programming in children's settings and will address issues which have an impact on the growth and development of young children. Chapter 1 will briefly describe the historical development of children's services in Australia and current issues such as the need for high quality services and government responses and responsibilities in this area. Chapter 2 will consider issues surrounding the importance of encouraging families to be involved in different aspects of early childhood settings, and how early childhood educators can work towards establishing a cooperative relationship with families. Chapter 3 sets the context for encouraging awareness and acceptance of the uniqueness of each individual, and the need for early childhood educators to provide an anti-bias approach throughout the setting.

1

SETTING THE SCENE

INTRODUCTION

As in many other industrial nations benevolent bodies have long domi-
nated institutional child care in Australia (Suransky 1982). The
Kindergarten Union of New South Wales, established in 1895, was one
of these bodies and it introduced kindergartens in 'working class' suburbs to provide appropriate environments for 'slum children' (Brennan
and O'Donnell 1986). While the focus within many organisations has
changed dramatically in recent years, these first early childhood settings
were established to *rescue* the children of 'working class' parents. This
reflected a growing concern amongst the 'middle' and 'upper' classes,
about life in inner city slum areas during the 1890s in Sydney as in
other major cities. This original belief that services for children under 5
years were only beneficial and relevant for the children of 'working class'
parents or 'slum children' has been perpetuated from the beginning of
the early childhood movement, both in Australia and other industrialised
nations. The belief was held that young children within these families
were poorly treated and environmentally 'deprived', therefore typical
development and learning would not take place unless some external
intervention occurred. This model of early childhood has become known
as the 'deficit' model and to some extent continues to be practised in
cases such as the Headstart program in the United States.

Institutional care and education were perceived, particularly by 'middle class' women's groups, as a positive alternative for these children
(Spearrit 1979). Whilst programs within these settings placed an emphasis on health, nutrition and socialisation, educational aspects were also
included. Much of this early movement was based on the educational
philosophy of Froebel, who proposed that, given a suitable environment,
typical growth and development of the child would be facilitated. As a
result, kindergarten was seen as a tool for social reform. Implicit in this
situation was the idea that this type of service was desirable, necessary

and rewarding — but only for a distinct group of children, rather than all children. Suransky (1982) describes the kindergartens of this era as setting a progressive alternative to the orphanage, incarceration, the asylum and the reformatory, which had previously catered for the child casualties of poverty.

THE BIRTH OF THE CARE VERSUS EDUCATION DEBATE

With the establishment of the day nursery or creche in the early 1900s a different brief was outlined by the Sydney Day Nursery organisation, which aimed 'to care properly for the babies of poor working women of Sydney during the hours when the mothers are forced to be at work; and the establishment of day nurseries in the needy sections of the city' (Brennan and O'Donnell 1986). This varied slightly from the initial 'deficit' model in that institutional child care was seen to be divided into services like kindergartens offering short hours care which prevented parents using them for child-minding (Brennan and O'Donnell 1986); and services such as day nurseries which offered parents longer hours for child care. This helped to establish the division, which can still be seen today, between services perceived to be offering education and services perceived to be offering care. Although attempts have been made to break down the division, the impact is still carried over into areas such as government policies, quality of service issues, working conditions for staff and community attitudes.

RESPONSIBILITIES AND RESPONSES: GOVERNMENT PROVISION OF EARLY CHILDHOOD SERVICES

The federal government's first involvement in children's services began with the funding of demonstration kindergartens in each state. This occurred as a result of the formation of the Australian Association of Pre-school Child Development in 1938 (Brennan and O'Donnell 1986). The Lady Gowrie Child Centres were established in each capital city, once more in 'working class' areas, thus continuing the existing benevolent approach in children's services. As a consequence of the changing demands of the community, these services have tended to mirror the general direction of children's services. That is, these services have now changed to provide long day care programs to meet the needs of children from birth to 5, as opposed to the original focus being family intervention and preschools catering for 3 to 5 year olds.

Further government involvement occurred during the years of the Second World War (1939–1945) as children's services began to meet the changing needs of this period. Many existing services were funded by the Department of Labour and National Service to extend child care operating hours, in order to encourage women to work in war industries. Despite these actions, women were not encouraged to remain in the workforce as men returned from service, and so returned to work in the home. Thus, immediately after the war these services returned to prewar operating hours and funding improvements were lost. However, the pressure for child care facilities continued through the efforts of 'middle class' women. This time the advocates emphasised public provision of services for their own children, rather than on behalf of children of the poor (Brennan and O'Donnell 1986).

In Victoria, in the postwar years, children's services were developing noticeably when the Health Department entered the field by offering grants to approved kindergartens. To receive funding, the centres needed the support of parent committees, which in turn lead to the provision of many services in 'middle class' areas due to the existing effective networks of women in these suburbs. This funding program, in addition to the influence of Bowlby's research into maternal deprivation, placed obstacles in the way of the expansion of long day care services (Brennan and O'Donnell 1986). This issue will be discussed in more detail later in this chapter. Consequently, most expansion of services at this time related to the establishment of preschool services. This showed the reluctance of governments to become involved in child care services and reflected the traditional community view that the care of young children is a family, not a community responsibility.

THE NEED FOR CHILD CARE

During the time after the Second World War, as women's participation in the workforce grew steadily, so did the need for child care. By 1970, when one third of all women (Spearitt 1979) were in the workforce, there were 560 child care centres operating throughout Australia with a capacity of 14 000 places (Brennan and O'Donnell 1986). Only 40 of these centres operated with assistance from state or local government bodies. The federal government's only assistance at this time was special funding to the Lady Gowrie Centres. The provision of child care centres was not adequate to meet the demand. Preschool facilities in most states at this time were also unequally distributed. Provision of preschool services varied widely in catering for the needs of eligible children. For example, the ACT catered for 50 per cent of eligible children, other states ranged between 27 per cent (Victoria) and 3 per cent (New South Wales) (Brennan and O'Donnell 1986).

In the 1960s, the provision of preschool facilities, that is, what was perceived to be 'education', remained a state government responsibility in terms of funding and policy. In several states, preschools are attached to various Departments of Education, whilst in New South Wales and Victoria other organisations such as the Kindergarten Union and the Free Kindergarten Association are large providers and managers of services. While, in the past decade this situation has improved, children in different states still have widely differing access to services. The availability and cost of preschool places in particular continues to vary dramatically between states. In Victoria for example, more than 90 per cent of 4 year olds have access to a (virtually) free preschool place. In NSW, the fees are much higher and places fewer (Community Child Care 1991). Aligned with the various government reactions to the pressing need for services, this division between education and care has continued to develop.

During the 1960s all levels of government were reluctant to take up the responsibility for long day care services, however state governments did provide some funding but this accounted for only a small proportion of funding in comparison to that received by the preschool facilities. The lack of involvement on behalf of the government indicates that long day care was not viewed as part of the education system for children, which is an interesting anomaly considering the worldwide concern for the first years of life previously mentioned.

In 1972, at the federal level, the Liberal–National Party Government began funding for the building of child care centres and included child care issues on the national agenda. The Child Care Act of 1972 allowed the federal government to make capital and recurrent grants to non-profit organisations and committed government funding to local groups (Hurford 1987; Brennan and O'Donnell 1986). Much of this was part of the submission model which will be outlined later in this chapter.

However, along with these initiatives, the government debate also included the 'need to research why women work, the need to counsel parents who wanted care for under 3s, and the provision of child care as necessary only when families fail' (Brennan and O'Donnell 1986; Cox 1983). So the century old notions were continuing — child care was a necessity for only those parents who had to work, not those parents who wished to work, and for children in 'deprived' environments.

A CHANGE IN GOVERNMENT ATTITUDE

Late in 1972, Whitlam, as leader of the Labor Party in his election speech (December 1972) indicated the emergence of new government responses to children's care and education. 'A women's choice between making motherhood her sole career and allowing another career in conjunction with motherhood depends on the availability of proper child care facilities...' (Brennan and O'Donnell 1986: p.24).

In attempting to support this policy, the Australian Pre-school Committee in 1973, recommended extended child care for 4 year olds in the form of preschool education and the development of family day care (Fry Report). Children's services groups saw these recommendations as limited and a result of the terms of reference, as well as the conservative composition and the lack of women's representation of the committee. These concerns lead to the Social Welfare Commission (1974) presenting its own report on child care matters at the request of the federal government. These recommendations were more in line with Labor's policy promises. The recommendations included establishment of the Children's

Services Commission to focus on the development of children's services through parent participation and the involvement of local government (Brennan and O'Donnell 1986). These recommendations were not realised due to the dissolution of the government in 1975.

The following Liberal–National Government (1975–1983) abandoned the Children's Services Commission and promoted a shift to predominantly state government funding of preschool and federal government funding of long day care. The Federal Office of Child Care was established to dispense funding to long day care services, and hence identified Child Care as a national issue. Despite these positive responses, the Spender Report of 1982 reduced funding dramatically, that is the 1982–1983 funding for children's services had decreased to a level 30 per cent lower, in real terms, than the Whitlam government's peak allocation in 1975–1976 (Hurford 1987).

Another important outcome of Liberal–National government was the introduction of the two fold 'needs-based' model of funding. Firstly, an economic subsidy went to families considered in need, leading to a reduction in fees. However, this tended to be ineffectual as the total amount of funding available was minimal. Secondly, the establishment of new services was considered on the basis of submissions (known as the submission model), based on the assumption that communities who needed children's services would be able to formulate appropriate submissions. One of the difficulties inherent in this approach was the inequity of service provision. In short, the model favoured articulate and well-organised communities over those in greater social and economic need who were not so able to state their case.

GOVERNMENT INITIATIVES — MEETING THE DEMAND

Due to the increasing demand for child care in the 1980s, the Hawke Labor government, on coming to power in 1983, aimed to increase the availability of quality child care for target groups within the community and to ensure that child care was affordable for those people who could get access (Hurford 1987). In order to do this, the government introduced an income related fee relief system; implemented needs-based planning concepts to better determine the location of children's services; specified priority of access guidelines with priority going to working parents; and developed a more cooperative arrangement with state and local governments related to the provision of services. This is commonly known as the Capital Works or the Services for Families with Children Program. Within this model there has been a rapid expansion of child care places for children under 5 years of age through, predominantly, the provision of long day care settings, family day care and the current move to increase before and after school care and occasional care.

ISSUES AND CONCERNS

After almost a decade of rapid expansion of service provision throughout Australia, both policy makers and professionals need to address many issues related to the impact of the Services for Families with Children Program on the quality and provision of services to children and families. As Clyde (1991) so clearly states:

> Where does that leave those people who are interested in child care as a children's service and who wish to particpate in the development, implementation and evaluation of such services? It leaves them with a trilemma...of balancing three often competing and contrasting variables; those of availability of services, afford-ability of services and quality of services. (Clyde 1991: p.23)

STAFFING IN EARLY CHILDHOOD SETTINGS

While the Capital Works Program has contributed much to the expansion of children's services in order to meet the needs of families with young children, other factors have impeded progress. One of these constraints, the lack of suitably qualified early childhood teachers, has not assisted the situation. This has occurred, particularly in NSW, where expansion has been greatest and licensing regulations require qualified early childhood teachers in long day care. Many services Australia-wide not only find it difficult to fill teacher positions, but any positions for qualified staff, such as workers with qualifications from Technical and Further Education institutions such as the Child Care Certificate and the Certificate of Child Care Studies (Ryan 1989).

The lack of early childhood trained staff may be the result of three possible factors. Firstly, the attitude reflected in the prospectus for one of the colleges in the early 1900s saw early childhood training as a preparation for marriage and child rearing:

> in choosing a means of livelihood for our girls, the fact must never be lost sight of that a woman's deepest instincts centre in the home... her natural place. (Spearritt 1979: p.13)

This belief is still prevalent in Australia today, although it is somewhat modified. Stonehouse (1988b) suggests that the field of early childhood suffers from its associated image with mothering and that this has reinforced the low status of the early childhood profession. The assumption implicit in this suggestion is that mothering is seen as not such a desirable profession. Many people in the community, including politicians and public servants, see that early childhood education as a profession requires little education or remuneration, as most women 'raise' children without training or payment. Duffie (1991) in her statement to the NSW Industrial Commission for improved conditions and salaries for early childhood teachers, points out, however, that while learning in the home setting does occur, 'within the group settings for young children, active steps have to be taken, to ensure that each individual child has the appropriate experiences necessary for their further development' (p.10).

A second factor is a widespread community perception that children's services are unnecessary for children when they can be cared for predominantly in the home and such traditional views may have played a role in inhibiting the development of child care services and the early childhood profession.

Finally, this staffing problem is perceived to be a result of fewer people being educated in this area (even though there have been two new Bachelor of Early Childhood Education courses begun in 1988 at the University of Western Sydney in New South Wales alone) and a reflection of the poor image and conditions of early childhood workers. Whilst improved salary conditions are presently being achieved, in an attempt to attract and retain staff within early childhood services, continued improvement in conditions is seen as an important link to promoting the status and image of early childhood workers.

This raises a further issue in that, while there has been a massive expansion in the number of services, there has not been a corresponding expansion in the number of early childhood qualified staff being trained. In this case the policies of different government levels (Commonwealth–Federal Children's Services Program and tertiary training, and state licensing controls and technical training) have not developed at an equivalent rate, thus causing a mismatch in policies. This has led to difficulties in filling positions in settings, and this, along with corresponding high staff turnover means that the quality of planning and programs also suffers. Another factor affecting staffing issues relates to the fact that each state has its own licensing controls which sets standards for the number and type of staff required for early childhood settings. This, in itself, causes problems for the quality of services in different states (discussed later), and also for staff wishing to work in settings throughout Australia, not only in their home state where they may have trained.

IMPACT OF GOVERNMENT POLICIES ON PROGRAMMING

Apart from the obvious influences of funding and availability of child care places upon programs as previously discussed, two other government policies have had major impact on programs — the design and size of buildings and the type of services available.

One of the advantages of the present federal program has been the potential for shorter building times for new centres due to the state and local government cooperation in the provision of building sites and the use of a standard building design (Hurford 1987). However, one of the outcomes of using the standard designs has been that services have felt locked into a particular style of program and number of children.

Although there are several designs from which to select, most designs tend to cater for 40 children from birth to 5 years and contain two distinguishable playrooms — one for under 3s and one for 3 to 5 year olds. While many early childhood educators, in relation to their educational philosophy or the directions in current research, might prefer smaller groups of children, or other criteria for grouping children apart from age, the building designs make these possibilities more difficult and less likely. While new services are able to request alternatives to designs, these are at the cost of the management/sponsoring group.

A further impact is that the financial viability of centres has become a major concern. One particular type of service — the Neighbourhood Children's Centre — has suffered changes as a result. Initially Neighbourhood Children's Centres catered more for smaller numbers of children than current service models and were established as an alternative to large group centres. It was believed that these centres were able to provide a more home-like environment to leave children in and would be more flexible to meet the needs of families for a wide range of care options such as occasional care, preschool and long day care (McCaughey 1979). However, with the major cuts to child care funding in 1986, neighbourhood centres were provided with transitional financial assistance whilst their budgets were restructured and future operations were assessed (Hurford 1987). In real terms this meant staff numbers were cut and settings were provided with grants to extend their services to cater for groups of 40 children, which was a viable number according to policy makers. This situation lead to neighbourhood centres operating only as long day care centres in order to receive funding rather than being able to meet the needs of the community at the time.

QUALITY VERSUS QUANTITY

This expansion of services, as well as changes in funding provisions, while attempting to meet the growing need for child care, has contributed greatly to the 'quantity versus quality' debate in children services. The current approach of the federal government is to create new child care places and services whilst seemingly withdrawing funds from existing services. As a result of amendments to the Child Care Act in 1986, users of child care were faced with huge increases in fees. Previously, federal government funded 75 per cent of licensed staff salaries, irrespective of the cost of qualified staff. The funding basis changed to an amount per child, which meant a decrease in overall funding, with the assurance of funding meeting costs of trained staff.

When this situation is considered in conjunction with different state government policies and licensing regulations, which may allow for less qualified staff, many concerns arise within the profession. The possibility exists that centres will not employ qualified staff due to lack of funding and increasing costs, with the lack of available trained staff increasing the risk of this occurring. As well, there has been a move towards the expansion and funding of family day care. This type of care, provided by community members in their own homes, is often seen as a cheaper alternative to long day care due to the very low wages compared to trained staff and low operational costs involved. While family day care should not be stigmatised as inferior, the service expansion of this form of care suggests a federal government not willing to expand child care places in centres as centre-based costs are greater.

Suransky (1982) found in a study in the United States that once high quality care is sacrificed due to economic factors, with child care becoming 'an industry' and privatised, little attention is then paid to the developmental needs of the child. She observed in several different child care centres that where the major concern was planning an economically viable service, the children's development was not fostered but rather, the main concern was how many children could be contained in a building with the smallest number of staff and for the least amount of money. Although the Australian situation has not reached the same extent of commercialism mentioned in Suransky's research, it is likely that negative influences may result from the emphasis in the present governmental policies and programs.

WHY IS QUALITY IMPORTANT?

The debate concerning whether child care is 'good' or 'bad' for children continually surfaces. In the 1940s and 1950s Bowlby's research in the United States considered attachment and bonding between mother and child, and suggested that day care would interfere with the consolidation of the attachment bond in the first 3 years of life. Although later research (Rutter 1982; Belsky and Steinberg 1978; Farran and Ramey 1977; Caldwell, Wright, Honig and Tannenbaum 1970) refutes these claims, the influence of this initial research lingers on in the community at large.

More recent research, in the past 20 years, has focused on whether day care is harmful for children. O'Connell (1983) collated ten studies and suggested that no significant difference in the mother–child bond was found between children in home or centre-based care. This report also suggests that infants whose mothers work full-time are somewhat more likely as 1 year olds to avoid their mother after brief separation, and later to be less compliant with their mothers and more aggressive with peers. This has lead to further suggestions that children in care are at risk emotionally (Clarke-Stewart 1989). However, Clarke-Stewart cautions that there are many issues to be addressed when studying attachment in young children. These concerns include whether the tools or research design used are valid or effective in the context and the need to take a broader approach to look at the family background variables. These include the possible non-availability of the mother due to both paid and unpaid work constraints and maternal attitudes to child rearing. Australian research currently being undertaken at the Institute of Family Studies (1991) comments that women who have two roles —

work and unpaid home duties — are under stress and may be less available to young children. This area needs to be investigated further, rather than only looking at the child in the centre situation.

This area may cause emotional difficulties rather than the fact that the child is in centre-based care. American research (Bredekamp 1987) cautions that early childhood education in industrialised nations promotes children's independence, assertiveness and non-compliance. It is difficult to then identify such children as insecurely attached because they do not cry when left by the parent!

The notion of different cultural practices needs to be considered in light of this research. Research does not acknowledge these differences. Research related to attachment seems to reflect North American culture (McCartney and Galanopoulos 1988) and findings are presumed to be similar in many western industrialised countries, including Australia. Within the Australian context, many different family practices exist in terms of child rearing, depending on the individual family. For example, many Aboriginal families share the care of children amongst kin, (Malin 1991). Exclusive child rearing, by mothers, in non industrialised countries is rare. It is more likely that care is shared with a wide range of relatives and siblings (McCartney and Galanopoulos 1988). Burns and Goodnow (1985) report similar patterns in child rearing in Israeli Kibbutzim, where the amount of parent–child interaction appears entirely adequate for emotional stability. So it seems that the situations in which young children are cared for vary, and the notion of exclusive parent care may not always be the case.

Perhaps the more important issue is not whether care is, in simplistic terms, 'good' or 'bad', but what can be done about improving the quality of services that are available to children and families in the community. Additionally, support for families using care in the form of ready access and a choice of high quality services, would go a long way to alleviate much of the guilt many parents go through as they place their child into care.

QUALITY PROGRAMS FOR YOUNG CHILDREN

The issue of quality programs for young children will lead the profession into the twenty-first century. Whilst regulations in each state set minimum standards or 'a floor on which to build', they in no way cover the components of a high quality service. The state regulations often place pressure on a service to meet a range of planning and programming aims related to children's growth and development with little in the way of clear guidelines for implementation and little staff preparation and support. This situation, along with the move towards dispensing federal government funds to wider sectors of early childhood service providers that commenced in 1991, indicates a need for the field to improve and monitor the quality of settings for young children.

Additional influences on the quality of services are seen in relation to the working conditions for staff in the two predominant settings — preschool and long day centres. Preschool conditions are customarily aligned to those in the school setting as opposed to long day centres where conditions are more closely aligned to the general workforce. This situation frequently contributes to high staff turnover in long day centres, subsequently affecting the quality of care (Ryan 1989).

High quality children's services are seen as an optional luxury by many, including some politicians, whether from federal, state or local governments. Some politicians who are under pressure to supply and extend services may have 'short-changed' efforts to improve the quality of services. The great shortage of child places is such that parents' choice of care is often quickly determined by the availability and cost rather than the quality of the program.

In earlier years, the components of quality programs were poorly explained, with limited definitions that included wide generalisations and assumptions supported by little evidence. The early definitions were global without any clear indicators of what actually constituted quality care. General definitions indicated that quality was:

> approximating what most people would consider a good natural homelike environment with the same goals as those that most parents want for their children. (Wills and Riccuiti 1975, in Patterson 1984: p.17)

Another definition stated that a quality service was:

> primarily a service to support the family unit in providing an environment which promotes the overall development of children. (Sebastian 1981: p.39)

Recent research in the United States has identified more clearly other indicators of quality care. Various researchers (Phillips and Howes 1987; Murray 1986; Bredekamp 1984) have classified these features under different categories. For example, Phillips and Howes have organised quality program indicators for day care into three main sets:

1. structural features, that is, group size, staff/child ratios, caregiver training, equipment, space;
2. dynamics aspects, that is, experiences and interactions; and
3. contextual features, that is, staff stability and turnover, type of setting.

From a collation of research findings it is clear that the provision of a high quality service is the outcome of many interacting factors. The presence of early childhood trained and experienced staff has consistently been linked to high quality interactions between children and adults, and as such is an important factor in the social and cognitive development of children in group settings. Small group sizes are another indicator of quality, as when children are placed in larger groups there is less adult–child interaction, less social stimulation, less active involvement in experiences and higher levels of apathy and uncooperative behaviour. Lower child:adult ratios are related to more positive interactions between young children and their caregivers, whilst higher ratios seem to lead to more managing and controlling behaviour on the part of the caregivers.

In response to this mounting evidence that high quality programs are more rewarding for young children and that poor programs adversely affect children's social, emotional and language development, there have been moves by the profession to establish some way of ensuring high quality in programs.

A global assessment tool has been developed in the United States (by the National Academy of Early Childhood programs) for the accreditation of high quality services (Bredekamp 1984). This tool is based on a set of criteria which evaluates the overall quality of a program. The criteria represents the current consensus of the early childhood field in the United States regarding definition of a high quality program for young children. It is based on the following indicators:

- interactions amongst staff and children;
- curriculum;
- staff–parent interaction;
- staff qualifications and development;
- administration;
- staffing;
- physical environment;
- health and safety;
- nutrition and food service; and
- evaluation.

The use of the tool involves a self-study phase, carried out by the staff and management in their centre; a validation observation carried out by independent early childhood educators; and consideration of accreditation of the particular centre as one offering a quality program by a Board of Commissioners.

This project has operated in the United States for several years and is currently being trialled in children's services in NSW. Other states such as Queensland and Victoria are trialling other accreditation procedures. The situation where services are trialling such evaluation procedures, in order to ensure high quality programs, is a positive step. In the 1991 federal budget, it was announced that $1 million will be allocated by the government towards investigating a national accreditation system for child care services. If a national system is established, it will be important that it ensures a high standard of quality service throughout Australia, not a 'dropping of standard' in some States, to create uniformity. Unless continued government financial support for quality programs is forthcoming, and the number of service choices available to families increase, many children will not be able to attend a high quality program.

THE CURRENT STATE OF PLAY

The Labor government's approach to children's services has been to increase the provision of family day care, long day care and out of school hours care. Whilst long day care has been identified as the strongest area of need, this provision is still inadequate. There has been no expansion of preschool services in the past decade, with additional funds available from 1990 for the establishment of occasional care and out of school hours care (as well as long day care). Due to the priority of access guidelines, set by the federal government, the first priority for places in long day care are children of working parents or those seeking work or retraining.

As a result of this the perceived division between care and education is extended, as many parents who are not working are unable to get access to centre-based programs for their children. This has sometimes lead to animosity in the community as some families believe they are disadvantaged as they choose not to do paid work.

This feeling is often exacerbated by the perception that families 'on welfare' get all the assistance as long day care centres receive funding from the Department of Health, Housing and Community Services and parents income levels are scrutinised by the Department of Social Security in order to obtain fee relief.

These perceptions that services are different has an impact on policy concerns and funding issues and also relates directly to the quality debate. Several states do not require early childhood trained teachers within long day centres, but require such training for preschools. This could be one of the contributing factors to parents transferring their children from long day centres to preschools when their child turns 3 or 4 years of age, after being on a waiting list for three or four years, which may in turn limit the availability of places for non-working parents in the preschool further.

Expectations in the community of early childhood services are continuing to change and increase dramatically. Duffie expands on this:

> discernible factors influencing these heightened expectations [of staff] would include growth in the knowledge base of the early childhood teaching profession, changes in society, pressure from consumers, the impact of the Centre Based Child Care Services Regulations (1989) [in NSW] and the impact of other reports, agreements, curriculum expectations. (Duffie 1991: p.10)

Children's Services in Australia are currently (1991) the subject of a National Review by state and federal governments. The purpose of this review, known as the Functional Review of Child Care, may have major implications for future funding arrangements for all types of children's services. The key purpose of the review is to determine whether funding and administration should be undertaken differently by governments in order to reduce duplication, and to improve services to users of services

(Community Child Care, August 1991). While this may be seen as a positive step towards rationalising policies, it is unclear as to the government's real agenda. Those in the profession are anxious that this will only lead to possible funding cuts.

Current policies reflect a government attempting to meet the need for child care places, perhaps at the cost of high quality care for those children with an existing place. With the dramatic increase in the number of services in the past 7 years, debate has continued within the early childhood profession in relation to the type of program most worthwhile for children in the early childhood years. As many children are now in an 'institutional setting' from 6 weeks of age, it is imperative that they have suitable programs. Programs suitable for preschoolers may not be equally as appropriate for a wider and younger age group who spend long hours in a service each day. Children are also entering the formal school system from a younger age, and the more formalised programs often experienced in schools may not be effective environments for children in the early childhood years. The perceived division between day care , preschool and school services is often reflected in the styles of programs offered within these settings and their status as understood by the community. The purpose of this book though is to suggest that while planning and programming will be different in each setting, due to the unique nature of that setting, there are many processes and principles that are equally applicable to children in various settings whether it be long day care, preschool, or school settings which cater for young children.

2

FAMILY INVOLVEMENT

INTRODUCTION

Family involvement in early childhood education has been reported by researchers to have potential benefits for all concerned. For the children, family involvement is related to increased positive self-esteem, fewer problems with discipline and an improved regard for learning and themselves as learners (Greenberg 1989; Galinsky 1988). Parents and children benefit from improved relationships, as well as from parents' development of a more positive attitude towards education and understanding of the education process (Brown 1989). Early childhood educators also benefit from the establishment of a partnership with families that has, as its focus, the best interests of the children in their care. Bjorklund and Burger draw on the work of Morrison (1978) and Nedler and McAfee (1979) when they note that:

> both parent (family) and teacher possess valuable information about the child's abilities, interests, likes, dislikes and needs. This information must be shared in a positive manner so that the best interests of the child can be served. (Bjorklund and Burger 1987: p.26)

WHY ENCOURAGE FAMILY INVOLVEMENT?

There are many reasons for promoting and supporting family involvement in early childhood services. Fundamentally, children do not live in isolation. To truly work effectively with children, we need to develop an understanding of each child and to respect them as individuals from a unique family.

To do this, we must avoid thinking of the family as 'the opposition'. Families care about their children, and show it in many different ways.

We risk alienating the family by making judgments about their parenting skills based on little information and stereotypes. By alienating the family, we also inadvertently alienate the child. The respect we show a child's family will directly affect the child's attitudes towards themselves in both the short and the long term (Greenberg 1989). This is discussed in more detail in chapter 3 — 'Accepting Diversity'.

Families are an ongoing factor in the child's life. They will continue to influence the child long after the child has left the early childhood service. The family's knowledge of, and positive involvement in, the child's continuing development is of paramount importance (Figure 2.1). The more the family is informed and involved, the more opportunity there is for positive experiences to carry through to the home environment, resulting in a more lasting influence upon the child's approach to learning and attitudes towards themselves as learners. It is certainly true to say that 'programs cannot adequately meet the needs of children unless they also recognize the importance of the child's family and develop strategies to work effectively with families' (*N.A.E.C.P. 1984*, cited in Powell 1989: p.9).

Families need to feel comfortable with the early childhood service in order for the child to feel truly comfortable. The child who sees positive communication and cooperation between staff and families, is less likely to feel anxious about the new surroundings. This can be a major factor

Figure 2.1: Encouraging parents to visit children throughout the day, as is possible in work-based child care services, helps build a trusting relationship between families and staff.

in helping to alleviate some of the anxiety felt by families when leaving their children in care. Parents suffer a high level of emotional stress when they leave their child. Particularly with child care, there is often guilt about the 'expected' role of parents, and how they are fulfilling that expectation. If the parent has a sense of comfort and trust in the early childhood educator's competence to care for their child, that burden will be lightened somewhat. It is a mistake though, to assume that it disappears totally. In a study conducted by Mann and Thornburg (cited in Powell 1989: p.72) 'mothers who reported more satisfaction with child care also reported feeling less guilt about leaving their child in out-of-home care'.

THINGS THAT HINDER FAMILY INVOLVEMENT

Family involvement in early childhood services is often talked about but not actively or effectively promoted. As Powell (1989: p.55) identifies, parent(family)/staff roles are not always clearly defined in early childhood services, and this can result in 'territoriality' over where the family's role begins and ends and where the early childhood educator's role begins and ends. The unfortunate result of this is displayed in 'guilt' on behalf of the family, and 'judgment' on the part of the early childhood educator (as discussed below according to Powell).

COMMON PERCEPTIONS OF EARLY CHILDHOOD EDUCATORS ABOUT FAMILIES

Common 'judgments' of families by early childhood educators are reflected in the following statements. These negative assumptions and prejudices need to be overcome if worthwhile family involvement is to be attained.

- *'If the parents were really interested in the child, then they would come and see me.'*

Parents often fear being classified as 'pushy', and do not wish to jeopardise the relationship between the early childhood educator and their child. On the other end of the scale, parents may feel that 'no news is good news', and that the early childhood educator must be pleased with their child's progress.

Other parents may not have confidence in their ability to communicate effectively with the early childhood educator. If the staff at the service have not welcomed parent initiative in the past, or written communication from the service has mainly been negative, communicating with the early childhood educator may be an alienating experience. 'This problem is likely to be many times compounded when the school and the parents speak a different language literally as well as figuratively' (Herrera and Wooden 1988: p.78).

A family's lack of involvement may be due to many things. Powell (1989: p.67) suggests that parental silence can be due to many things: from a 'lack of interest in the program and/or the child...[to] a lack of trust in the centre staff'.

■ *What is perceived as a problem by the early childhood educator may not be seen as a problem by the parent.*

Early childhood educators and families often have different expectations of children as well as different methods of doing things. Where each is not aware of what the other is doing or trying to achieve, tension can result.

Both staff and families are functioning on the basis of their current understanding of children and how they grow and develop in all areas. The past experiences of the early childhood educator and the family members will influence how they perceive their child's development, therefore effective communication of these perceptions is vital. This closely relates to the next point.

■ *The early childhood educator may not agree with, or approve of, the parenting style adopted.*

There are definitely differences between families and early childhood educators and their values, expectations of how children should behave and the way adults should interact with children (Powell 1989). Placing children in conflict situations where home values and behaviours are criticised is detrimental not only to the family-service relationship, but also to the child's ability to function, socially and academically, within two vastly different worlds.

In one study, parents and early childhood educators have been found to agree on what makes good parenting (Galinsky 1988), however, they disagreed on the assessment of the skills of the parents involved in the program. Early childhood educators typically believed that parents were less skilled than the actual parents thought they were. Fairly clearly, this can be a source of considerable tension.

Kantos and colleagues (cited in Powell 1989: p.68) has investigated the perceptions of staff and families about child-rearing competence. Their findings correlate with those of Galinsky in that 'staff rated the child rearing practices of their center parents lower than their own (staff) standards of good parenting'. The question that arises from this is 'what criteria are staff using to judge the abilities of parents?'.

Those parents who were reported by Galinsky (1988) to be held in the lowest esteem were low-income families, single parent families and families of minority groups — surely those that need the most support and understanding. A vital point for early childhood educators here is the necessity to avoid judgment of childrearing practices until infor-mation is gathered regarding each individual family and situation.

- *The early childhood educator may be regarded as an 'expert', who should be able to give immediate answers and solutions to problems.*

Early childhood educators need to feel comfortable when they don't know how to solve a problem, or when they have to seek out additional information. The idea that parents are also experts, particularly in regard to their own children, must also be accepted.

A joint approach to problem solving will help to dissipate this perception. A situation can be discussed utilising both parent and staff knowledge and perceptions of the child and other relevant factors, with a joint series of strategies developed. This allows both the early childhood educator and the family the opportunity to discuss and analyse the situation and to feel competent in their ability to act on the decided strategies.

- *Early childhood educators see parents' involvement as important, but only in fundraising and volunteer work.*

Ebbeck (1979) refers to this as 'peripheral' involvement rather than a real or meaningful involvement in decision making or management. Cunningham (1985 cited in Stonehouse 1989: p.10) also refers to this when it is noted that 'the professional hands over some responsibilities and values parents, but allows them to contribute in a restricted way so as not to diminish the professional's control'.

Early childhood educators may feel that they have the necessary early childhood training, background and the experience, and that it is their responsibility to make decisions about what the children should be learning, as well as how and when this learning should occur. This represents a very narrow view of learning and does not take into account all that occurs outside the early childhood service.

- *'Parents have got many commitments already, they don't have the time to be really involved.'*

Parents do have many and varied demands on their time, however, being actively involved doesn't necessarily mean an extensive time commitment — there are many different ways that families can be involved. Greenberg also reports that:

> The amount of work a parent does for her child's school is probably not important. It's the amount of colleagueship and mutual respect that matters — an attitude of teamwork. (Greenberg 1989: p.62)

- *Early childhood educators don't feel that parents value their work.*

People who greet early childhood educators at the end of a long and tiring day with words like 'Did you have a good day playing with the children? I wish I could give up work and do that some days', don't show an understanding of the nature of the work of an early childhood educator. Understandably, early childhood educators can feel that their training, experience and skills are not valued.

It is also common for early childhood educators to undervalue the work of parents, or to become judgmental about the parents' choice to work. Some early childhood educators who work with young children make it known to parents that they disapprove of leaving the child in care, and that they certainly would not be doing the same for their own children.

- *'I would spend more time talking to _____, but she only wants to tell me her problems.'*

Sometimes communicating with families does involve actively listening to their worries and concerns — not all of which may relate specifically to their children. Often this is a family member's method of initiating contact with staff and assessing their receptiveness to them as individuals, before addressing other concerns about their child or the program. After assessing the situation, and if this is not the case, it is important that the early childhood educator be aware of their own limits, and know when and how, to refer families to other professionals. Early childhood educators don't have to try to be everything to everybody.

- *'I really like ____'s parents; they never complain.'*

It is easy to like parents that don't rock the boat. Parents who want to know detailed information about the staff, the program and policies can give the impression that they don't trust the early childhood educator. However, were the early childhood educator in the role of the parent, they would undoubtedly want the same, and maybe more, information. It is imperative that the early childhood educator place themselves in the parents' position, looking beyond the displayed behaviour of perhaps aggression or 'fussiness' and translate these into the driving force — concern!

It is unrealistic to think that potential conflicts with parents will never arise. We know that, even for young children, conflict situations can result in problem solving and creative thinking. It can be the same for adults. When ideas or approaches are openly questioned, discussed and changed whenever appropriate, tensions can work as positive forces.

STAGES OF RELATIONSHIPS

In developing relationships with families, Gonzalez-Mena and Eyers (1989: pp.193–4) describe three stages that many educators pass through. They do not suggest that these stages are universal; rather, that recognising some elements of each of these and working to overcome them, may help develop better family involvement in early childhood services. The stages listed are:

1. The 'saviour' complex, where early childhood educators are concerned with saving children from their parents. Comments like 'Don't they know what they're doing to their child?' would fit under this category.
2. The second stage is when parents are viewed as clients. This stage marks a growing understanding of parents and parenting, yet there is still a sense of the caregiver as the 'expert' who now turns to educating the parents about what is important for young children.
3. The third stage involves supporting parents rather than trying to change them. Only on achieving this stage do early childhood educators see parents as partners in the care and education of the child.

At each of these different stages, early childhood educators perceive parents, as well as themselves, differently. The perceptions held can, and do influence the interactions that occur as well as the expectations that are formed. Overcoming some of these perceptions, that are often inaccurate, is a task for all early childhood educators.

FAMILY PERCEPTIONS OF EARLY CHILDHOOD EDUCATORS

Just as educators have different perceptions and views of families, families have differing views of early childhood education and educators. These views can be dependent on many things, such as the reasons for enrolling their child, the availability of choice of early childhood services, their initial experience with the particular service or previous experience with similar services.

Within the service, parents may view staff in many different ways. Staff may be seen as:

- *A threat*, where the early childhood educator is seen to be taking the place of the parent, so setting up an atmosphere of competition between educator and parent/s;
- *An expert*, who seems to know what to do all the time, and who is thought to be judging the parent's own ability as a parent;
- *A model*, from whom different approaches can be learnt;
- *A novice*, who may lack credibility if not also a parent;
- *A support*, who can offer advice, a sympathetic ear or even a possible solution to a problem;
- *A partner*, who expands the number of caring people in the life of the child and the family and who uses their professional skills in conjunction with an understanding of the individual family.

Every service will have a range of families, with parents who will identify with one or more of these perceptions at different times.

FAMILY EXPECTATIONS OF EARLY CHILDHOOD EDUCATORS

Basically, parents expect that early childhood educators will provide the best possible care and education for their child. Parents will always want the 'best' for their children, however, families and early childhood educators often have different definitions of what is 'best'. Some families may expect food, shelter, discipline and love, while others will expect these plus variety, stimulation and insight. Still others will expect results, products and displays of 'knowledge' from their children.

The expectations of families will vary dramatically. These may also be very different to the expectations of the early childhood service, and many potential conflicts may arise because of this. Questions like; 'Why are my children always untidy and dirty when I collect them?' and 'When is my child going to learn the alphabet and to recognise shapes?' should not be ignored by early childhood educators. Rather, the need for open discussion and effective communication becomes clear. As early childhood educators we must recognise our accountability to families and balance our training and personal values with those of each family and child.

WHAT IS THE AIM OF FAMILY INVOLVEMENT?

The aim of involving families in early childhood services has often been to develop a 'partnership', where both parties contribute to the well-being and overall development of the child. Stonehouse (1989) suggests that such a partnership has a number of characteristics. These include a mutual respect and trust of both families and early childhood educators; an open approach to communication which works both ways; the establishment of common goals; a sense of equality in the relationship, where the contribution of each party is recognised and valued; involvement in shared decision making; a sensitivity to the perspective of the other; a teamwork approach, where there is no competition between parties; and the sharing of valuable information about the individual child.

This notion of a partnership goes far beyond the idea of parents as fundraisers and volunteers. It embraces a view of parents and families as a valuable aspect of early childhood services, with much worthwhile expertise to contribute.

WORKING TOGETHER

How can families and early childhood educators work effectively together? Though each family is unique, and each family is likely to respond in different ways to efforts to involve them in the early childhood service, there are some basic assumptions from which we can work in considering this. These are that:

Figure 2.2: Family members can contribute and participate in many ways throughout the day.

- Families and early childhood staff are working towards the same goal, that is, in the best interests of the child.
- Families and staff believe in their approaches to child rearing.
- Families are involved and do have an 'important role to play in their child's development.
- Early childhood educators do not work solely with children, they work with families.

ENCOURAGING FAMILY INVOLVEMENT

Effective communication with families is the most important step in family involvement. Communication can take many forms, from very simple, to quite complex, one-way or two-way, spontaneous or planned. What is important is that communication is regular and meaningful. Some initial communication is important, such as in an enrolment interview, where the early childhood educator can begin to learn about the family; share information about the service; establish some ongoing communication channels and provide a welcoming atmosphere. The importance of a non-judgmental approach to the family at this time cannot be stressed enough, as it 'sets the scene' for future interactions.

The communication that follows is usually a combination of one-way and two-way processes. Berger (1987) describes **one-way communication** as that which involves the circulation of information from one source, such as the early childhood service. It could involve the following approaches:

- Developing a regular newsletter or noticeboard (Figure 2.3). Newsletters and noticeboards can inform families of what is happening or about to happen, and can also include useful information. Children can contribute to the newsletters with drawings, pictures or stories. A truly successful approach would be to involve families in the development of the newsletter and its production.
- Sharing spontaneous events with families. Notes to parents about what has happened during the day or what was said or done, can be communicated to parents through a daybook or diary for each child, a quick comment as the parent arrives, or even through a phone call when appropriate.
- Having a regular section in a local paper, where special events can be reported.
- Sharing information through a variety of other means, such as a video, displaying photographs, making the service program available.
- Making use of information from the family, such as having a suggestion box, where families can write — anonymously — any suggestions, concerns or words of praise. If successful, this can be a very effective source of feedback for the early childhood educator.

One way communication is important, but it really is only involving one party in the communication process. To have families effectively involved in early childhood services, **two-way communication** must occur. In this process, both families and staff are actively involved in the sharing and discussion of information. Berger (1987) lists several strategies to facilitate this. They include:

- Having an 'open-door' policy, where parents are always welcome. When families feel comfortable about approaching an early childhood service, without having to make an appointment, or having to abide by set consultation times, many issues can be solved before they become problems. It also encourages communication when there are no problems. This policy also recognises that 'many basic educational processes take place in the family...thus necessitating close school-community contacts' (Powell 1989: p.55).
- Making an effort to get to know families soon after children enrol. In some cases, this can even occur before children are enrolled, where parents and children are encouraged to visit a service.
  Knowing the names of family members, and how they prefer to be addressed, is an important initial step towards treating them as individuals and encouraging open communication. If appropriate for the service and the family, home visits are also a starting point for developing a relationship between home and early childhood services.
- Periodically surveying families about their expectations and desires for their children within the early childhood service. Not only does this

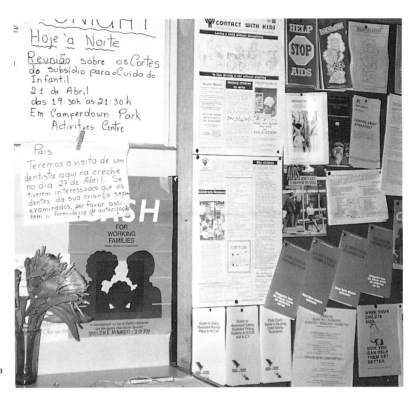

Figure 2.3: Noticeboards are a form of one-way communication.

provide valuable information to the early childhood educator regarding family perceptions of the service, but it also allows families a non-threatening introduction to true participation within the program.

■ Utilising communication books for individual children. Through regular written communication relating to individual children, families can provide valuable routine and one-off pieces of information the early childhood educator requires to truly be in tune with and understand the children in their care. It also provides a regular forum for the early childhood educator to record any special incidents throughout the day, as well as routine information.

■ Issuing invitations for families to visit. Family members can be issued with special invitations to either share a special skill or interest, or to spend the day interacting with the children.

■ Involving families in shared decision making. This is most clearly seen in parent management committees, however, it is not restricted to these situations. Parents can, for example, be consulted about the sort of equipment that should be purchased, or the priorities to be set for maintenance of the premises, as well policy formation, decisions about approaches to grouping children and program decisions.

■ Having regular conferences with parents. With young children, such conferences are usually between parents and early childhood educators, however, there should always be the opportunity of involving the child in such conferences. Successful conferences are those that show:
— sensitivity to parents' needs and priorities;

— reflective listening;
— open responses;
— the use of understandable language;
— positive emphases, rather than negative;
— shared decision making; and
— preparation.

Such conferences are not held whilst trying to supervise a group of children; rather they are planned to suit the parents' availability, to ensure privacy and to promote effective communication. They are not conferences where the educator does all the talking from behind an imposing desk; rather they are times when parents and educators can share their concerns and develop joint decisions regarding strategies for their child's development — within the early childhood service and the home environment.

FAMILY EDUCATION

A further feature of family involvement in early childhood services involves family education. It is essential that early childhood educators view this as a positive process, not as an opportunity to purely 'impart knowledge' to parents. Families bring many varied and sometimes 'hidden' talents as well as knowledge about growth and development from many different perspectives. In a positive light, the focus on parent education can see the development of:

- resource books, articles, magazines and similar material being available for parent use;
- information regarding political and financial influences upon early childhood services and avenues for advocacy and lobbying for change;
- a parents' room, which can act as a meeting place, a chance to talk with people or time-out. When a room is not available, it is still important to provide some space for parents to talk, leave things, collect things and so on, indicating to parents that they are accepted and valued;
- a notice board for parents to place messages, interesting articles, advertisements and the like. This recognises that parents are also valuable sources of information for each other, as well as early childhood educators;
- a toy library; and
- parent nights, which can include things relevant to parents' interests, workshops about specific topics, guest speakers.

In approaching parent education, it is important to see parents as partners, and as significant educators of their children. We can do this by:

- focusing on parents' interests and concerns;

- helping parents feel competent;
- developing links between informal and more formal approaches to education;
- providing a clear rationale for what we do;
- providing clear demonstrations of practices we see as important; and
- giving positive feedback to parents.

One of our roles as early childhood educators is to help parents understand early childhood services and approaches, and to help them feel competent in helping their own children. Practice, participation and discussion are more helpful than notes or newsletters about what parents should or shouldn't do.

REFLECTING ON FAMILY INVOLVEMENT

The early childhood educator must be prepared to critically assess the degree and type of family involvement that exists within a particular service. If there is not a true partnership between staff and families, all early childhood educators need to ask 'why not?' and to be honest and open in their answers. Responses to the following questions may provide part of the answer:

- Are we judgmental about families?
- Are we possessive of the children in our care, not wanting to share information with families?
- How do we communicate with families? Are written forms of communication usually negative, such as a reminder to pay fees?
- Are we comfortable with the idea of out-of-home care for young children? If not, do we communicate this, either in body language or in words, to families?
- Do we provide a welcoming environment?
- Does the environment we provide reflect the diversity of the wider community?
- Are we aware of the impact our relationship with families has upon the children?
- Do we recognise family members as individuals and utilise a variety of communication techniques to cater for this?
- What time do we allocate for parent meetings, questions etc.?
- Do we accept that individual families will be comfortable with different levels and types of involvement?
- Do we understand that individual family members may be naturally drawn to different staff members, and have we strategies to facilitate this?
- Do we recognise the importance of communication at transition times, such as arrival and departure?
- Do we respect the family's right to privacy and ensure that professional ethics are maintained?

There are many other questions to ask, and to continue to ask, about family involvement. These questions relate to all early childhood services, as the opportunities for, and encouragement of, parent involvement should continue well into the school years. Asking ourselves these sorts of questions is part of the process of working towards developing a true partnership with families. There are many strategies and approaches that can be implemented to facilitate family involvement, some of which are listed in this chapter. Each situation and service and family and staff member will be different, however, when all can work together and value the contributions made by others, everyone benefits.

USEFUL RESOURCES

Berger, E.H. (1987) *Parents as partners in education: the school and home working together* (2nd edition). Merrill: Columbus, Ohio.
Galinsky, E. (1990) Why are some parent/teacher partnerships clouded with difficulty? *Young Children*, 45(5), 2–3, 38–9.
Stone, J.G. (1987) *Teacher–parent relationships*. Washington, DC: NAEYC.

3

ACCEPTING AND PLANNING FOR DIVERSITY

INTRODUCTION

Although there are many similarities amongst Australians, there are also many differences. Diversity amongst the peoples of Australia has always existed. Differences amongst Aboriginal groups have always existed in terms of language, Dreamtime stories and lifestyle, although there are many similarities in their view of the world. Over the last 200 years migration has brought considerable changes to the ethnic make-up of Australia. In the early years of white settlement the vast majority of settlers were of English, Irish, Scottish and Welsh descent (when taken together known as Anglo-Celts). In the second half of the nineteenth century Chinese, Pacific Islands, Lebanese, Indian and Afghan settlers began to arrive. However, the 'White Australia Policy' was also introduced at this time and this, along with the rapid decline in the Aboriginal population, resulted in a predominantly Anglo-Celtic population. By 1947 Australia was made up of nearly 90 per cent Anglo-Celtic (Price, cited in Jupp 1989: p.6).

This strong British influence is still very much in evidence, although since the Second World War the patterns of migration have changed.

Inter-marriage amongst ethnic groups within Australia, as well as the postwar influx of migrants from non-English speaking backgrounds (N.E.S.B.), has also increased the cultural diversity within Australia. While many newly arrived migrants do not wish their children to marry outside their ethnic group, as a means of maintaining their culture, there are also high levels of mixing amongst ethnic groups. Price (cited in Jupp 1989: p.7) notes that two thirds of third and later generation Greeks, Italians and Germans in 1981 were of mixed ethnic origin. Mixture of ethnic groups has in fact been in operation since 1788. Most Australians, if they trace their family histories, will find that they have mixed ethnic origins, whether they are English–Irish or some other combination. None of us are 'just Australian'. In fact, 7 million Australians have three or more ethnic ancestries, another 4 million have four or more, with some having as many as eight (Price, cited in Jupp 1989: p.6). Most of us, in reality, are multicultural.

This reality has largely been ignored over the last 200 years by the legislation and institutions of Australia, including our educational institutions. It was only in the 1970s that governments in Australia became committed to policies such as multiculturalism and Aboriginal self-management. Aboriginal education and multicultural policies do now exist in schools and training institutions have introduced relevant courses on Aboriginal and multicultural perspectives.

Early childhood educators, like other teachers, have mostly been educated in a monocultural rather than a multicultural system. Traditionally our education system has focused mostly on white, middle–class, Anglo-Celtic values and beliefs and seen only English as the language of communication. This has not prepared early childhood educators for the diversity they will experience, both inside and outside of early childhood settings. If we are to be effective early childhood educators, we need to broaden our thinking and help to broaden the thinking of children and families we work with.

We need to recognise the diversity that exists within Australia and within our settings. As early childhood educators we should help children become aware of the many differences between people:

- culture;
- race;
- beliefs;
- language;
- lifestyle;
- age;
- ability; and
- gender. (Derman-Sparks 1989)

While awareness of diversity is important, we need to go beyond this and help children to understand, accept and value diversity in all its forms. The importance of adults as role models here cannot be underestimated.

FAMILY BACKGROUNDS

Each child has their own unique culture, strengths and knowledge based on their own particular family background. It is important that we recognise and value these differences, rather than expect all children to conform to the same standards. Some of the differences amongst children will be obvious, such as speaking a community language other than English, or practising a particular religion, while others may be more subtle differences. These may include:

- Learning styles: While some children learn best through verbal inter-actions and a question and answer technique, others may be used to learning through non-verbal means such as observation and imitation or trial and error.
- Communication styles: In some cultures questions are used to elicit a display of information, for example 'What's that', 'a dog'. In this case the person asking the question usually already knows the answer. In other cultures questions may be used more to find out new infor-mation, to encourage others to talk about similarities and differences between objects or people, or as an invitation to tell a story.
- Family expectations: The extent to which children are expected to be independent, and at what age, varies amongst families. The age at which children are expected to feed and dress themselves will differ, as will the age at which children should be toilet-trained.

As early childhood educators we need to remember that the way that we were brought up is not the only way. It is also important to note that much of the research into child development theories and what is expected behaviour for children at different stages of development is based on British and North American research where the subjects were mostly of Anglo-Celtic middle-class background. However, child-rearing practices vary amongst groups and no one way is the right way.

Traditionally 'the family' consists of a mother, a father and one or more children. In reality there are many different family structures. Grandparents, aunts, uncles and cousins may all make up the child's immediate family and share the responsibility of child-rearing as well as or instead of the biological parents.

Some children will come from single parent families, some from com-munal households where a number of adults share the parenting, some will be parented by homosexual couples and some will come from tradi-tional two parent families. Some parents will be in their 40s while other parents may be in their early teens. These issues should all be acknowl-edged when interacting with children and their families and in planning an early childhood program.

GOALS

In the past 20 years the main emphasis has been on multicultural and Aboriginal perspectives, and on developing positive identity and self-esteem in young children from diverse cultural backgrounds. Terms such as multicultural are now being replaced with cross-cultural, anti-bias and multi-racial to reflect a broader perspective. As both Ramsey (1987) and Derman-Sparks (1989) note, all aspects of diversity need to be included in a program: race, gender, age, differing abilities, lifestyle variations, language, religion and sexual preference. Learning about one's own cul-ture and developing positive self-esteem are important, but no longer enough. It is also necessary to promote acceptance, in both children and adults, and positive interpersonal relationships amongst people from diverse backgrounds.

An early childhood program should aim to help children develop the skills to resist negative attitudes, aimed at them or at others. In promoting acceptance, the early childhood program is considering individual rights, and thus human rights.

Regardless of whether you use the term multicultural, anti-bias or cross-cultural, the goals of the program need to reflect all aspects of diversity and address the issues of bias. Some people choose to use the term multicultural as it is a generally well accepted term and may be less threatening to others than terms such as anti-bias or multi-racial.

In *Teaching and Learning in a Diverse World*, Ramsey suggests that the goals of a multicultural program should be:

1. To help children develop positive gender, racial, cultural, class and individual identities, and to recognise and accept their membership in many different groups.
2. To enable children to see themselves as part of a larger society; and to identify and empathise with individuals from other groups.
3. To foster respect and appreciation for the diverse ways in which other people live.
4. To encourage in earliest social relationships an openness and interest in others, a willingness to include others, and a desire to cooperate.
5. To promote a sense of social responsibility, and an active concern that extends beyond immediate family or group.
6. To empower children to become autonomous and critically analytical with the skills that will allow them to resist and challenge bias and unfair treatment.
7. To support the development of educational skills that are needed for children to become full participants in the larger society in ways most appropriate to individual style.
8. To promote effective and reciprocal relationships between schools and families.

(Ramsey 1987: pp.3–5)

These goals will not be achieved through a 'token' multicultural curriculum that focuses on the national dress, food and festivals of particular countries, or approaches each country as a theme. Underlying a valid multicultural program is an ongoing understanding that children have the right to feel confident, competent and proud of who they are today and of their family history. This cannot be achieved in a one week theme, or by focusing on 'exotic' differences. The continuity of multicultural programs and the integration of multicultural perspectives into every aspect of the curriculum is the key. As Ramsey notes:

> Multicultural education is not a set curriculum, but a perspective that is reflected in all decisions about every phase and aspect of teaching. (Ramsey 1987: p.6)

Multicultural perspectives should be reflected in the content and the processes of the curriculum, the materials and experiences that we offer children, and the teaching strategies that we adopt. The potential exists for introducing a multicultural approach in all areas of the curriculum.

If the majority of children in our classroom or centre come from the same cultural or racial background, or come from the same social class, then it is equally, if not more important, to introduce them to the concept of diversity. These children need to be presented with people, materials and experiences that will broaden their view of the world. Children who are not presented with diversity in their local community or in the early childhood setting are likely to grow up with the unrealistic view that all people are like themselves.

As children in early childhood settings learn through experience, they need concrete, hands-on opportunities with a variety of materials that are different to those in their home environment. They may use a variety of cooking implements, clothing and tools; listen to music with different rhythms; paint on a variety of materials; and be exposed to a variety of children's literature.

Rather than 'tell' children about difference, the early childhood educator's role is to encourage children to express feelings about diversity and respond appropriately.

THE ROLE OF ADULTS

Adults in early childhood settings play a major role in influencing the way that children see themselves and each other. We need to be aware of the ways that we respond to children and their families, and of the messages that we are giving about their value and worth. As Phillips (1988) points out, it is not differences themselves that are 'the problem' but the way that we respond to these differences. As early childhood educators, it is essential that we are aware of the ways that we respond to children and their families and the impact that these responses have on children's developing self-concepts.

Often the messages that we give to children are unconscious, and reflect our own personal values and beliefs about what is desirable and appropriate. All adults working with young children should be aware of the verbal and non-verbal messages they are giving to children. We need to critically examine our responses and become aware of our own values, beliefs, prejudices and biases.

Early childhood educators, like everyone else, have grown up with their own particular prejudices and biases. Sometimes we unconsciously make assumptions about children and their families that reflect the stereotypes and prejudices of our family and friends or those portrayed by the media.

WHAT IS PREJUDICE?

Prejudice literally means pre-judgment, making up our minds about something or someone without sufficient information. Prejudices are usually negative, and can relate to differences in lifestyle, language, gender, religion, age, and abilities, as well as race and culture.

When we are faced with someone who is different to ourselves, we usually identify them as a member of a particular group. This may be because of their facial features, or the way they dress, talk or act. Once we have assigned them to a particular group, we then make judgments according to the attitudes and beliefs we hold about that group. We do not necessarily need to have met anyone from a particular group to hold a prejudice against them. When we pre-judge people we label them, and those labels are usually based on the stereotypes that we hold about particular groups of people.

WHAT ARE STEREOTYPES?

Stereotypes are generalisations, usually fixed, about different groups of people. When we stereotype, we do not take the time to find out about an individual's characteristics, but assume that 'they' are like 'all the rest'. Stereotyping results from judging too soon, generalising from one person or incident to the whole group and/or forgetting the realities of variations within groups. This is not to say that *all* generalisations should be avoided, but that they should be considered as tendencies. Generalisations may be used as a starting point for finding out more information about individuals and their families by getting to know them. We simply do not know enough if we rely on the views of others and written information. Each family is different and individuals within families will also vary.

When we assume that 'all Asian children are quiet and well-behaved' or that 'all Aboriginal children avoid eye contact' we put up barriers to effective communication. Stereotyping is also harmful because it often results in selective perception — we only see what we want to see (those things that confirm our stereotypes), and refuse to see, or disregard as an exception, any information that conflicts with our stereotypes. Self-fulfilling prophecies may also result from stereotyping. Others may be pushed into behaving as we expect them to behave, and into perceptions of themselves as we perceive them.

HOW DO STEREOTYPES AND PREJUDICES DEVELOP?

As children, we become used to the ways of behaving and the beliefs of those around us; firstly our family, and later our friends and the media. We usually grow up believing that 'our way' of doing things is 'the way', or at least 'the best way' or 'the natural way'. We tend to feel threatened by differences and only see things from our own perspective.

As early as the age of 3 or 4 children have begun to develop prejudices and biases (Ramsey 1987; Derman-Sparks 1989). Children 'pick up' prejudices through contact with those around them, and assume the attitudes and values of the group they are surrounded by.

There is a natural tendency for all groups to see their own ways of doing things as best, and to view any differences as inferior or deviant. We tend to then divide people up into 'us' and 'them'. Seeing 'them' as inferior makes 'us' feel better about ourselves, or as Cole puts it:

> Since we are all right and they aren't like us, then...we're sure glad we're not like them! So we build a filter that brings us together and lets us see them, while protecting us from questioning ourselves. (Cole 1990: pp.20 23)

Sometimes we look through the filter at others and see what we fear, or what we have been told to see. This reinforces our anxiety about how different 'they' are and we feel even more threatened.

When we filter people and see something that does not fit our preconceptions, we tend to build an even stronger filter. We may meet someone who is different to us and does not behave as we expect them to behave. Because stereotypes are often so strong, we often discount our own personal experience and follow the stereotypes, eventually refusing to see anything that does not fit the stereotype. The stronger the filter becomes, the harder it is to step out from behind it and to get to know people as individuals.

The filter often helps us deal with problems and conflicts within our community by giving us someone to blame, for example 'I can't get a job because of all the Asians that have been allowed in'. Using the filter also prevents us seeing others' suffering or needs and being confronted by examples of oppression or discrimination. If 'they' have problems, then it must be 'their fault' — 'they asked for it', 'what would you expect from them', 'they're always like that' (Cole 1990).

When living and working in a diverse world we, as early childhood educators, need: to look more objectively at our own values and beliefs, and to accept that 'our way' is not 'the only way'; to see differences as something positive and as an opportunity to learn; and to be able to accept multiple views of reality without feeling threatened by them. To do this we must recognise and challenge our own prejudices and stereotypes, take the risk and step out from behind the filter.

If we do not identify and respond to differences in an open way, we will not be able to recognise and discuss feelings, fears and prejudices related to these. Children need to experience other ways of doing things, with the aim of becoming less fearful of the unknown and realising that differences are valuable rather than threatening.

CONFRONTING PREJUDICE AND BIAS

When early childhood educators are aware of their own attitudes and biases, they are better able to work with children, parents, other members of staff and the community in promoting the acceptance of diversity. If adults are uncomfortable with differences, children's discomfort is reinforced and differences are mystified.

One of the first steps in implementing an anti-bias approach in an early childhood setting is for the staff to be aware of and confront their own biases (Ramsey 1987; Derman-Sparks 1989). This can sometimes be a painful process if we have grown up with years of learning stereotypes. Our immediate reaction may be to claim that 'I'm not prejudiced' or 'I treat everybody the same'. Years of filtering others has probably resulted in a lack of knowledge and understanding of diversity and of the oppression and victimisation of minority groups. We may have had no experience with people who are not from the same cultural, social and language background as ourselves in our years of social interaction and education. We may deny that we have any prejudices because we feel embarrassed to admit that we do.

It is essential that staff support each other in exploring stereotypes and in developing strategies to deal with them and change them.

> Only open dialogue and self-examination can clear the air of your own fears and misconceptions about each other...(Phillips 1988)

It is not until we have opened up to each other that we are able to work effectively with children, parents and community members. 'Exercises for confronting prejudices and biases' are useful for generating discussion about stereotypes.

EXERCISES FOR CONFRONTING PREJUDICES AND BIASES

These exercises can gradually be worked through with staff in a supportive environment, and may also be useful with parents.

■ We need to recognise that we all have prejudices and biases and openly share that 'no one escapes learning and believing some of the stereotypes and biases'. (Derman-Sparks 1989: p.112)

■ Discuss situations where you feel that you have been discriminated against. Why do you think this occurred? How did you feel? What did you do in this situation? How did this make you feel?

■ Share aspects of your own individual culture that are important to you. Discuss similarities and differences amongst group members.

■ Discuss how similar and/or dissimilar your attitudes are to those of your parents, or other members of your family. What beliefs and behaviours were you brought up to believe were

important? What do your family members consider to be
acceptable practices? What do they consider to be unacceptable behaviours and to whom? Why? If you think differently to
other members of your family, how did you come to think this
way?

■ What events or environments in your experience have caused
you to form further prejudices and biases? Were your responses
based on fact or were you making generalisations? What role
did family, friends and the media play in your responses?

■ Identify the children and families that you feel most comfortable with and relate to most easily. Discuss why you think this
is the case. What are the similarities and differences between
you and the child/family?

■ Identify and share with others which children and families you
feel least comfortable with or feel that you cannot relate to.
Why? In what ways are they similar and different to you?

■ Talk to each other about your feelings in relation to particular
families or groups. This will help you to clarify why you feel this
way and help you to approach the family and child with a less
clouded view. Make a conscious effort to acknowledge the differences and extend information on these. Do not judge on
the basis of perceived differences, but get to know the family.

ACCEPTING OTHERS' POINTS OF VIEW

Parents have many different ideas as to what is appropriate for children
at different stages of development, of the value of play, of what is seen
as educational and so on. These may be different to the values that you
hold. It is important to be able to listen to others' points of view, regardless of how different their beliefs may be, and to establish and maintain
communication. We need to actively listen to parents, respect their point
of view and respond to what they are saying, without forcing our own
views on them. Only then should we present an alternative view. Early
childhood educators need to:

> be able to view issues from many perspectives and to see people's
> behaviour as rational responses to the challenge of their environ-
> ment. This process requires a remarkable commitment and an
> ability to see one's own biases, to suspend judgment, and to resist
> polarization. (Ramsey 1987: p.185)

It is important to find out about each individual child and their family
rather than make generalisations. There are as many variations within
cultures and among families as there are between cultures. We cannot
assume that all Greek-Australian, all Vietnamese-Australian or all Anglo-
Australian families are going to be the same. When parents feel that

their values and beliefs are respected by the staff, they will be more likely to share information about their individual family culture and their expectations for their children with staff. In this way a partnership can be developed where there is a two-way exchange of information.

Staff may also have different beliefs about child-rearing practices, education and discipline, according to their own culture and family background. It is essential to acknowledge and work through these differences as a staff. Again it is vital to establish an exchange of ideas and to recognise that we do not all have to do things the same way.

Open channels of communication are essential both between staff and between staff and parents. The goals of the program need to be agreed on by both staff and parents to be effective. Participants need to recognise that there may be many different paths to reach those goals. By talking with families and staff about their beliefs and incorporating these as best we can within the program, we acknowledge the value of their input, and at the same time enrich the program.

Parents' desires for their children should be respected and incorporated wherever possible. If we feel uncomfortable with a parent's request for their child, we need to ask ourselves if this is because we feel that the child's physical or emotional well-being will be threatened, or is it simply that their request does not correspond with our ideas of what is appropriate?

If parents and staff are going to exchange information, then we need to make parents feel that they are welcome in the setting. By reflecting diversity in the physical environment, the menu, the languages spoken by staff and displayed on notices and posters, and the music played, we take the first step towards truly welcoming families from diverse backgrounds. The channels of communication should enable all families to participate. Notices should be displayed in community languages that are appropriate to the families using the service and interpreters should be provided where necessary. Staff should acknowledge that families will have varying levels of literacy. Communication should be spoken and pictorial as well as written to cater for the needs of different families.

By utilising every possible situation and means to welcome, understand and get to know individual families, we model cooperation and sensitivity to diversity. We also convey to children that their family is valued by others, which is crucial for young children's developing self-esteem. The material resources that are present in early childhood settings give hidden messages to children about their worth as a person. If there are no resources, or only a few tokens that reflect the child's family background, what message does this give to the child?

ACCEPTING EACH CHILD AS AN INDIVIDUAL

As stated previously, accepting young children for who they are, means accepting their culture, language, values and beliefs, and abilities, and reflecting this in our program. When early childhood settings are sensitive to children's individual differences, this promotes each child's feelings of self-worth and develops increased pride in their heritage.

> Child care centres should not be wresting the child from the culture of the home and immersing them as quickly as possible in the culture of the centre. Instead, the role of the centre should be to enhance the cultural and social background of the child, teaching the new without forcing the repression of the old and familiar. (Hopson 1990: pp.5–6)

All early childhood settings should aim to maintain and strengthen the skills and experiences that children bring from home. Early childhood educators need to recognise that there is no 'common set of experiences' that all children bring to the setting. Even when children may appear to be 'all the same' and come from a cultural and social background similar to our own, we cannot assume that we know and understand the background and experiences of each child. We need to observe each individual child and note their developing skills and interests. We need to talk with the child and with their family and find out specific information relating to that child and their family. This is essential for all children, but particularly for those children who come from cultural and social backgrounds different to our own.

If we are to reflect each child's background in the program, we firstly need to know the family, going beyond our initial impressions, and perhaps biases and prejudices. For instance, from what we know about Aboriginal child-rearing practices we may assume that the Aboriginal child in our centre has had different experiences to non-Aboriginal children. The reality may be that the child has an Aboriginal father that she has not seen since she was 12 months old, and has been brought up by her non-Aboriginal mother with no exposure to Aboriginal culture or lifestyle. On the other hand, there may be a child with red hair and freckles who we assume comes from an Anglo-Australian background, whereas in fact the child has an Aboriginal heritage and is part of an extended family where independence and self-reliance are encouraged.

As Hopson (1990) points out 'cultural heritage is learned'. It is not something that we are born with, but rather something that we learn as we take part in everyday family life. We need to keep this in mind and avoid making judgments based on appearances.

Only by communicating with parents can we obtain accurate information on each child's background. Although workshops and written information on issues such as child-rearing practices of different cultural groups are very useful, we should avoid making generalisations. We should also be aware that cultures change. The beliefs and practices of a family in their country of origin will most likely change when that family migrates to a new country. For example, Greek culture in Greece may be quite different to Greek culture practised in Australia. Each family makes their own decisions regarding the extent they wish to assimilate to the culture of the new country. Some aspects of the original culture may be strengthened after migration, while other aspects may be modified to different degrees.

Communication with parents needs to be ongoing and informal.

Finding out about individual families and their values and beliefs takes time and sensitivity. Rather than 'interrogating' parents on enrolment day, build questions into everyday conversations about their child. If you have regular interviews with families to discuss their child's progress, these will also provide an opportunity for families to share information about their child and their expectations.

SOME AREAS WHERE INFORMATION COULD BE COLLECTED FROM FAMILIES

- country of origin of families
- language/s spoken by various family members
- language/s read and written by various family member
- parents' competence with oral and written English
- eating/sleeping pattern
- attitudes to play
- family rules, discipline, affection
- expectations held for the child

(For a more comprehensive list see Hopson 1990: p.13)

PLANNING FOR DIVERSITY

Through ongoing interactions with each family we can find out about individual family cultures and reflect these in the setting. Then, rather than having saris in 'home corner' that 'come from India', we may have saris 'like the ones that Laxmi's mum wears sometimes'. Rather than describing the flat bread for afternoon tea as 'Lebanese bread' we may talk about the fact that 'Abdul eats this bread sometimes at home, and his family are Lebanese-Australians.'

When selecting resources and experiences it is essential that these reflect the everyday lives of family and community members. Posters, props for dramatic play, music, literature, cooking experiences and so on should represent contemporary, rather than traditional culture. Search out resources that represent families' everyday cultures, rather than those that focus on the exotic and traditional. Resources can be obtained from families within the centre or local community or you can make your own. It is better to have authentic photos of local people and events that are relevant to the children's lives rather than glossy posters and pictures that present stereotyped images.

STAFF

The staff within the setting should also reflect the backgrounds of the children, as staff act as important role models for children. Where children come from a wide variety of backgrounds, it may not be possible to reflect each child's culture, language, religion or race in the staff. In this case, utilising family and community resources is important. Invite parents and community members into the centre to share aspects of their culture with the children. Also tap into the local resource centres and support networks, both formal and informal.

Staffing for diversity should, as far as possible, include a full range of human differences — age, gender, race, culture, beliefs, language, lifestyle, physical and mental abilities. Regardless of the backgrounds of the children, staff should reflect the diversity of the wider community as far as possible. The consideration of diversity should be an integral part of staffing procedures for each setting.

In many settings there will be Equal Employment Opportunity (E.E.O.) guidelines. In this case you will be participating in procedures that relate to social justice and equity, where all people regardless of background, have equal employment opportunities. It is important in any situation to base selection of staff on valid criteria, relevant to the work to be done, and to seriously consider the skills of each applicant.

Numerous studies have shown that young children can readily identify and label people according to racial groups. Katz (1976) found that infants noticed racial differences and that by 3 or 4 were able to assign racial labels of 'black' and 'white' to people, dolls and photographs. In this study Katz also found that evaluative comments were developing alongside children's racial awareness, and that these comments tended to reflect the prevailing attitudes of the child's family and local community. A staff with diverse skills and backgrounds can help children to see differences as normal, acceptable and of value. As Deardorff has pointed out:

> there is no substitute for personal contact with people who are 'different' to help children realize that they aren't really very different at all. (Cited in Neugebauer 1987: p.71)

As well as children learning about diversity within the setting from the 'different' adults they come in contact with, staff also learn much about human differences and similarities, and begin to be able to see things from others' perspectives.

MORE THAN ONE LANGUAGE

The languages that children bring from home, whether a community language other than English, or a variation of English, should be accepted in the early childhood setting. Acceptance of each child's language and communication style is important for that child's developing self-esteem and for their acquisition of skills in the Standard Australian English dialect.

Wherever possible a bilingual approach should be implemented, maintaining and developing the child's first language or dialect. Although this can be achieved to varying degrees with the assistance of bilingual staff, SUPS workers, interpreters and family members, it is crucial that the child and their family see that their first language or dialect is acknowledged and valued in the setting.

QUESTIONS TO EVALUATE HOW AND TO WHAT EXTENT
WE DEMONSTRATE THE ACCEPTANCE OF EACH CHILD'S
LANGUAGE/DIALECT

- Are we familiar with greetings and everyday words (e.g. toilet) in the child's first language/dialect?
- Are enrolment forms and information booklets printed in relevant community languages other than English?
- Is there environmental print in the setting in languages other than English?
- Are stories, poems, chants and songs shared by parents and staff in a variety of languages? Are those that are shared in English originating from a variety of cultures?
- Do children have the opportunity to teach each other stories, poems, chants and sayings from their own family and a variety of cultures?
- Have we learnt to pronounce the child's and the family's names and to use the appropriate forms of address?
- Are there opportunities to monitor the child's language development in their first language for developmental records?
- Have we communicated to parents the benefits of maintaining and extending the child's first language at home?
- Have we asked the child's family about the language/s spoken at home, and by whom, and whether the child has other avenues of first language development (e.g. community language school, Saturday school)?
- Do we have enough knowledge of the child's first language to help us recognise the developments that the child is making in gaining control of the English language system?
- Is the child's first language used as a grouping criteria for some part of the day to promote language maintenance?

As Ramsay (1987) and others have pointed out, it is the role of the early childhood educator to support the development in children of the skills needed to participate in the wider society in whatever way they choose. This means that they do need to acquire skills in the dialect of Standard Australian English, but not at the expense of their home language or dialect. If children are forced to drop the language or dialect of their home this can result in a breakdown of communication with their family and local community. In fact, children can develop skills in communicating successfully in both languages or dialects and need help in identifying which is appropriate in which situations. This is particularly the case when there may be more subtle differences in terms of dialect.

Harris (1990) suggests that early childhood educators, and all teachers, should clarify the different expectations of home and school for children, rather than expect them to learn this by osmosis. Differences should be pointed out in a way that does not denigrate the ways of the home, but instead values them. By making clear the language, communication styles and ways of behaving that are appropriate for success in the school system and in much of the wider community, children are able to develop the skills to function in these environments as well as their local community and home.

DIVERSITY OF PATTERNS

1. COMMUNICATION STYLES

We need to observe the children within our setting and the ways in which they behave, and to communicate this information to each other. Rather than assuming that all children come into the setting sharing our values, we need to recognise that there will probably be many differences. We do not necessarily need to agree with the values of the home, but we need to understand them so that we can work together with families. We need to respect that these different ways of behaving may be functional in the home and local community, and indeed even necessary for survival, and to explain the reasons for our different views to children and families.

SOME AREAS WHERE DIFFERENCES MAY OCCUR, AND THAT SHOULD BE CONSIDERED BY EARLY CHILDHOOD EDUCATORS

- Physical closeness: Are there some children who like to be in close physical proximity to others and need lots of physical touching while others maintain their distance and avoid being touched?
- Loudness: Are some children loud and active while other children speak quietly and prefer more passive activities?
- Obedience: Do some children automatically comply with your requests, while others seem to ignore you?
- Sense of order: Do some children respond readily to requests to keep their belongings tidy and return equipment to the shelves and others seem to always be 'untidy'?
- Use of equipment: Are there some children who have experienced the play equipment of the setting at home and others who may not have seen this sort of equipment before? Are there some children who need to be shown the basic uses of equipment?
- Concepts of time: Are there some children and families who are used to a structured day and strict adherence to time, while there are others for whom time is more flexible? Are there some children and families who are used to planning ahead and making appointments and others who live more for the here and now?
- Communication style: Do some children seem to constantly interrupt or talk while others are talking yet remain silent when nominated to talk in front of the group? Does this reflect what are considered to be acceptable practices in the home?

Source: Adapted from B. West Children are caught — between Home and School, Culture and School in B. Neugebaur (ed) *Alike and Different.*

2. VALUES AND BELIEFS

Values, beliefs and social practices should also be respected within early childhood settings. It is necessary to find out about each family's religious beliefs, taboos and celebrations and to honour these. The families and individuals who have different philosophies need to be acknowledged and understood just as much as the families with traditional religious beliefs and practices.

When planning menus, staff need to acknowledge and accommodate the dietary practices of each child and their family. This should be done in a sensitive way so that particular children are not singled out as always having special food. As often as possible, try to incorporate special needs within the menu for all of the children, for example, by having vegetarian meals some days.

If you include celebrations within your program, remember that none of these are universal and that for some children 'celebrating' may be against their family religion. As well as the traditional Anglo-Australian celebrations of Easter and Christmas, it is essential to acknowledge significant events and celebrations for other groups — for example, Ramadan, National Days, New Year, Hannukah. At times such as Easter include a variety of traditions to help children explore diversity.

Visits to important places within the community such as temples, mosques and churches encourage staff or family members to share particular stories that are a meaningful part of their religion or philosophy.

To help broaden children's understanding of different religious and social beliefs, we need to talk about people's everyday practices and of the meanings behind symbols, rituals and celebrations. If we do not do this we run the risk of only presenting children with a 'postcard impression' of the world.

SOME RESOURCES TO CONSIDER WHEN PLANNING FOR DIVERSITY IN EARLY CHILDHOOD SETTINGS

- Does your staff library contain 'readable' background material on religious and social practices which could offer general background information in preparation for investigating and discussing each family's customs?
- Does your planning calendar offer reminders of important events for the various groups in your setting and the local community?
- Does your excursion calendar include visits to local places of worship?
- Do you have the necessary dramatic play props to provide children with the opportunities to replay important religious and social events in their lives such as birthdays, weddings, christenings and name days?
- Is there a variety of children's literature that reflects different religious and social beliefs that staff and families can share with children?

> ■ Do you program times for family and community members to share their religious stories, beliefs and particular foods associated with celebrations with the children either at the centre or in the family home?
> ■ Do you consider different family structures when events such as Mother's Day and Father's Day come around?

3. VARYING ABILITIES

Children of differing abilities are part of every early childhood setting and need to be catered for in our planning. We need to accept each child's developing skills and provide opportunities for each child to succeed at their own level and at their own pace. To help each child feel competent it is vital when programming that we focus on each child's individual strengths, rather than what we perceive as weaknesses.

Each child deserves the right to explore their environment and extend upon existing skills without being hindered by adults fears for their success. The adult's role is one of support, not 'protection'. Be available and provide suitable encouragement for positive attempts and make this meaningful and sincere, based on each child's individual progress.

A suitable environment will provide experiences that cater for all developmental levels. We should encourage each child to spend as much or as little time engaged in an experience as they feel necessary, and allow them to utilise their existing skills without hinderance.

By providing an environment where each child may experience challenge and success, we are increasing the likelihood of each child internalising feelings of competence and having the confidence to positively approach new experiences.

When special needs children are integrated within your setting help all children to accept and interact positively with these children. Often other children will be initially apprehensive about someone who looks different to themselves. It is necessary to allow all children to express their feelings about children with differing abilities and to ask questions. The early childhood educator and all of the children need to explore differences in an open way, and at the same time explore the many similarities amongst the children.

Children with differing abilities need to see images that they can identify with around them, just as all children do. Resources in the early childhood setting need to represent people with visual and hearing impairments, physical and mental disabilities and people of different physical characteristics, e.g. height and weight. The physical environment and material resources may also need to be adapted so that all children can be actively involved.

Whether there are special needs children integrated in your setting or not they should be represented in the resources available and displayed in the setting. This may include equipment such as books, dolls, puzzles and posters. These resources can be used as discussion starters with children to explore similarities and differences.

BROADENING CHILDREN'S PERSPECTIVES

While it is important to promote children's pride in their own heritage and to help children develop a positive self-identity and self-esteem, it is equally important to help children to be comfortable with diversity. Particularly if the majority of children come from a homogeneous background, it is important to present positive images of people from a variety of racial and cultural backgrounds and with a variety of abilities, ages and lifestyles.

Some children may be exposed to diversity as part of their everyday lives, while others may grow up only seeing and mixing with people from similar backgrounds to their own. For children who have only experienced white Anglo-Celtic Australian middle-class, mono-lingual culture, their version of reality can be very distorted. It is essential that these children become aware of the diversity in the wider community within Australia and recognise that diversity is all around us.

We need to evaluate the environment that we are presenting to children within our services, both in terms of resources and our responses to diversity. The fact that there are no children in your service — or you believe that there are none — from different backgrounds, is no excuse for a lack of attention to issues of diversity. There do not need to be 'multicultural children' or Aboriginal children in the service before multicultural or Aboriginal perspectives are introduced.

Recognising diversity needs to begin with the differences that exist amongst children within the early childhood setting and local community and work outwards from there to encompass the diversity existing in the wider community around us. Planning for diversity needs to go beyond the mere provision of 'a black doll' and Chinese bowls in home corner, to being integrated across all curriculum areas.

DO THE RESOURCES IN YOUR EARLY CHILDHOOD SETTING REFLECT THE DIVERSITY OF CHILDREN, THEIR FAMILIES AND THE WIDER COMMUNITY?

- Are there books, puzzles and posters showing people of different races, cultures and abilities?
- Are the images representative of people going about their everyday lives or are they stereotyped images that present purely exotic differences?
- Do the resources reflect people of differing lifestyles, such as single parent families, multi-racial and multi-ethnic families and communal families?
- Are there images of people engaged in a variety of occupations, both skilled and unskilled and resources depicting both men and women in non-traditional roles?
- Are cultural, religious and social practices portrayed as universal or as some of the many ways that people engage in everyday practices?

- What values are portrayed in the choice of colours for furnishings and decorations? Are there earthy tones as well as bright primary colours?
- Are there displays of artwork such as textiles, sculpture, pottery and paintings from a diversity of ethnic and racial groups and that depict both men and women?
- Are there images of people of mixed race and ethnic background and paints that represent a variety of different skin tones?
- Do dolls reflect the full spectrum of skin tones, rather than just black and white? Are there dolls that are authentic representations of Aboriginal groups, Pacific Islanders, Vietnamese as well as Anglo-Celtic groups? Do the dolls represent the main groups present in your centre and in Australia as a whole?
- Is there a variety of music that is heard by children throughout the day? Do children have the opportunity to move to music with different rhythms and to sing and listen to songs in a variety of languages?
- Does the literature presented to children come from a variety of sources? Are there some books that are bilingual? Is there environmental print such as labels, notices and posters in a number of different scripts?
- Do children have the opportunity to see and hear different language systems such as sign and Braille?
- Are there a selection of materials for children to manipulate and construct with that include figures that depict diversity in race, ethnic group, gender, physical abilities, for example, lotto games, construction sets and block accessories? Do posters displayed alongside children's construction areas include women as well as men as builders, carpenters and mechanics? Do posters depict a variety of types of housing, not just suburban housing?

Lack of appropriate resources and budgetary constraints may make it difficult to present children with authentic resources in all curriculum areas. However, there are many libraries and resources centres where equipment can be borrowed. Parents and community members may also be able to lend materials to the centre, and you can also make your own.

Stereotyped resources should be removed from the children's daily environment or adapted for use. Books or posters that have stereotyped images or that only present a limited view of the world can be changed by adding pictures of differently abled people and people from different backgrounds, and by posting new pictures over the old stereotyped ones (Derman-Sparks 1989: p.15).

The resources that we use with children need to be included on a daily basis, not as a one week 'theme'. They also need to be utilised by staff in a positive discussion of diversity. Staff are a major influence on children's developing understandings and acceptance of differences. Staff may intervene where appropriate to draw children's attention to resources and follow through on the children's observations of, and interactions with resources. The ways that staff members respond to resources, both verbally and non-verbally, are important cues to children about our attitudes and biases. It is of no benefit to children to provide them with dolls that have different kinds of disabilities, if we are too embarrassed to talk about these; or provide them with black paint and play dough, if we have negative attitudes about this colour ourselves.

ATTITUDES

Attitudes are an important part of children's development. With prolonged observation and interaction with individual children we can identify attitudes that they may be developing towards people in the community. These observations can inform us of the effectiveness of our Accepting Diversity program and may pinpoint issues that need addressing immediately (such as name calling, stereotypical comments and repeated myths) and issues that need addressing in the long term in working with parents and involving them in the program.

Early childhood educators need to provide children with experiences that challenge their stereotypes and myths. This may include bringing people into the setting who directly challenge these myths, such as an Aboriginal doctor, a woman carpenter or a teacher who uses sign language. Storytelling and the use of persona dolls can increase children's knowledge and understanding of unfamiliar people and situations and help them see the other person's perspective, particularly if we talk about how others may feel in particular situations (Derman-Sparks 1989).

Opportunities need to also be provided for all children to interact with a range of children within the setting, increasing 'their interpersonal skills, awareness of others and range of contacts' (Ramsay 1987: p.193). Experiences can be planned that encourage children to mix with others who may have different social or language backgrounds to their own. Providing opportunities for children to work and play cooperatively and allowing them to solve their own problems and resolve their own conflicts will help develop children's acceptance of each other.

DEALING WITH UNFAIR BEHAVIOUR

The anti-bias approach differs from other approaches in that its goals include developing critical thinking about bias and the ability to stand up to unfair behaviour.

> Children learning to take action against unfair behaviours that
> occur in their own lives is at the heart of anti-bias education.
> (Derman-Sparks 1989: p.77)

It is not possible to create a bias-free world or unbiased children, but it
is possible to point out to children when behaviour is discriminatory,
and to talk about why behaviour such as name-calling is unfair.

Early childhood educators can help children to explain why they
think something is unfair and help children develop the skills to resist
bias. Part of developing positive feelings about yourself is to tell others
when their behaviour is hurting or upsetting you. For children to develop
respect for the feelings and rights of others they need to be able to
recognise injustices.

> Teaching for the fundamental feelings of self-esteem and em-
> pathy/sympathy cannot begin too early. Feelings are skills and
> specific feelings have to be encouraged and taught for in a very
> active fashion if they are to become an effective part of a child's
> emotional, moral and behavioural vocabulary. (Pettman 1986: p.3)

The development of self-esteem and a sense of identity with others is
crucial for developing cross-group interactions and acceptance. When
this occurs, children are able to become activists on behalf of others.

The development of these skills needs to begin with children's daily
experiences and interactions with peers. Children need to learn from an
early age to express their feelings, be assertive and appreciate the rights
and feelings of others.

Ways that early childhood educators can foster this development can
be planned for with experiences such as those using personna dolls
(Derman-Sparks 1989) although often the experiences will occur spontaneously as a result of children's interactions or verbal expressions.

AS STAFF MEMBERS DO YOU...

- Encourage children to verbalise their feelings towards one
  another and to work through their own emotions and conflicts?
- Model positive conflict resolution with other staff members,
  demonstrating how acknowledging and discussing differences
  can produce positive results?
- Help children to verbally express their feelings if they are
  becoming frustrated or verbally or physically aggressive?
- Discuss feelings with children when they are the victim of inci-
  dences such as name calling, e.g. 'How do you feel when
  someone says that to you?'
- Respond immediately to name calling or misconceptions mentioned by the children by stating the situation? e.g.
  Child: 'There's new kids next door. Mum says not to play with
  them — they're coons.'

> Adult: 'Did you know that those people like to be called Kooris or Aborigines?'
>
> ■ Assist children to be assertive and say 'I don't like that' or 'Don't be unfair'? Do you help children to be in control and recognise their capabilities by saying 'No' to behaviour they don't like?

Many situations arise in day-to-day interactions with children where a child may be told:

'You're a girl, you can't play here.'

'You talk funny. Go away.'

'You're stupid. You can't do this.'

'You look funny.'

'You smell.'

and so on. It is essential that we point out to children that using these words, and excluding children from play on these grounds, is unfair and unacceptable behaviour in our classroom or centre. Ignoring or excusing this behaviour ('She didn't really mean it'; 'He doesn't understand what he is saying'), is only reinforcing prejudice and lowering the self-esteem of the child who is the target.

As well as responding to the immediate situation, early childhood educators should plan steps to deal with these issues in the longer term. Often children's responses are based on their fear or discomfort with the unknown. These feelings need to be dealt with sensitively by adults through giving children developmentally appropriate information about unfamiliar people and situations they may be faced with and by giving specific and relevant information in answer to their questions.

HOW CAN WE IMPLEMENT AN 'ACCEPTING DIVERSITY' APPROACH?

The first step is to identify and describe the current situation, considering children's backgrounds, family involvement, staffing procedures, learning experiences and resources. (See chapter 6 for further discussion of the evaluating process.)

Whilst we may be very keen to introduce all sorts of changes in terms of diversity issues, it is important to move slowly and ensure that everyone involved understands the policies and practices being introduced. Derman-Sparks (1989) talks of the Anti-Bias Curriculum as a journey, rather than an overnight change. It is essential that this journey be taken together rather than imposed from above. The rapid introduction of the desired policies and practices may result in changes at a superficial level, rather than changes in thinking. As Derman-Sparks has noted, what is required is a change in consciousness not just in curriculum.

At times it can be frustrating to move slowly, however it is necessary to recognise that not everything can be done at once. Selecting a particular focus for diversity implementation is a useful strategy as staff are involved in policy development, implementation and the evaluation of practices. The selected focus may be identified in the situational analysis (see chapter 4) or from observations. Whatever focus you choose, you need to consider the children's backgrounds, needs and interests and the issues that affect them (Derman-Sparks 1989: p.116).

In selecting a focus, begin with something that is achievable and that is least threatening to the group you are working with. Open discussion of anti-bias issues in a non-threatening atmosphere can help break down barriers and fears and result in a strong support group. Developing support groups and allowing sufficient time to explore issues will result in a greater understanding and commitment to change than implementing overnight changes.

Changing attitudes and beliefs takes time. Remember that each individual needs to start from where they are at and to change at their own pace. Not everyone may be ready for change. Start with those who are ready and work from there.

The overall message is one of valuing each individual for the skills and the background they have — this includes their family background, race, beliefs, language and so on. Each individual sees the world through their own perspectives and with assistance, through the perspectives of others.

This can only be achieved over a lengthy period of time and with ongoing evaluation of our own attitudes, the environment we provide (human and physical), the diversity within our staff, children and families and with an acceptance of the diversity within our changing Australian society.

USEFUL RESOURCES

Stonehouse, A. (1991) *Opening the Doors*, Sydney: Lady Gowrie Child Centre.

Hopson, E. (1990) A Cross-Cultural Anti–Bias Approach, Sydney: Lady Gowrie Child Centre.

Part 2
PROCESSES OF PLANNING AND PROGRAMMING

INTRODUCTION

The approach taken to planning in a setting involves staff making decisions as to what they consider to be appropriate for the particular setting they are in. These decisions will be based on a number of factors such as the type of setting, the setting's philosophy and overall goals, the skills and interests of the staff and family members, and methods of evaluation. Evaluation is a key component in the planning process, as we need to gather information in order to be able to reflect on daily practices and to ensure that they reflect our philosophy. It is important that we continually evaluate what we are doing and why, and that we are able to make changes to the program where necessary.

As well as the program being appropriate to the needs of a particular setting it is also essential that it is developmentally and individually appropriate. The needs of individual children and ways in which the program can promote each child's unique development must be the basis of daily programming if we are taking a child-centred approach. The way that we organise the environment so that it is able to meet children's needs throughout the day is the focus of this section.

This section considers the overall planning process and ways that children's needs can be met in the daily program. Chapter 4 looks at philosophy development and analysis of the needs and constraints of the setting as the starting points of planning. Chapter 5 then considers ways of reflecting these in the goals of the setting and the approach taken to planning the whole day. Chapter 6 focuses on the steps involved in planning for the strengths, needs and interests of individual children within group settings. In Chapter 7 a variety of grouping strategies are explored along with ways of analysing the effectiveness of grouping methods used within a particular setting. Resources and ways of organising environments to meet the needs of all participants in the setting are discussed in Chapter 8. While the importance of on-going evaluation is stressed throughout this section, Chapter 9 focuses on the purposes and processes of evaluation and ways of designing evaluation tools to meet particular needs.

4

GETTING STARTED

INTRODUCTION

This chapter focuses on starting points in the planning process, both in broad terms and setting specific contexts. We will discuss developing a personal and collective or team philosophy and undertake a situational analysis of our setting.

PHILOSOPHY

WHAT IS A PHILOSOPHY? WHY DO WE NEED ONE?

Put simply, a philosophy is another word for a vision, or a 'great plan'. It's rather like a master plan that sets the direction in which we plan to move.

Having a vision of the early childhood service we want to develop is very useful. It involves thinking about the kinds of programs that we consider valuable, the kind of staff development and participation that is possible and the kind of family involvement that would strengthen the centre program. If we have 'a picture' of where we are headed, it is more likely that we will get there. Although when starting out some aspects of the philosophy or vision may seem like 'pie in the sky', it is essential to provide a clear direction for all working and associated with the early childhood service.

WHERE DO WE START?

To develop a vision or philosophy, starting points need to be identified. This usually takes place as we clarify what knowledge, values and assumptions we consider important to early childhood education and to our own particular setting. This means that as individuals we need to be aware firstly of our own personal philosophy, in order to articulate it to other members of the team and to be able to assist other team members to identify their own visions before developing a setting philosophy together.

In any program design, decisions need to be made about the 'overall' philosophy. Each staff member and parent has a particular vision, a set of knowledge, beliefs, assumptions and values about early childhood education and care which are reflected in what they do each day. These are the core of ideals or 'impossible dreams' at the centre of our daily practices. In some areas these features are known as ideology. However, sometimes we are not aware of our vision or ideology, of its patterns, its inconsistencies or its paradoxes and how this influences our behaviour and expectations; it may be implicit. Making our philosophy explicit through discussing it and writing it down gives us a set of reference points or framework for conscious decision making (how to behave and act). Being aware of our philosophy can guide us to make better decisions in the 'nitty gritty' of daily practices.

HOW CAN WE CLARIFY OUR PERSONAL AND EDUCATIONAL PHILOSOPHIES?

As there are so many influences contributing to a vision, it is important and extremely useful to clarify and refine our *personal* views on education and care before we work together with other staff and families to develop a setting philosophy. The vision we refine will affect many aspects of our work; including our perceptions of our role in the early childhood setting, the way we set up the environment and the way we plan. The vision will also influence the type of experiences we provide, the resources we use and the atmosphere we create. Other areas reflecting our philosophy include the way we perceive the roles of others — staff, families and management — and why, how and what we evaluate.

There is no recipe for a philosophy to suit every individual and every setting. Each setting varies — service, children, families and staff. The process of developing or revising a philsophy needs to be worked through as a joint effort with familes and staff in that setting. As a consequence the philosophy will be relevant, valued and most importantly owned and understood by all participants.

There are various influences on our educational and personal philosophy. These include a range of different kinds of information such as:

- our knowledge and understanding of children's growth and development;
- our knowledge and values about the ways children learn;
- our knowledge and understandings of children and families within a particular setting;
- our own understandings and views of the world;

- our own education, skills, expectations, dispositions and experiences; and
- our understanding of interpretations of philosophies, policies, practices and expectations of outside organisations (for example, the management body — local, state and federal government departments like Kindergarten Union, Children's Services, Department of School Education, Department of Community Services and Health).

THE PROCESS OF DEVELOPING A TEAM PHILOSOPHY FOR A SERVICE

Once each individual has clarified their personal philosophy, we need to work together to develop an 'overall' service philosophy.

As each setting is unique, there is no 'one' philosophy which is suitable to every setting. However the process used may be similar in different settings. This process also needs to allow for group members to investigate possible constraints for the setting and develop a program which will best reflect their ideals in response to these constraints.

The issues that need to be addressed in the process of developing a philosophy are outlined in figure 4.1 and are discussed in the remainder of this chapter.

WHO SHOULD BE INVOLVED?

All of those who will be affected by the philosophy adopted and who will have an impact on its implementation should be involved in the development. Some of these groups may be:

- families;
- staff;
- children;
- government bodies;
- management bodies; and
- communities.

All staff and families associated with the service, need the opportunity for involvement in the development of the setting's philosophy. This process is a worthwhile development experience. Where staff have contributed to philosophy development they are more able to translate aspects into daily practice, spot inconsistencies and conflicts in daily experiences and become concerned about working through other ways to meet a particular philosophical statement in a sound and consistent manner. Once the setting's philosophy is clarified, decision making for relevant daily planning becomes much easier. As a result of participating in team philosophy development, some families will gain a better insight into the importance of components of high quality programs whilst other families will contribute significantly to ideals espoused in the philosophy.

Through this involvement, families will be providing input so that their needs are met and reflected more readily within the program.

Management groups, community and government organisations also play an important part in the development of the philosophy of a setting. If the early childhood service is to reflect the needs of the community and take into account policies that may affect the philosophy's implementation, there should be some consideration of these issues and representation from these groups.

This is often possible through the establishment of sub-committees with diverse representation which can feed back into the larger group i.e. a group may include one or two staff members, family members, representatives from management groups, and community and government organisations where appropriate.

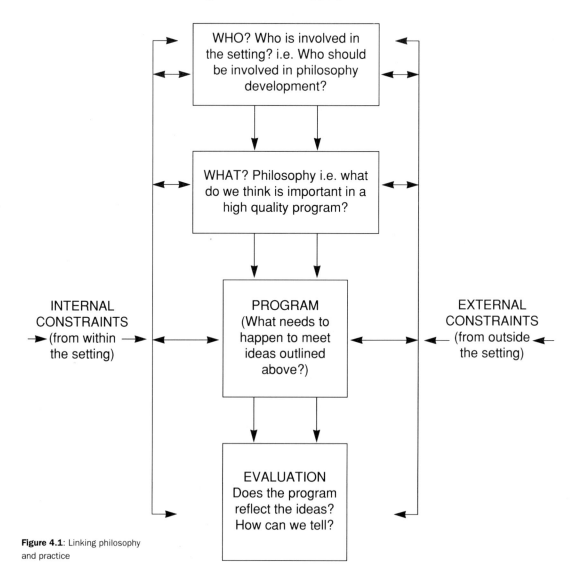

Figure 4.1: Linking philosophy and practice

In addition to these groups, the needs and development of the children in the setting will also impact on the philosophy and should be taken into account of the development phase.

WHAT DO WE THINK IS IMPORTANT IN A PHILOSOPHY?

There are many factors that will influence what we consider important in a high quality program. We need to incorporate ideas into our philosophy that relate to known components of high quality programs. From our experiences and knowledge-base — reading, own beliefs and values, awareness of issues like the Code of Ethics, membership of various professional organisations like AECA, attendance at inservice courses, seminars and discussions with network of peers — particular components of high quality programs for young children will be identified for each setting. Features of currently recognised high quality programs concern developmentally appropriate learning experiences for children, the importance of adult–child interactions, relationships between home and the centre, recognition of the diversity of peoples, and the role of evaluation as an integral aspect of all programs. These aspects are explained further in the chapter 1. Over time and in light of further research, these desirable features may be refined or emphasised differently. This underlines the need for the early childhood educator to be continually involved in professional development.

Members of the different groups in each setting need to work together through what they consider important in a high quality program to be able to use it to form a base for their own philosophy. One possible process to develop ideas towards the philosophy within a setting is outlined in 'Process of developing a philosophy'.

PROCESS OF DEVELOPING A PHILOSOPHY

1. Raise the issue with staff, families and management at a meeting.
2. Ask members to brainstorm issues they think are important in a setting.
3. Draw and detail a representation.
4. Display the representation in the communal area of the setting like the foyer for several weeks and invite different group members to add what they think is important under various headings.
5. Collate the ideas to develop philosophy statements as illustrated in the following example:

    To provide a flexible service which meets the differing needs of the surrounding community.

    To provide a caring supportive environment which reflects individual and cultural diversity for everyone at the centre.

cont...

cont...   To ensure that the program caters for individual needs and developmental levels of the children.

To encourage as much family involvement as possible for the individual.

To foster a team approach where all staff are respected as individuals as well as a valuable part of the team.

To provide a stimulating environment to encourage creativity, exploration and investigation across all areas.

WHAT ARE THE CONSTRAINTS? WHAT HAPPENS BETWEEN PHILOSOPHY AND PRACTICE?

Often, we have lots of ideals but our practice does not always reflect these beliefs. This situation often occurs due to the many constraints that impact upon settings. Constraints are considered to be any feature which presents an obstacle to or an influence on practices.

HOW CAN WE WORK WITHIN THE PRESSURES AND CONSTRAINTS PLACED UPON US?

Sometimes, once we have clarified our 'overall' service philosophy, implementation does not always easily follow. The first step is to acknowledge and identify those pressures impeding our implementation.

What are the internal and external pressures that may affect the implementation of philosophical ideals? Some are suggested in figure 4.2.

WHAT HAPPENS WITH CONFLICTING PHILOSOPHIES?

Members in each setting need to identify pressures. Having identified and clarified these conflicts, we can then think of a range of ways to meet these conflicts and so still be able to implement the philosophy.

In some cases possible solutions will be specific to only one setting and in other cases they will be similar across settings. Some constraints, like the lack of suitable resources for infants will be easy to overcome, others will require negotiation with team members and some will instigate a plan within the setting to overcome these pressures over time — like staff development for the use of developmental records. It's important to keep these issues in mind but be clear, as early childhood educators, what our bottom line is for achievement of high quality programs. With this in mind we can keep a firm but gradual direction for improvements based on our setting philosophy.

If one of our beliefs is team work, active encouragement for others to contribute to the philosophy is important. Similarly, if we believe in family involvement we will find ways to authentically involve *families*. As others — staff and *families*, can be involved in developing the philosophy,

INTERNAL	■ Children's diverse needs and stages

■ Building design — Childrens' Services Program
   — two play room design building
   — renovated building/house
■ Staffing difficulties e.g. availability of qualified and experienced staff
   — high staff turnover
   — lack of time; no planning meetings together
■ Lack of resources
■ Expectations of families, community, staff, management
	EXTERNAL
	■ State licensing regulations
	   — poor staff–children ratios
	   — different interpretations of regulations
	■ Funding issues
	   — lack of funding
	   — different funding guidelines
	■ Management
	   — lack of understanding of children's services

Figure 4.2: Internal and external pressures.

their awareness of implementation of philosophy into daily practice is also developed. A philosophy which does not include family involvement would seem tokenistic as a setting philosophy. In terms of team work, we need to remember that as we have a personal philosophy, so do others, and we need to be able to respond creatively and positively to this at all times.

HOW CAN PHILOSOPHY BE REFLECTED IN PRACTICE?

There are many elements in the program where philosophy can guide daily practice. Once we are aware of our philosophy, we can undertake the following process to integrate philosophy and practice.

We need to think about what the philosophy will mean in practice, that is:

If we believe... (philosophical statement)

Then we will... (range of ways for practical implementation)

Planning this translation from philosophy into practice can be done with staff and other team members in brainstorming sessions to which all members can contribute. One way of doing this is to use a very large sheet of paper, and develop a matrix (see figure 4.3) listing features of the program and philosophical statements along each axis, with large spaces for suggestions from the *team*. The matrix can give the opportunity for the *team* to explore all potential implementations of philosophy in this way.

HOW DO WE EVALUATE WHETHER OUR PHILOSOPHICAL IDEALS ARE OCCURRING IN PRACTICE?

Once we have developed a philosophy we need to evaluate annually in three ways. Firstly implementation of the current philosophy needs to be evaluated. This may mean examining the philosophy and checking whether all service users are addressed, i.e. children, families, staff, self, community. Each philosophical statement needs to be considered for all the possible ways of implementation throughout the program and whether reasonable progress is being achieved.

Secondly we need to evaluate the philosophy in terms of current knowledge and understandings. Keeping up with readings in journals, attending workshops, conferences and seminars and networking may provide more relevant and practical ideas which can be implemented as well as keeping in touch with major shifts in knowledge that informs our philosophical bases, for example, research concerning separation, transitions, small groups etc.

Thirdly we need to evaluate for future action. This includes recommendations for forward planning, i.e. it is an ongoing process as we return to see how modifications and changes can occur and we commence the process of development again. This means reassessing the relevant 'who', and 'what' etc., in terms of future modification and changes.

SETTING PRIORITIES

It would be difficult to instantly implement all aspects of the philosophy in an effective way (figure 4.4). In order to make the implementation possible and successful, priority foci need to be set and decisions made regarding the priority of certain components of the philosophy. Where a team/setting has just recently developed a philosophy and awareness of implementation directions in say, consideration of all children as individuals through a focus–child approach and during small group learning experiences, consequently less stress may be placed on parent involvement to the degree the philosophy initially indicated. Setting a time-frame chart for implementation of various aspects of the philosophy can make this procedure clearer and more manageable. In this situation for three months the focus may be for staff to develop expertise in focus children and small group experiences along with general communication with families. Then the focus expands to include another area — concentrated communication with parents. The constraints of time and energy on all staff members should be firmly acknowledged, but also balanced to allow for establishing and working through priorities. There are always aspects of philosophy to be seriously considered later in the year as well as the following year!

SITUATIONAL ANALYSIS

While philosophy development provides a broad direction for the team to aim towards, staff need also investigate aspects of their setting on a regular basis. This is known as situational analysis — a collection of detailed information regarding the setting. The second part of this chapter

PROGRAM ELEMENTS	PHILOSOPHY	IMPLEMENTATION
	Aims and Goals: If we believe......	Practice: Then we will......
■ Organisation of daily environment	■ Children have individual needs	■ Offer sleep and rest experiences ■ Offer child initiated experiences ■ Offer a flexible daily schedule
■ Learning experiences		
■ Groupings	■ Children learn and interact best in small groups	■ Offer small group experiences throughout the day ■ Use small groups in transitions ■ Offer small group music and literature experiences
■ Routines and organisation of the day		
■ Adult/child interactions		
■ Family involvement		
■ Planning		
■ Children's behaviour		
■ Adult role and utilisation of staff		
■ Individuals		
■ Diversity of individuals and families		
■ Evaluation		

Figure 4.3: Philosophy into practice

considers situational analysis as an important way to assist staff to develop a program reflecting both the philosophical basis and needs of the particular setting in detail and identifying the possible constraints to be worked through.

Similar to developing a philosophy, developing a situational analysis, is a particularly worthwhile team effort. The process helps all involved in the service

- become more familiar with the people involved;
- understand more about the setting in terms of resources — human and material, as well as policies, regulations and funding guidelines;
- understand more about centre philosophy — and learn more about the children and families attending the setting.

A team effort is required to collect and collate much information in confidentially ethically ways. This includes completing and reading enrolment forms, interviewing parents, conducting surveys, examining regulations etc. The team then needs to collate and transform this information into a readable and useful document or set of documents. *The team effort is essential in order to manage and present this information and will make the task all the more possible.* As in philosophy development, the experience of being involved in the situational analysis process makes informed decision making all the easier in planning an appropriate program and learning experiences for the children. Once the basic situational analysis has been developed, it is likely that staff will need to revise and adapt some aspects each year so it remains a current and useful document.

The kinds of information which may be collated include the following details — under three main sections — as shown on figure 4.5.

Perhaps the worth of situational analysis can best be demonstrated through considering some questions that may be used to guide its development, looking at two examples and predicting some of the implications for planning. These examples will focus on settings for young children — one for children aged from birth to 5 and the other for children aged 5 to 8.

From the examples of situational analysis in figures 4.6 and 4.7 it can be seen that formats vary slightly in different settings. One example presents how a situational analysis for an early childhood setting with children aged from birth to 5 stresses the Centre and Planning Implications sections. Here, aspects of the centre program are explored in detail whilst the children's section is not presented in as much detail, as individual developmental records and planning will depend on each centre's approach and is a *key* feature in the setting itself. This is not a reflection of importance but the fact that the individual child aspect will be dealt with following the initial situational analysis.

The other example, a situational analysis in a school setting, shows a variation with the inclusion of another section of information — the classroom. In this school example the most detail is to be found in the classroom and children's sections and the corresponding sections of

1993											
J........F..........M.........A..........M.........J...........J..........A.........S ..........O.........N.......D.........											

Focus Child — to be implemented over the whole year

  — establishment of developmental records
     through observations

General Parent Communication

  — high priority from beginning of year
  — involvement of bilingual staff

April

Staff Development — Small Group Experiences

  — using information from
     developmental records
  — strength, needs, interests

July

Parent Involvement

  — investigating range of ways parents can
     participate

September

Staff Development

  — evaluate methods of
     small grouping
  — introduce mixed age
     grouping for part of the
     day and to evaluate the
     outcomes

Figure 4.4: Setting priorities

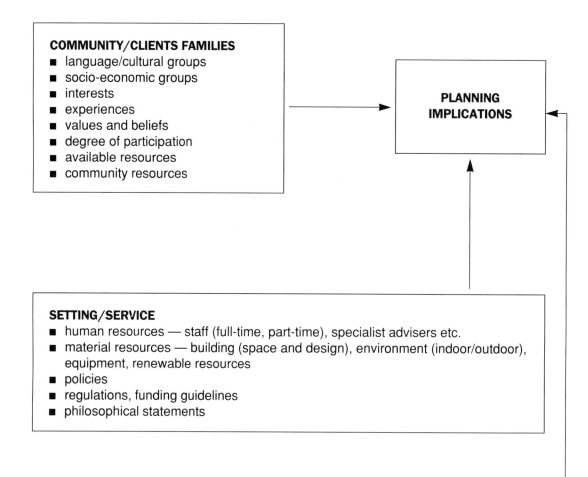

Figure 4.5: Situational analysis

implementation due to most planning taking place within the classroom context. One of the resources that may be available in a school context, is a school-based situational analysis developed by the staff which describes the community/client families and resources — human and material, for the school as a whole.

Another way of looking at the differences in situational analysis between the two contexts is to consider the similarities and differences.

**SOME GUIDING QUESTIONS WHEN DEVELOPING A
SITUATIONAL ANALYSIS COMMUNITY/CLIENT FAMILIES**

- Which language/cultural groups are represented in the community?
- Which language/cultural groups attend this setting?
- Do language/cultural groups maintain their first language at home?
- How do language/cultural groups have the opportunity and the need to learn English?
- What are important general child-rearing practices held by families in the community?
- To which socioeconomic groups do families presently belong?
- Are families supported by social services?
- Which interests do families spend time and energy on? — study, sport, travel, house and garden, community events etc.
- What are important past experiences for the families? — migration, unemployment, housing difficulties, study etc.
- What particular values do families regard highly? — 'clean' play, non-sexist roles etc.
- What kinds of time, energy, talents and presence can families contribute towards setting?
- What resources are available in the community? — parks, shopping centre, other early childhood settings, senior citizens centre, resource centres etc.

SETTING/CENTRE

- What staff are available — full-time, part-time, occasional?
- What experiences, talents and interests do staff currently have?
- What is the nature of the building/s?
- What is the indoor/outdoor environment like?
- How is the setting resourced with equipment?
- What consumable resources are available?
- Which policies are important to the setting?
- Which are the relevant regulations and funding guidelines for the setting?
- Which philosophical statements are important in the setting?

CHILDREN

- Who are the children?
- What is each child's dialect/language/s and cultural background?
- What is each child's developmental stage, strengths and needs?
- What is the nature of each child's current interests, experiences and attitudes?
- What is the size of the group?
- How are levels/stages (infants, toddlers, preschoolers, schoolers) distributed throughout the whole group?

Figure 4.6: Situational analysis — inner city under-5 setting

Community
- Range of Anglo-Australian, Greek-Australian, Macedonian-Australian and Chinese-Australian families
- Most families speak their first language at home
- Mostly two parent families with both parents working
- Parents engaged in factories, retail, restaurant and office work
- Most parents live close to work, close to centre
- Most families from low socioeconomic group, some families, from middle socioeconomic group
- Many parents have recently migrated, other parents migrated to Australia as children
- Most Anglo-Australian parents interested in travel, house renovations, family
- Range of beliefs — Buddhism, Taoism, Christian, Humanist — held by parents
- Range of child rearing practices
- Various levels of parent participation in centre, but all parents show support in some way
- Local community is highly urbanised and is a light industrial area
- The environment has many busy roads and few small parks

Centre
- Human resources
  - 6 full-time staff
    - 1 director/teacher — working in the centre 3 years, with an interest in special needs
    - 1 teacher — newly graduated, bilingual
    - 3 trained CC workers — two child care workers (TAFE), one interested in anti-bias issues and one working closely with families and one mothercraft nurse
    - 1 untrained worker — interested in upgrading qualifications, strong music talents
  - 4 part-time staff
    - cook — currently completing a nutrition course
    - 1 clerical — bilingual
    - 1 cleaner — interested in cooking
    - 1 special needs teacher (2 days per week) — interested in integration
- Material resources
  - children's Services Program building
  - outdoor environment — basic lawn and trees — some shady patches where lawn doesn't grow
  - sufficient range of play equipment
  - consumable resources — butcher's paper, ingredients for paint and paste, reverse garbage supplies, factory offcuts — woods, computer paper
  - centre philosophy
  - regulations
  - funding
- Program
  - centre open 7am–6pm
  - community-managed centre
  - staff currently work in set rooms with particular groups of children

Children
- 40 children
  - 10 Anglo/Australian
  - 7 Greek/Australian
  - 7 Macedonian/Australian
  - 16 Chinese/Australian
  - 2 Malay/Chinese/Australian
- Distribution
  - 6 infants
  - 14 toddlers
  - 20 preschoolers
- Groupings — stage related
- Individualised information on developmental records
  - developmental summaries, strengths, needs, levels, interests experiences and attitudes

Figure 4.6: Continued   Both examples contain sections relating to *Community/Client Families,* *Setting/Centre/School and Classroom, Children* and *Planning Implications.* In the setting for children from birth to 5 years of age the *Planning Implications* refer to the way the total program will operate, i.e. several aims/goals for the setting involving all children and staff. *Planning Implications* in the setting for children aged between 5 and 8 years, pertain only to individual children within the classroom, not to the total setting.

IMPLICATIONS FOR PLANNING —

Community
- Interpreters to translate and assist in improving and extending parent communication
- Visual displays — posters, photos etc. to communicate aspects of program to parents e.g. messy play, baby/adult interaction etc.
- Staff members to survey and interview parents (where time and languages permit) about their families child rearing practices
- Staff to organise informal and short family meetings which are social and informative and fit in with parent's working day
- Staff to involve interested parents in sharing aspects of their family culture

Centre
- Promote staff development with details and funding of seminars, workshops, professional reading
- Utilise staff skills and interests more effectively
- Encourage staff to explore various ways of grouping children (large/small/overall centre)
- Evaluate implementation of philosophy in second half of the year
- Introduce anti-bias program in meet childrens' needs
- Evaluate resources — books, posters, art prints, dramatic play accessories, music, musical instruments in light of children's cultural backgrounds
- Try to develop outdoors areas

Children
- Continue to use developmental records as a basis for planning
- Introduce mixed age grouping for part of the day to promote evaluation of outcomes of grouping methods
- Assess more effective ways to meet individual needs
- Use a focus system for planning

Figure 4.7: Situational analysis — suburban school setting

Community

- Mostly Anglo-Australian families with some Tongan-Australian and Spanish-Australian families
- Tongan-Australian and Spanish-Australian families speak first language at home. These parents have different degrees of competency in English
- Families are mostly from low socioeconomic groups, some families from middle socioeconomic groups
- Range of single, two parent and same sex families
- Families live in a mixture of public and private housing
- Some parents in manufacturing, building and retail work
- At nearby regional centre. Some parents work in the home, some parents are on social security benefits
- Some parents are interested in participating in the classroom. A few parents have shown interest in parent meetings

IMPLICATIONS FOR PLANNING — Community and Families

- Translations required for parent communications in Spanish and Tongan
- Requests for families to pay cost of 'extras' needs to be minimised
- Family cultures need to be reflected in classroom
- Involve interested parents in daily experiences
- Provide informal and social family gatherings which may appeal to 'less' interested parents
- Promote families' understandings of learning through play

School

- Human resources
  - 27 Classroom Teachers
  - 2 Teacher Aides
  - 2 ESL teachers
  - 1 Librarian
  - 1 Ethnic Aide
  - 1 Relief from Face to Face Teacher
  - 2 IM Teachers

- Material resources
  - mixture of old brick and new demountable buildings
  - large concrete and lawn playground
  - new library building
  - rich children's literature supply
  - much concrete maths equipment
  - sufficient audio/visual equipment
  - school based documents for all key learning areas
  - school policy document

IMPLICATIONS FOR PLANNING — School

- Consult Supervisor regarding funding for extra play equipment
- Consult ESL teacher regarding timetable and co-operative planning and evaluating cycle
- Integrate children from pre-school located in school grounds with pre-school 3 times a week for 1 hour in the afternoon, plan with teacher

Kindergarten classroom

- Human resources
  - 1 class teacher
  - ESL teacher 5 x 1 hour per week parent 5 x 30 min per week
  - librarian 1 x 30 min per week

- Material resources
  - classroom at end of demountable building
  - access to playground — steps
  - sufficient storage space and children's furniture
  - adequate range of play equipment

- Renewable resources
  - newspaper, butcher's paper, computer paper
  - ingredients for paint and dough

- Personal Philosophy of Education and Care

- School Based Curriculum Documents, State Documents

- School Policies

IMPLICATIONS FOR PLANNING — Classroom

- Extend own expertise in devising and maintaining a workable system for development records
- Implement focus child approach — 3 chn per week, 30 covered in a 10 week cycle
- Plan literature and social studies units with ESL teachers and IM teacher which focus on children's interests and current experiences

Figure 4.7: Continued

Children
- ■ 30 children
  - — 23 Anglo-Australian
  - — 5 Tongan-Australian
  - — 2 Spanish-Australian

    23 children ESB
    7 children bilingual learners
- ■ Most children have not attended preschool — some children have attended playgroups
- ■ All children are enthusiastic and keen about starting school
- ■ Families are very interested and supportive of children in their first year at school
- ■ Summary of Areas of Development

SUMMARY — Children's development areas

Language Development
Most children are happy to interact with each other. Some Spanish-Australian (John, Maria) and Tongan-Australian (Tomara, Junior) are confident in their first language, they often talk quietly with a peer. Most children have had some book experiences at home and most children show interest in writing.

Emotional Development
Although Kindergarten is the first large group setting in which the children have been involved, they are mostly happy and content. Caroline, James and Toni sometimes show their anxiety about leaving their family in the morning. Several children (Chris, Sandy, Allan, Sean, Marcus) seem to find it difficult to decide which learning centres to play in.

Social Development
Most of the time children interact well with each other individually and in small groups. Sometimes there are disputes over turn-taking of special equipment and insufficient spaces at popular learning centres.

Cognitive Development
Most children sort and classify materials. Most children seem interested in problem solving, predicting possible solutions and suggesting why. Carla, Michael and Andrew in particular, often ask searching questions.

Physical Development
The whole group of children demonstrates control of gross motor skills in running and jumping. Several children — Josh, Carla, Kate, Stuart, Neil, Tom — are presently learning to skip. Fine motor skills are developing in all children.

IMPLICATIONS FOR PLANNING — Children

Language Development
Promote bilingual children's first languages with their parents reading and story telling with small groups
Tape reading of books in first languages
Use language/culture as a grouping criteria
Organise small group experiences whenever possible to promote peer interaction
Spend time talking individually to children whilst engaged in learning experiences
Introduce U.S.S.R. (Uninterrupted, Sustained, Silent Reading) for short periods
Set up literacy dramatic play corner e.g. newsagent, office
Demonstrate reading and writing daily

Emotional Development
Structure predictable routines to promote children's confidence e.g. children hang up bag outside and choose which play experiences to become involved in, first thing every morning
Promote children's decision making at all times — variety of experiences to choose from

Social Development
Encourage children to turn-take
Promote sufficient variety of learning centres so all children are satisfied
Continue using small groups for learning experiences
Set up dramatic play areas that relate to children's experiences — shop, hairdresser etc.

Cognitive Development
Model open-ended questions, prediction and confirmation in discussions
Investigate Carla, Michael and Andrew's interests further with a view to integrating their interests within learning centres

Physical Development
Encourage use of climbing equipment during P.E. times
Provide opportunity to skip with appropriate music
Provide access to scissors, paste, playdough, fingerpainting, manipulative play equipment, computer keyboard within learning centres

These examples illustrate the procedure of adjusting the notion of situational analysis to the individual setting, and of identifying significant information and drawing out planning implications which are integrated into daily practice.

CONCLUSION

This kind of planning — developing a philosophy and situational analysis — is not necessarily time-consuming in the long run. By putting in the initial time and effort, we can gather information that is important for future planning. Team approaches to clarifying and developing philosophy as well as collating information associated with the situational analysis are essential to staff development and the direction that the service is taking. Rather than constantly adjusting our program and being continually surprised by 'new' information, planning in the manner outlined in this chapter enables us 'to get it right' the first time.

USEFUL RESOURCES

Lambert, B., Clyde, M. and Reeves, K. (1987) *Planning for Individual Needs in Early Childhood Services*. Watson, ACT. Australian Early Childhood Association.

5

APPROACHES TO PLANNING

INTRODUCTION

There are various approaches to programming and planning in early childhood settings. The approach to planning that is chosen by each setting is influenced by a wide range of factors, such as the type of setting, who is involved in the planning process and the philosophy/ideology of the setting. This will include aspects such as what staff perceive is important in early childhood education, and beliefs as to what constitutes learning.

SEVERAL APPROACHES TO PROGRAMMING

Stonehouse (1988a, p14) outlines various approaches to planning. These include:

1. The egg carton curriculum — where the novel or unusual art and craft approach may be chosen because of staff interest or to impress parents with colourful displays. The emphasis is usually on the 'end-product', rather than the processes involved. Often all of the 'products' look the same and there is little opportunity for children to use their own creativity.

2. Acceleration — which is based on getting the child ready for the next step, whether that be school or an older group, rather than recognising the stage each child is at and providing appropriate experiences for this stage.

3. Fill-in-the-blanks — or the 'activity-based' model of planning, where the activity provided becomes the focus and fills in the blank on the planning format. Experiences may be set up by the staff because 'we haven't had this for a while', rather than to meet the needs of individual children. This approach also tends to miss out on the vast learning potential of a wide range of experiences, such as routines, that may not appear on this type of planning format.

4. Themes — which use as their basis a particular idea or concept to 'hang' planning on, such as seasons, colours, shapes or people in the community. While there is nothing inherently 'wrong' with planning experiences around an idea, difficulties occur when the program is fixed on these ideas, and may tend to follow a set format year after year. For example: 'We do "the self" first, then "people in the community", then in September we do "Spring" (because its Spring!)'...and so on.

The thematic approach does not allow for the fact that children may not be interested in the idea at the time. With this approach, children's individual development and interests may be overlooked, and many children may become bored when all of the puzzles, art and craft experiences, books and songs relate to the current theme. For children who have spent up to five years in the same setting, do they 'cover' a core curriculum for each group and then move on?

Lastly, Stonehouse refers to:

5. Non-programming — which provides no guidelines for planning for individual needs, but staff state that the program is 'flexible' with lots of free play. This may lead to children's needs and strengths being overlooked and staff lacking direction.

A CHILD-CENTRED APPROACH

The alternative to these approaches is a program that is designed to build on the unique strengths and interests of each child. Staff constantly observe individual children, and prepare the environment based on these observations, developing a program that is centred on each child's needs. Each experience provided is matched to an individual child's developing skills and interests. A program that is child-centred is able to take advantage of children's natural curiousity and motivation to learn. Experiences are mainly child-initiated, or self-selected: that is children are able to choose from a range of experiences and to follow their own interests.

Materials and experiences that are provided are mostly open-ended, enabling children to develop creativity and problem-solving skills and to construct their own knowledge. Adults structure the environment to encourage verbal interactions amongst children and the sharing of ideas, then join in and extend children's play where appropriate (figure 5.1).

WHAT INFLUENCES APPROACHES TO PLANNING?

The approach to planning and programming used in a particular setting will be affected by many issues. Influences may include:

- the philosophy/ideology of the setting;
- information from the situational analysis of the setting, including the size of the setting, age range of the children, hours of operation, and so on (see chapter 4, 'Getting Started');

Figure 5.1: Adults structure the environment to encourage children to choose from a range of experiences and to follow their own interests.

- policies relating to the setting, such as those formulated by government bodies, management committees, and staff;
- the level of family involvement;
- who will be involved in the planning process;
- the basis (as outlined on previous pages) for the planning approach and how it will be documented; and
- the evaluation processes.

WHAT IS EARLY CHILDHOOD CURRICULUM?

The term curriculum is often avoided by early childhood workers who see it as a primary/high school based term which usually refers to what is going to be taught: that is the content or the 'intended curriculum'. In early childhood education it tends to relate to more than just what is going to be implemented. It relates to both why and how as well. It tends to become the total planning process throughout the entire day, with a prominent focus on individual children.

ACCOUNTABILITY

In early childhood education, particularly in 'under five' settings, staff are given a great deal of autonomy over the decision making in programs. While in certain settings, such as schools, staff are clearly accountable to some person or body, accountability can sometimes be forgotten in other settings.

In schools, staff need to be aware of school-based curriculum documents and overall state departmental policy documents. In other settings, such as preschools and long day care centres, staff need to be aware of the various government policies and regulations, whether federal, state, or local, as well as those of the relevant management body, such as the community group or local council. Often though, the staff in individual settings are left very much on their own to develop their program. As early childhood educators, we have a major responsibility to plan and program effectively. We also have a great deal of power and influence which should not be misused.

As early childhood educators we are accountable to the children and families who use our setting, and to the early childhood field. To be perceived as professionals, our approach needs to reflect current research and ideas in early childhood education, and be evaluated constantly to ascertain its effectiveness.

THE PLANNING PROCESS

There is no 'blanket' method of planning that will be suitable for every setting. Each setting is different and will have different needs, strengths, and resources. If we think of each setting as a 'cake', then we consider the many different types, which have different ingredients, with different methods for being made, before the final result is achieved. If the 'cake' does not turn out right the first time, we try to work out why, and try a different ingredient or method. In addition, the size of the cake may mean we use different ingredients or methods to produce the result. This idea is illustrated in figure 5.2.

While each 'cake' is different, there is a general process that can be followed to achieve results, and the same is true for planning in early childhood settings. Planning is necessary for effective management of a program. It is a means of ensuring that the decisions we make concerning our organisation are helping to achieve the goals, aims and objectives developed by the setting and by government funding bodies.

Planning for each service will be different, but the steps in developing planning will be reasonably universal. These steps are outlined in figure 5.3.

Figure 5.2: The early childhood cake

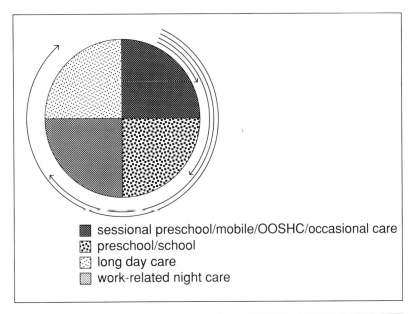

■ sessional preschool/mobile/OOSHC/occasional care
▨ preschool/school
▦ long day care
▩ work-related night care

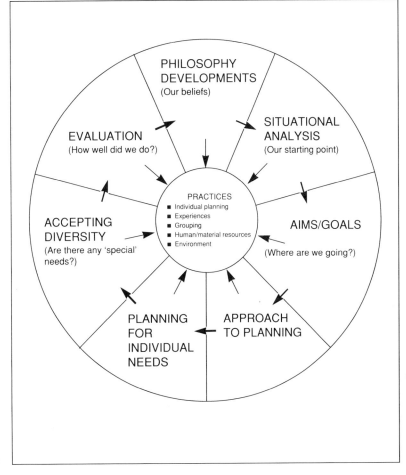

PHILOSOPHY
DEVELOPMENTS
(Our beliefs)

SITUATIONAL
ANALYSIS
(Our starting point)

EVALUATION
(How well did we do?)

PRACTICES
■ Individual planning
■ Experiences
■ Grouping
■ Human/material resources
■ Environment

ACCEPTING
DIVERSITY
(Are there any 'special'
needs?)

AIMS/GOALS

(Where are we going?)

PLANNING
FOR
INDIVIDUAL
NEEDS

APPROACH
TO PLANNING

Figure 5.3: The planning process

WHAT IS THE PLANNING PROCESS?

The planning process needs to have direction, which begins with philosophy/ideology. The first step in the process is to consider what type of program or 'cake' we would like (philosophy), and what ingredients go into making up that 'cake' (situational analysis). The philosophy of the setting will provide the broad direction for the program. The goals and aims should reflect this philosophy and the situational analysis, while also providing more detail about the direction of the program in a variety of areas, such as the types of learning experiences to be provided and methods of grouping children.

WHAT DOES PLANNING INVOLVE?

- A vision of what we want;
- A knowledge and understanding of the needs and wishes of the client group and the local community;
- Knowledge of the resources available;
- Awareness of the existing constraints;
- Accountability, in terms of responsibility for future directions; and
- Negotiation with major interest groups about desired outcomes and the means to achieve them.

Based upon this set of assumptions and an understanding of what is involved, we can then move onto developing goals for our particular setting.

SETTING GOALS

A goal (or aim) is a statement of broad direction (or purpose) based on identified needs and values. When a pursuit or need becomes purposeful, a desired place or objective can be worked toward by an individual or group. While goals may be idealistic and rather general, they are statements which establish direction. Formulating goals helps us to clarify our principles and confirm what is valued by the individual or group.

In an early childhood setting, group goals become important, as 'teamwork' is an effective way of working towards meeting goals. A goal needs to be desired by enough members of a group to get the group working towards its achievement.

WHY DO WE NEED TO HAVE GOALS WITHIN A SETTING?

Within an early childhood program it is important that everyone is working towards the same goals or aims in order to provide for consistency and cohesion in program implementation. We need to ensure that we have the support and involvement of families, staff, children and other groups such as management to achieve these goals. If goals are not fully understood, or are resisted, within any of these groups it is generally very difficult to achieve successful implementation.

Goals help to:

- reflect the philosophy in more concrete terms;
- reflect the issues raised in the situational analysis;
- provide the structure from which the program is developed; and
- assist us in evaluation.

The goals that we develop should state in general terms what the program is trying to achieve.

HOW DO WE FORMULATE GOALS FOR THE PROGRAM?

After the development of a philosophical basis and analysis of the situation, we should look at the needs of all groups connected with the setting and that impact on the program. These include the children, staff, families, local community, management and government.

Before considering a program for a particular setting, we must first look at the needs, strengths, attitudes, skills and knowledge that all of these groups bring to the setting. Then we should consider the characteristics of a high quality service and try to match the two to formulate our goals. The process of developing goals should involve input from all of the groups connected with the setting. This may be a lengthy and time consuming process, involving much discussion and some negotiating, but is essential if all of the various interests and needs of the group are to be truly considered. By involving everyone in the process of developing goals for the setting, we also help to ensure that there is a commitment from all to meeting these goals.

It is essential when developing goals that we are realistic about our situation and the resources that are available. Ambitious plans will fail without adequate resources. When formulating goals we need to take into account financial, staffing and time constraints, as well as the impact that our decisions may have on staff, children, families, and the local community, including other children's services.

HOW DO WE ACHIEVE THESE GOALS?

Goals alone are not enough. To achieve our goals we need to devise strategies, or a plan of action, to enable our goals to be reflected in the daily program. When strategies have been outlined, then a reasonable timeline for achieving each goal should be worked out, with tasks perhaps being assigned to particular people to make the implementation of each goal more manageable.

Priorities should be set. It may be more productive to focus on one or two areas at a time, rather than attempting to work on everything at once. If our energies are spread over too many areas at the same time, we may not achieve any of our goals.

QUESTIONS TO ASK WHEN GOAL SETTING

- What is the existing situation?
- Can time currently be organised to take this on?
- What does it really mean if we don't take this on?
- What would happen if we did take this on?

A decision to drop the goal or to keep going is taken.

If we decide to keep working on this goal:
- What would we like to see happen in this area?
- What information do we have to address this situation?
- What factors are influencing the situation (for example the setting, structures, staff, parents)?
- Given these influences, what extra information is needed?

Assessing information thus far, is this likely to be:
1. a priority goal?
2. short term goal?
3. long term goal?

- What steps might be taken towards this goal(tasks)?
- What are the current and projected time constraints?
- What is a possible timeline for when this might be achieved?
- How might we timetable towards this date?
- What do we do next week to start on this goal?
- How will we evaluate our progress?

(*Source:* Developed by Community Child Care Cooperative, NSW, 1987)

WHAT SHOULD HAPPEN WITH THESE GOALS?

Once goals have been developed they should be shared and discussed with all those involved in the setting. This can be accomplished in a variety of ways including both spoken and written means of communication. Once this is done, we need to ensure that the goals are reflected in the program and used as a basis for planning. As well, all members of the planning team should constantly reflect on the goals of the program as part of the evaluation process. We need to critically evaluate — on an ongoing basis — whether we are achieving our goals. An example of this process is outlined in figure 5.4.

OVERALL GOAL: to encourage family involvement in the program	
Implementations	**Evaluation**
■ After hours informal meetings for parent committee Aim: for parents to get to know each other and the staff	
■ Encourage all staff, parents and support services to have input in planning the program	
■ Get to know each child and their family by talking with them on an individual basis. Include pictures, puzzles, books, dolls, food that reflect each family's backgrounds	
■ Use newsletters and information boards, as well as arrival and departure times to communicate with families about program	
■ Discuss individual plans for children with their family	

Source: Forbes, French, Stacey, Wade, UWS Macarthur students, 1991

Figure 5.4: Format for evaluation of implementation of goals on a regular basis

QUESTIONS THAT MAY BE ASKED IN THE EVALUATION ARE:

■ Are we still aiming at the same goal/s? (Often goals change without us realising it!)

■ If we are still aiming to achieve the original goal/s are the strategies that we are using successful? If not, why not?

■ Are they the best strategies or does performance need to be reviewed?

■ Are we resourced sufficiently?

■ Is communication of the strategies effective?

■ Are there any problems? If so, what are they? Can they be overcome? How?

■ What needs to change in order to achieve the performance we want?

■ Can any aspect of the implementation plan be improved? At this point look at what is being done and who is doing it. Are they the best actions and people for the job?

■ Should this goal be higher or lower down on the priority list? Does it therefore need more or fewer resources? Are we doing the most important things first?

■ Is this goal working for the organisation generally? (*Source:* Lady Gowrie Child Centre, 1989)

FOCUS FOR PLANNING APPROACH

The focus of our approach to planning should reflect the program's values. We should clarify the difference between personal values and the program's values (which have become the focus for our philosophy and goals).

> Would you tell me please, which way to go from here? asked Alice. That depends a good deal on where you want to get to, said the cat. (Lewis Carroll, *Alice in Wonderland*)

Much of what goes on in the program reflects our values. One important aspect of developing a philosophy and goals for a service is that the processes undertaken help those involved to clarify their values and to establish which of these are shared by others. Many arguments about educational practices and policies are based on value differences. For example, the extent to which emphasis should be placed on academic skills as opposed to the acquisition of personal relationship skills and the development of creativity, is one issue that is often debated.

An example of the way that different values are reflected in programs may be seen by comparing programs that may be classified as formal with those classified as informal. The values underlying different programs may not always be openly articulated, however they are evident in the types of experiences implemented on a daily basis.

By comparing formal programs with informal programs the difference in reflected values is illustrated. (See figure 5.5).

Many aspects of planning will be affected by our focus, including the type of structure within the setting, the role of the adult and the types of experiences provided. One example of the potential for different approaches to an early childhood setting is the extent that the environment is structured by the adult. The organisation of the environment can be mainly adult-directed or it can be child-directed. The influence this has on the child's interaction with equipment, in turn influences the experience within the setting (see figure 5.6).

Settings will also vary in the extent to which the learning experiences are directed by the adult. Adult-directed, or teacher-directed, experiences usually require the adult's presence as the focus is on 'getting the content across' or on getting an 'acceptable' (in adult eyes) end-product. This may be a wall-hanging for the playroom or a craft item to take home, or the end-product may be measured in terms of skills or behaviours. Often adult-directed experiences are also adult-initiated, so the adult selects the children to take part in the experience, or 'directs' all children to the experience.

Child-directed experiences are generally ones children can partake in without an adult's presence being necessary. These are experiences that focus on the processes involved rather than on the end-product. Children are free to experiment with equipment and to solve problems, and to direct their own play. An adult may become involved as an

Formal setting underlying values	Informal setting underlying values
■ Acquisition of skills and knowledge important ■ Content important ■ Children need external motivation ■ Direct instruction is necessary so that children learn what they need to know ■ Children should meet set standards of achievement and behaviour	■ Exploring the environment and curiosity important ■ Processes important ■ Children are internally motivated ■ Children will choose what they need from a wide range of experiences ■ Development of independence and self-esteem emphasised
Practices	**Practices**
■ Emphasis on skills such as counting and letters of the alphabet ■ All children required to complete set activities ■ Focus on large group experiences ■ End-products that conform to adult standards valued ■ Large amount of time spent in direct teaching	■ Children encouraged to develop at their own pace ■ Children choose own experiences and complete to their own satisfaction ■ Focus on individual and small group experiences ■ Creativity and problem-solving valued ■ Adult seen as facilitator and guide

Figure 5.5: Formal versus informal settings underlying values and practices

observer or may join in children's play, extending an individual child's thinking or language where appropriate. Child-directed experiences are usually also initiated by the child, so that the child selects the experience he/she is interested in.

Sometimes settings are referred to as 'unstructured' or 'non-directed', whereas they are often actually structured by the child and child-directed. For children to feel some control over their lives and build a sense of competence and positive self-esteem, they must have choices about what happens in their day. Early childhood educators should provide opportunities for children to make choices and to engage in self-initiated play. This does not mean that the adult's role is to stand back and never initiate experiences or never take a major role in children's play for fear of interfering. A balance is required with the sensitive early childhood educator carefully observing children's play to determine the appropriate points to enter children's play or propose specific experiences (figures 5.7, 5.8 and 5.9).

Structured by adult	Structured by child
Adult decides on equipment	Child decides on equipment
Adult decides on place for equipment to go	Child decides on where equipment is to go
Equipment stays in one place	Children are free to move equipment around
Equipment set up with a particular concept in mind, e.g. classification	Children interact with equipment spontaneously

Figure 5.6: Structure of the learning environment.

Figure 5.7: An adult may join in children's play, or become involved as an observer.

Figure 5.8: A major part of the day for young children, particularly children under 3, is spent in routines and transition times. Objectives for children can be met during experiences such as meal times.

Figure 5.9: If children are to feel some control over what happens in their lives and to build a sense of competence as well as a positive self-esteem, then they need to have choices. It is important to explain to families and community the importance of choice for children.

WHAT MAKES AN 'EFFECTIVE' DAY FOR CHILDREN?

The effectiveness of a child's day will differ depending on the nature of the service and the child themselves. It is important, however, irrespective of the type of service, to have a balance throughout the day. Programs that are too adult-structured and are too adult-directed are inappropriate for young children. Such programs tend to stress the acquisition of knowledge and the mastery of skills while ignoring the child's interests. On the other hand, programs that provide too little structure from the adult and that are too child-directed are also developmentally inappropriate, as they may not give the stimulation and guidance from staff necessary for the child to grow and learn within a group setting.

The structure of the day should not be too rigid or merely instituted for the benefit of the staff. There should be a framework that provides for flexibility and individuality.

When trying to decide if there is too much structure in the day, look for children who:

- stay playing at an experience when it is time to pack away;
- ask if they can go outdoors/indoors when the 'program' tells them they are meant to be in a certain place;
- frequently ask if they can take equipment to other parts of the setting; and
- don't want to be where **you** want them to be.

An 'effective' day in any early childhood setting, whether it is preschool, long day care, family day care, school, or any other setting, is one that provides balance and caters for the needs of individual children. Throughout the day there should be alternating periods of quiet and active experiences, both in the indoor and outdoor environment, and a reasonable pace so that children are not constantly being hurried from one activity to the next. We should try to make the day flow as smoothly as possible for children and to make sure it is not full of stressful changes. Children should be provided with opportunities to select their own learning experiences and direct their own play, as well as enough time to fully explore and repeat experiences. This should be balanced with opportunities for small group experiences that may be initiated by an adult or by the children.

A major part of the day for young children, particularly for children under 3, is spent in routines and transition times. These times form a large part of the curriculum and should be planned for as much as any other part of the day, if not more so. Objectives for children can be met during any experience, including morning teatime or nappy change time. We should consider the learning potential of all experiences and make the most of the one-to-one and small group interactions that many routine and transition times provide. In this way routine times can be used effectively to meet individual children's needs.

Arrival time — Are children and families shown recognition? Is there someone available to greet children and families? Are families able to spend time in settling their child?

Self-selected experiences/Free play — Are children able to follow their own interests? Are children given time to relax into the setting? Does the program provide opportunities for individual and small group play? Can children choose between quiet or active experiences indoors and outdoors?

Transitions/Morning tea — Do these times cater for individual needs? Are these times planned tor'?

Self-selected experiences/Free play — Are individual children's needs being met? Are there opportunities for small group times with staff as well as individual experiences? Do you need to change over experiences from indoor to outdoor (or vice versa)?

Transition/Lunch time — Do these times provide for child choice, individualised pace, social interactions, and language development in small groups? Do adults spend time sitting down with children? Are these times used to meet individual children's objectives? Are these times planned for?

Transition/Rest time — Do routines take into account individual differences? Are short-sleepers and non-sleepers planned for? Are there quiet experiences available for these children? What is the atmosphere?

Transition — Does the program cater for children who wake up differently and at different times? Are there opportunities for interacting with children on a one-to-one basis?

Self-selected experiences/Afternoon tea — Does the program consider the amount of time children have spent in the setting and the time of day? Are individual differences and children's feelings catered for?

Packing away — Are children given 'warnings' prior to the time to pack away? Is this time viewed as a learning experience?

Quiet play/Small groups — Are children able to choose experiences and to choose whether to participate in group experiences? Again, are children and families shown recognition at departure times?

Figure 5.10: Questions to consider when planning effective days for young children

7.30	Children arrive, **quiet time, free play**, indoors (or more active play, outdoor play depending on children's energy levels and weather)	
8.30	**Free play** — indoors and outdoors, children choose based on interest **Morning Tea** set up — children eat when ready	**Small groups** – throughout morning different children may participate in small groups with adult for up to 30 minutes
11.30	**Pack away/transition** to lunch for younger children	**'Special' experiences** for older children
12.00	**Lunch** for younger children	
12.30	**Lunch** for older children	**Transition/sleep** for younger children
1.00	**Sleep/rest time** — children sleep/rest as needed, quiet activities for non-sleepers Gradually get up, quiet time (indoors or outdoors)	
3.00	**Afternoon Tea** set up — children come when ready **Free play** — indoors and outdoors, child choice	
5.00	**Pack away** — children involved as much as possible **Quiet play** indoors — individual/small group Gradual departures	
6.00	**Close**	

Figure 5.11: An example of a balanced day-long day care

Depending on the type of service, different factors such as the length of the day, the building design and the number of staff, will need to be taken into account when organising the day. The weather may also be a consideration, so that there may be a summer and winter program. Whether the setting is long day care, occasional care, pre-school, or the first years of school, it is important to think about what the day is like for children. Think about the time frame and what the focus of the program is and ask questions to help to design an 'effective day'. Does the organisation of the day reflect your philosophy and goals for the children? Does it provide balance?

When examining the structure of the day that we provide for children, we must consider the 'whole day'. Figures 5.10 to 5.13 and ideas can be used as starting points for discussion with staff in planning a day that reflects a child-centred approach.

9.00	Children arrive, family members free to stay if choose **Free play** — indoors and/or outdoors, child choice individual/small groups
10.00	**Morning Tea** — small groups, with staff
10.15	**Free play** — indoors and/or outdoors **Small groups** with staff throughout morning
11.45	**Pack away** Gradual **transition** to circle time (whole group)
12.00	**Circle time**, gradual **transition** to lunch
12.30	**Lunch** — small groups, with staff **Quiet activities** as children finish eating
12.30	**Gradual transition** to sleep/rest for those who need it
1.00	**Sleep/rest** **Quiet activities** for non-sleepers Limited free play choice for children as they wake up
1.30	**Free play** — indoors/outdoors, child choice
2.30	**Pack away**, gradual transition to indoors Limited free play choice
3.00	**Home**

Figure 5.12: An example of a balanced day-school

9.00	Children arrive, parents/carers stay if choose **Free play** — playgroups
9.15	**Transition** to classrooms **Developmental play** — indoors and outdoors Small groups/individual
9.45	Pack away/gradual **transition** to whole group

10.00	**Housekeeping**
	English Workshop:
	■ Uninterrupted Sustained Silent Reading
	   demonstrations, literacy experiences
	   (small group/individual; optional/compulsory)
	■ **transition**/whole class sharing/transition to recess

11.00	**Recess** — free play outdoors
11.15	**Transition** to classroom **Integrated unit/key learning area workshop:** ■ demonstrations, learning experiences (small group/individual; optional/compulsory) ■ whole class sharing
12.15	Pack away/**transition** to lunch
12.30	**Lunch, free play**
1.20	**Transition** to classroom
1.30	**Uninterrupted Sustained Silent Reading or rest**
1.50	**Integrated unit/key learning area workshop:** ■ demonstrations, learning experiences (small group/individual; optional/compulsory) ■ whole class sharing
2.50	■ **Packaway, housekeeping, rest**
3.10	■ **Home**

Figure 5.13: An example of a balanced day-school

The daily routine for each setting should be appropriate for the type of setting and the developmental needs of the children. The following is an example of the daily routine of the Magic Pudding Child Care Centre, Sydney, that provides extended hours care for forty children from birth to age 5.

7.30–8.00: Preparation time. One staff member is on duty to prepare the room and equipment in the small playroom. Children may arrive at this time but parents must remain with them until the centre opens at 8.00 a.m..

8.00–8.50: Indoor activities in the small room. Parents are asked to inform the staff of any changes to the child's normal routine. Any messages from parents should be written on the whiteboard. Staff greet children and family members on arrival and interact with children. As more staff arrive, outdoors is set up with children who wish to help.

8.50–10.00: Indoor/outdoor self-selected experiences. The children may move freely between the playground and the small room. At 9.00 a.m. morning tea is served and children eat in small groups with a staff member. Children are free to choose to eat or not and to leave the table when they are finished. At 9.30 two staff members change and toilet children as required.

10.00–11.30: Small groups occur, based on the developmental needs of children and skills of staff. Throughout the morning individual children's toilet, food and sleep needs are attended to by staff on that roster, and recorded for staff and family information.

11.30–12.00: Children help with packing away, setting up tables for lunch or putting out beds. As children are ready, they wash their hands and move to the lunch area.

12.00–12.40: Lunch time. Children sit in small groups of mixed ages with an adult at each table. Children serve and feed themselves and clear their place when finished, with adult assistance if required. As they are finished, children go outdoors.

12.40–1.30: Small groups of children are brought inside and assisted in getting ready for rest or sleep. Space is arranged to cater for long sleepers, short sleepers and resters. Each group of children is settled before another group is brought in, with resters being last to come inside.

1.30–3.00: Those children who had a morning sleep or who are not sleeping participate in quiet experiences either indoors or outdoors, depending on the weather. As children wake up they join in these experiences.

3.00–6.30: Indoor and/or outdoor self-selected experiences . Children move freely between the playground and the big playroom. Experiences are provided to cater for individual needs and spontaneous small group experiences occur. Afternoon tea is served when all of the children are awake, usually around 3.00 p.m. The outdoor and then the indoor area are gradually packed away, and children are encouraged to assist. A late snack is provided. Day care finishes at 6.30.

5.00–6.30: Indoor evening care. A separate room is set up to welcome the evening care children, away from day care children being collected to go home.

6.30–10.00: Dinner is prepared and day care children who are staying for evening care join the group. Older children may help to prepare the meal if they wish. Children eat in small groups with staff. After dinner children follow the routine indicated by their family, with some children participating in experiences, while others are doing homework, watching television or sleeping. Children are collected by 10.00.

TRANSITIONS

As shown in the above examples, transitions and routines form a large part of the day, and are therefore a large part of the learning process. Transitions can be classified as a passage, a change from one place, state, act, or set of circumstances to another.

Major transitions children may deal with are separating from care-givers, moving to a new house, going to hospital, child care or school. Transitions within settings usually deal with moving from one situation to another, such as freeplay to lunchtime or rest time. These times of the day are often classified as routines, things which happen each day at regular times.

Each individual reacts differently at these times. Some children will cry, some are withdrawn, and some react with behaviour that may seem inappropriate. This may be their way of coping.

Within our planning, it is important to consider what we want to happen at these transition times. Do we want the child directing and gaining control over his/her own behaviour or do we want the adult dominating?

Some factors to think about when trying to ease transition times are:

- How will movement occur?
- How can we prepare children for the transition? (perhaps by giving a prompt that it will be pack-away time soon)
- How will children probably be feeling at this time? (are they likely to be tired or active?)
- How many adults are available to ease the transition and assist children?
- How can we use the environment to lessen the need for transitions? (for example, can experiences remain set up, can there be a permanent meal area or sleep area?)

Transition times will be less stressful for children and adults when we involve children in the transition rather than direct them to do things and when we move children individually or in small groups. Gradual transitions in small groups result in waiting time for children being minimised and makes 'crowd control' unnecessary. Transitions can be kept to a minimum by planning large blocks of time and providing for individual and small group transitions.

BRINGING IT ALL TOGETHER

The overall planning *format* that a service uses should 'bring it all together' and include ways of incorporating the needs of individual children and small groups. The planning format may be a daily or weekly format; the way the setting records its practices.

WHY WRITE DOWN PLANS?

An important aspect of the planning process is documentation. When we write plans down it helps us to clarify our goals and articulate more precisely to others what we are doing and why. As plans can be available to other staff (including relief workers), families, and visitors, we are able to communicate our goals to others and maintain accountability. Written plans also help us to evaluate and make changes to our planning, by providing us with ongoing information about children and the program which can be used for future planning.

HOW CAN WE PLAN EFFECTIVELY AND EFFICIENTLY?

We need to plan for a wide range of aspects within an early childhood setting, including individual children, small groups and the total environment (other chapters within this book devote in-depth sections to planning within each of these areas). How can we record these plans for the total environment and involve all members of the team?

Each setting should develop a planning format that suits the needs of the setting and that staff feel comfortable working with. Some of the issues that should be taken into account include the method of planning (individuals or teams), staff skills, the style of the programme and the way the environment is used.

Each setting will have a different format or model for planning, but there are certain criteria or organisers that should be considered and incorporated in a planning format. These include:

■ the focus of planning (that is, the main feature of the planning format as outlined below);
■ the use of time throughout the day, including routine times;
■ the use of space and the total environment (indoor and outdoor space, room arrangements and so on);
■ use of resources, including both material and human resources;
■ learning experiences;
■ methods of grouping children throughout the day;
■ individual children's needs; and
■ evaluation.

The overall design of the planning format will reflect the philosophical base from which the setting is planned, so that the major focus may be: the child; the experiences; curriculum or developmental areas; the physical environment or another feature considered important in the philosophy of the setting.

A setting may choose to use several different formats, depending upon the needs and style of the program. The type of format will also be affected by the staff involved. It is important to develop **planning methods** that everyone can use. Make them simple and to the point! See figures 5.14 to 5.25.

WHAT WILL INFLUENCE THE TYPE OF FORMAT/MODEL USED?

One of the issues that will influence the planning format adopted by a setting is the amount of preparation time available for planning, and whether staff plan individually or in teams. The skills and personal preferences of staff should also be established, as staff bring a variety of skills to a setting and will have preferences for certain planning formats. For example, some staff may prefer to use diagrams rather than formats set out in columns. Staff turnover may also be a factor determining the most appropriate planning format, as high staff turnover may limit the effectiveness of some formats. If staff turnover is high, the format will need to enable new members of staff to fit in easily.

The type of planning format that is most appropriate for a particular setting is likely to change as circumstances change. Ongoing evaluation of the effectiveness of the selected planning methods is essential to ensure that they are meeting the needs of children, families and staff.

WHEN CAN WE PLAN?

It is essential that staff are given the necessary time to plan effectively as written plans cannot be done adequately when there is only 5 minutes allocated at the end of the day, or staff are expected to plan in their breaks.

Staff need sufficient planning time to be able to:

- add to developmental records;
- formulate objectives;
- draw up plans for individual and group experiences;
- include these aspects on the overall planning format; and
- evaluate planning.

Planning time may be allocated for one member of staff at a time, or for a planning team, depending on the method of planning utilised by the setting. Planning teams may be organised around developmental stages, ages, spaces (for example, one team plans for indoors and one team plans for outdoors) and so on. At least an hour a week planning time should be allocated to allow staff time to reflect and evaluate, as well as to formulate and write up plans for the week ahead.

HOW CAN WE MAKE CHANGES TO THE PROGRAM?

Evaluation is an important aspect of planning. If the program is not working effectively, modifications may need to be made. Regular evaluation usually means that only minor changes are required; for a yearly evaluation, major changes may be needed. As we all know, it is more difficult to bring about major changes.

Change is a source of stress and the magnitude of the change will determine the amount of stress that is generated. When looking at introducing innovative approaches we need to be aware of the obstacles to change and to devise strategies to help everyone view change as positive. Sometimes, in our enthusiasm to introduce new ideas, we may forget that not everyone else will see things the way that we do and be so interested in change.

Changes are taking place all the time in early childhood settings. These may be changes in staff or in the children and families we work with, or changes in government regulations and guidelines. Often people are resistant to change, and see it as something threatening. This may be the case when staff are asked to make changes in their daily practices and do not see the need for these changes. They may feel that: 'This is the way we have always done things and it works'. Often negative feelings towards change result from a feeling of powerlessness. People may feel that these changes are imposed upon them.

WHAT MAKES CHANGE DIFFICULT?

Greenman (1988) outlines three major reasons why change is often so difficult to introduce.

1. People do what they know how to do, and most of the time they believe in what they are doing. A change can be seen as a personal threat, perhaps resulting in the person no longer feeling that they are valued by the organisation.

2. In an institution, each individual's actions and desires are meshed with the actions of others, so that if one staff member makes a change, this will affect others. It requires more than one staff member to be motivated, and to be receiving training, for change to be successfully implemented.

3. Change takes time. People need time to think, meet, and plan, and to work through any problems that arise. For changes to persist, stability in staff and material resources is often needed.

HOW CAN WE COPE WITH CHANGE?

Some people have the ability to adapt to change better than others. Those who are open to challenges and exploring new ideas, feel secure within the situation and willing to take risks, are more likely to see change as an opportunity for growth. When introducing changes we need to plan them carefully, taking into account what we know about the staff and the existing situation. Below are some ideas for assisting staff to cope with change (based upon a range of sources including Schrag, Nelson and Siminowsky (1985)).

BUILDING A CREATIVE STAFF

Staff need to feel that their ideas are valued, and to feel comfortable in offering ideas and sharing information and skills. Open communication is an important factor in developing creativity. We need to foster an atmosphere where all ideas are given a hearing and taken seriously. Staff members need a supportive environment where they are given recognition for their ideas and the necessary resources to draw upon to generate innovative ideas. A creative staff are more likely to see change as a challenge rather than a threat.

AVOIDING BLIND SPOTS

It is important that we try to understand the concerns of others and to see the situation from their perspective. Our enthusiasm for a new idea can often blind us to the feelings of others and prevent us from seeing what is really happening. We must ensure that there are opportunities to explore each person's feelings about the proposed change and the time to be able to work through these.

KEEPING OTHERS INFORMED

Both staff and parents need information about what is happening and why. Fear of change is often fear of the unknown. Much of the anxiety about change can be dissipated by keeping others informed both before and after any change. Discussing any changes that are going to occur, what has prompted these changes, and the impact that they may have will help people adapt to changes. When changes are seen to be meeting the goals of the organisation, they are likely to be supported by others.

INVOLVING STAFF IN THE CHANGE PROCESS

When staff are involved in a planning change they have a vested interest in seeing that it succeeds, and will put a great deal of effort into ensuring that their plan works. For staff to be able to participate effectively in decision making they need to be able to clarify what the task or 'problem' is and to have the opportunity to offer suggestions. Participation only works if those asked to participate feel that they are contributing and not just being asked for a rubber stamp approval. Change should be viewed as a participatory process and acknowledgment given to the fact that if people do not see change as necessary then it probably won't work.

ALLOWING TIME

Staff need time to experiment, give feedback, ask questions and revise plans if changes are to be more than surface changes. Time should be allocated for staff to visit other settings to make observations and interact with other staff. Change involves learning. We need to remember that learning takes time and that staff are individuals and therefore will react differently and learn at their own pace.

Figures 5.14 to 5.25 are examples of formats that have been developed to meet the unique needs of individual settings.

Figure 5.14

DATE: DAY:

Morning focus	Table 1 Green mat	Table 2 Green mat	Table 3 Green mat	Table 4	Table 5	Large mat	Green mat

Outside focus	Veranda activities Green area	Yard activities	Sand area

Afternoon focus	Table 1 Green mat	Table 2 Green mat	Table 3 Green mat	Table 4 Other	Table 5	Large mat	Grey mat

Source: Cavendish Street Child Care Centre, Sydney 1990

Figure 5.15

| PROGRAM FOR THE WEEK ENDING... GROUP .... |

TIMETABLE	ROUTINE	ORGANISATION/STAFF

CHILDREN FOR INDIVIDUAL CONSIDERATION:

EVALUATION/FUTURE PLANNING:

Source: Furry and Whitters, 1990

Figure 5.16

STIMULATION	STAFF/CHILD	PROCEDURES/ACTIVITIES
Language		
Self		
Perceptual		
Sensory		
Fine/Gross motor		
Set-up – Clean Up		
Arrival/Settling		
Changing		
Feeding		
Sleeping		

Source: Furry and Whitters, 1990

Figure 5.17

	MONDAY	TUESDAY	WEDNESDAY	THURSDAY	FRIDAY
EARLY					
EVALUATION:					
AM					
EVALUATION:					
PM					
EVALUATION:					
LATE					
EVALUATION:					

Figure 5.18

Investigation	Language and Literature	Creative Arts	Physical	Children
				To observe
				To plan for
				To observe
				To plan for

Figure 5.19

DAILY PROGRAM

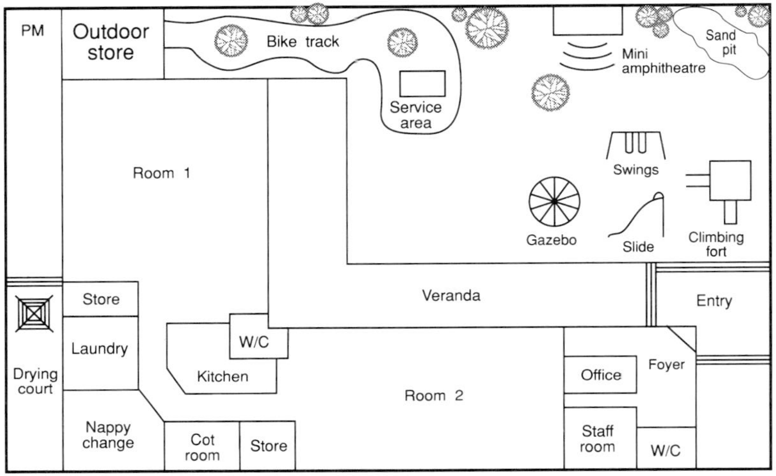

AM

Sand pit
Mini amphitheatre
Swings
Slide
Climbing fort
Entry
Gazebo
Office
Staff room
Foyer
W/C
Veranda
Room 2
Bike track
Service area
Outdoor store
Room 1
Store
Laundry
Nappy change
W/C
Kitchen
Cot room
Store
Drying court

PM

Sand pit
Mini amphitheatre
Swings
Slide
Climbing fort
Entry
Gazebo
Office
Staff room
Foyer
W/C
Veranda
Room 2
Bike track
Service area
Outdoor store
Room 1
Store
Laundry
Nappy change
W/C
Kitchen
Cot room
Store
Drying court

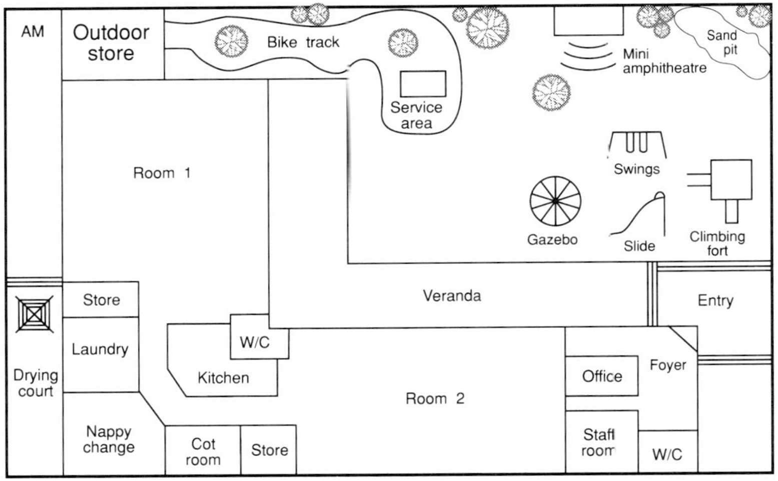

DATE:.............	ACTIVITIES	RESOURCES
STAFF 1. 4. 2. 5. 3. 6.	AM	AM
PROGRAM	PM	PM

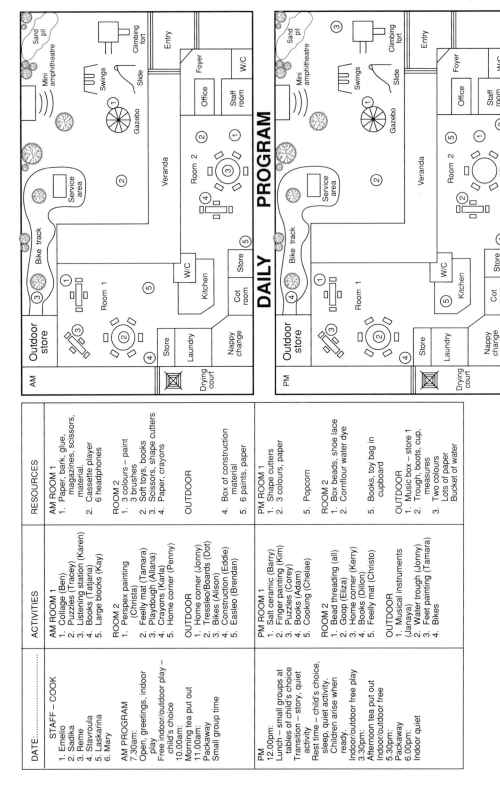

Source: Richards, UWS-Macarthur Student 1991

Figure 5.20: A working example of figure 5.19

Figure 5.22: Evaluation of planning in figures 5.19 and 5.20.

EVALUATION... DAY .... DATE		
EXPERIENCES	RESOURCES	TIME

(Richards UWS-Macarthur student 1991)

Figure 5.22

BIG ROOM SETUP
Date 20th – 24th MAY 91
Time AFTERNOON
Staff JENNY & TONI

Resources
BABY MAT — A frames, boards
tyres, pillows, PLAYDOUGH, Rice
BRIGHT GREEN.

Construction
M Poly M
T Struts
W Polydron
T Animals
R Large Lego

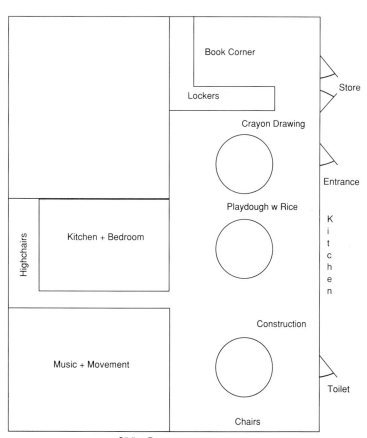

Rationale
BABY MAT – GROSS MOTOR — gives opportunities to provide a low gross motor mat to allow E. whos learning to walk to pull to stand on A frames etc.
MUSIC + MOVEMENT — during last week's program I noticed children L., J., H., involved in music + movement. I want to extend this activity by involving all children by using the Wiggy Woo tape.
PLAYDOUGH + MIX + MESS — A soothing activity for M.to extend her eye-hand coordination and social skills.

Source: Magic Pudding Child Care Centre 1991

Figure 5.23

OUTDOOR

Date 20th – 24th May

Time Morning

Staff Mary, Lolita, Caitlin (student)

Resources Musical, string, balls, cooking equipment, block corner, obstacle course.

Rationale Will provide activities to encourage involvement from Mimi, Nina, Alex and Jana who all are a little anxious and unsettled at the present time. Have noted when these children are engrossed in play, they relax and get on with their business. Will endeavour to provide plenty of opportunity for this to happen with the children.

Source: Magic Pudding Child Care Centre 1991

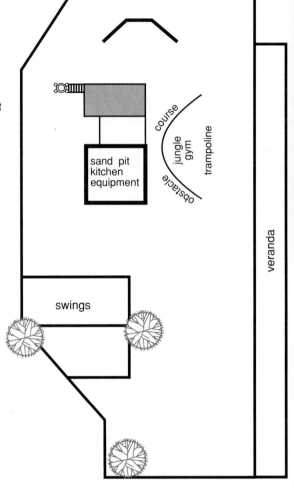

Figure 5.24: Evaluation of planning in figures 5.22 and 5.23.

OBSERVATION/EVALUATION — COMMENTS Area evaluated	Signature and Date
....	....
....	....
....	....
....	....
....	....

Source: Magic Pudding Child Care Centre 1991

Figure 5.25

	Any reminders of things to follow up.

DATE
    Any special events such as visitors, birthdays, notes to send home etc.
 	
EARLY AM
    Activities planned for this time, any special notes re-communication with parents and children.
 	
MORNING TEA
    Any special plans or set up.	

	EVALUATION

AM SESSION — MIXED AGED GROUPING

Layout of indoors
with individual focus resources
listed

Outdoors set up with individual focus.
Resources briefly listed if necessary.

SMALL GROUPS

TIME   PLANNED

If staff wish to utilise room,
"book" it to avoid clashes of
use of room and resources.

FORT
Any activities
occuring on
fort

SAND
Resources
listed for
sand play

LUNCH
    Any special activities, set-up individual focus.

REST/SLEEP
    Any individual focus.
    Activities set up in older room.
    Any special activities.

PM SESSION

YOUNGER
    Layout of activities, individual
    focus, resources.

OLDER
    As above

Any changes for afternoon.

FORT

SAND

AFTERNOON TEA
    Any special set-up, changes, individual focus.

LATE PM
    Activities planned, any special features such as communication with parents etc.

Evaluation, any special features, changes for next time. Individual observations written onto children's records.

Source: Smith, UWS-Macarthur Student 1990

EVALUATING AND MODIFYING

Close and continuous monitoring of the changes allows the centre or school to gauge the effects on staff, children and families. To be truly innovative and open to change we need to be constantly evaluating and making modifications where necessary. Any plan for change should be structured to allow for evaluation and flexibility to modify when things are not working.

HOW CAN WE PLAN FOR CHANGE?

Planning for change involves analysing the existing situation and recognising staff needs, developing goals and devising a sequence of planned steps. The following models may assist in planning changes.

MODEL 1

Problem/Objective	What problem do we want to overcome? What do we aim to achieve?
Resources/Opportunities	What time, staffing and equipment do we have available?
Constraints	What constraints exist? How will these affect the methods of change?
Achievements	Did the change meet existing needs? Did it overcome problems? Can it be extended?

MODEL 2

Methods of change:

1. Objectives	■ Goals to be established
2. Consensus	■ Discussion of alternatives
3. Group project	■ Resources available ■ Roles for each group member ■ Visits to other services/staff ■ Inservice
4. Evaluation	■ How will we know if goals are met?
5. Implementation	■ What is the agreed upon period?

MODEL 3

Step 1:   Develop a goal statement.

Step 2:   Collect information.
Consider: *What is hindering movement towards this goal?*
What is helping?

Step 3:   Generate options. Brainstorm to come up with as many options
as possible.

Step 4:   Select preferred option/s through informal discussion or developing
a chart with the advantages and disadvantages of each option.

Step 5:   Develop a plan of action.

Step 6:   Implement the plan.

MODEL 4

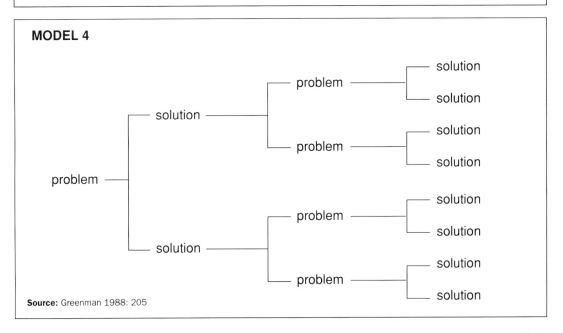

Source: Greenman 1988: 205

The more people you involve in this process, the more ideas will be
generated. When problems are shared with others through meetings,
photographs, and copies of plans on the noticeboard and in newsletters
a wide ranging pool of ideas, drawing on a variety of past experiences,
can be called on to help generate solutions and to forsee possible
problems.

Sharing information and exchanging ideas with other early childhood
settings can help in creative problem solving and with the analysis of
issues. Visiting other settings, writing articles about changes introduced

and the processes involved, and talking with others can help facilitate change. Networking is helpful, as others are likely to have faced similar problems. Others can benefit from learning about the successes and problems, creative solutions, and ideas that did and did not work and why, within our setting.

In conclusion, what is likely to contribute to making the child's experience in an early childhood setting a positive and high quality one is when the selected planning approach is responsive to and tailored to the philosophy and values of all participants. That is, not only the children, but the families and staff, as well as the contextual features of the setting itself. For a planning approach to be implemented effectively, it needs to be developed through co-operative team efforts within the setting.

USEFUL RESOURCES

Greenman, J. (1988) *Caring Spaces, Learning Places: Children's Environments That Work*. Redmon, W.A. Exchange Press Inc.

Harison, L. (1990) Planning Appropriate Learning Environments for Children Under Three. *Australian Early Childhood Resource Booklet*. ACT. Australian Early Childhood Association.

Lambert, B., Clyde, M. and Reeves, K. (1987) Planning for Individual Needs in Early Childhood Services. *Australian Early Childhood Resource Booklet*. ACT. Australian Early Childhood Association.

6

PLANNING FOR INDIVIDUALS

INTRODUCTION

If we value each child as a unique individual, with their own strengths, needs, interests and past experiences and their own unique family background, then we should plan experiences that foster that individual development. In any early childhood setting, individual children should be the starting point for program planning. As early childhood educators, we must find out about each child in our setting, by talking with the child's family, and by undertaking regular observations of the child in a variety of situations throughout the day.

All planning should start with observations of each child's behaviour and developing skills, and the professional interpretation of these. Once information is gathered relating to family background and parent expectations, the implications for future planning can be considered and long term objectives formulated. Each long term objective can then be broken down into short term objectives and appropriate learning experiences and teaching strategies planned to meet each child's needs. Ongoing evaluation of each child's development towards meeting objectives and continuous observations are used to review objectives and teaching strategies and to plan suitable follow-up experiences (figure 6.1).

THE FIRST STEP — OBSERVATIONS

Ongoing observations of individual children, and the recording of these observations, provide insights into each child's developmental strengths. Detailed observations of behaviour and skills over time enable early childhood educators to build up a comprehensive 'picture' of the 'whole child'. We can observe the child's behaviour when playing; we can see what a child is doing during an experience, with the equipment or in

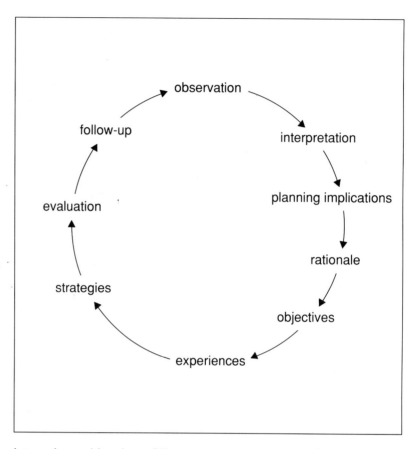

Figure 6.1: The planning cycle

interactions with others. We cannot see processes such as 'thinking', 'wondering' or 'reasoning'. Processes cannot be directly observed as they are internal — they can only be inferred based upon what we observe and then interpret. This happens after we collect information about the child through observations.

A range of observation methods should be used in a variety of different contexts, to gain specific information about each child's strengths in all areas of development. These observations of events in a child's day are also valuable to share with family members on a daily basis. Detailed, descriptive accounts of each child's interactions with their peers and the environment will provide a much sounder foundation for planning and for discussing a child's progress with families, than relying on checklists and rating scales. Checklists and rating scales do not indicate how a child responds in different situations or provide specific examples. This can result in children being placed in a testing situation in order for the checklist or rating scale to be completed.

To assist decision making about which observation method may be most appropriate for different children and situations, the following questions may be useful:

■ Why do you want to observe the child/situation?

- Who will do the observing?
- Who/what will be observed?
- Where will be most appropriate?
- When will be most appropriate?
- What type of method will be most appropriate based on above information?

WAYS TO OBSERVE CHILDREN

ANECDOTAL RECORDS

This type of observation is a 'story', or anecdote, about the child's behaviour. The observation starts when the child begins to participate in an experience, an interaction or with equipment, and ends when the child finishes participating. Therefore, this type of observation may be short or long depending on the incident. These observations can be maintained with a card file or folder for each child, where anecdotal information is recorded on a regular basis (figure 6.2). Anecdotal records should record details of what the child said and/or did during the period of the observation. As much detail as possible should be recorded, including the child's tone of voice, facial expressions and so on. In this way a picture of the 'whole child' can be built up over time.

A quick method for recording in a setting may be having a notebook handy, for example hanging from a hook in an accessible place.

CHILD'S NAME:	OBSERVER:	DATE:
D.O.B.:	SETTING:	TIME:
TIME FINISHED:		

Figure 6.2: Anecdotal records

SAMPLES OF WORK

Each child's 'work' in a variety of areas can be collected over a period of time, and compared at a later date. Work collected could include samples of the child's art and craft, writing samples, audio tapes of oral language or reading, and photographs or sketches of construction. One of the advantages here is that the child is not being compared with external standards, but with their own standard of progression (or perhaps re-gression) from earlier work.

TIME SAMPLES

Recording behaviour at regular time intervals — for example every thirty minutes, or every ten minutes, or at routine times — can be used to document a child's behaviour at a certain time of the day — for example on arrival, or at meal times — or to give a 'whole' picture of the child's day. Time samples can indicate the play experiences that a child is most interested in and the amount of time they spend at each experience. Time samples may focus on a particular area of behaviour, such as the child's interactions with peers (figure 6.3).

CHILD'S NAME:	D.O.B.:	OBSERVER:
TIME COMMENCED:	TIME INTERVALS:	DATE:
10.00		
10.30		
11.00		
11.30		
12.00		

Figure 6.3: Time samples

DIARIES (RUNNING RECORDS)

A diary records everything a child says and does during a set period of time. The time should be recorded regularly during the observation to aid in later interpretation. A diary is a method of faithfully recording actions and dialogue by describing what happens as it is happening (figure 6.4). Therefore a diary record tends to be for a short time span, for example, five minutes.

Diaries can also be recorded in visual form (as illustrated in figure 6.5), and this may be useful for tracking a young child's movements over a prescribed time period.

SOCIOGRAMS

These can be used to examine the patterns of social interactions of a particular child or group of children. Sociograms can record who the child interacts with, as well as the frequency of interactions, initiations and responses. They can also provide details about the adult's behaviour and interactions with a group of children (figure 6.6).

CHILD'S NAME:	D.O.B.:	OBSERVER:
TIME COMMENCED:	TIME FINISHED:	DATE:
SETTING:		
9.30		
9.31		
9.32		
9.33		
9.34		
9.35		

Figure 6.4: Diary (running record)

INTERVIEWS, SELF-REPORTS AND QUESTIONNAIRES

These methods are useful with older children who are able to contribute a great deal of information about themselves — what they are doing and why. These do not have to be formal and can involve children interviewing and reporting to each other as well as to an adult.

AUDIO AND VIDEO RECORDINGS

Using a video camera, individual children can be observed throughout the day to obtain a picture of the child's 'typical day', or children can be observed engaged in a learning experience (such as sand play), or during routine times. The advantages of using video cameras are that recordings can be shared with the child's family and can also be used by staff to gain further insight into a child's interactions. Audio recordings can capture language, giving a full record for later interpretation. Detailed analysis is time-consuming so close examination of carefully selected excerpts is recommended.

CHECKLISTS AND RATING SCALES

These offer a systematic way of recording specific behaviours or actions. Checklists and rating scales can be useful in focusing attention on a particular aspect of the child, the adult or the program. One problem with

CHILD'S NAME: D.O.B.:   OBSERVER:

TIME COMMENCED: TIME FINISHED: DATE:

SETTING:

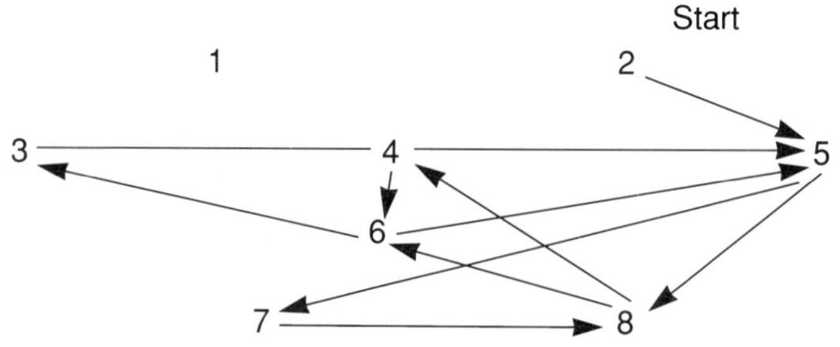

KEY: 1 = book corner; 2 = puzzles; 3 = family corner; 4 = easel painting; 5 = play dough; 6 = bathroom; 7 = farm animals; 8 = block area

Figure 6.5: Visual form of a diary

adopting a list or scale developed by others is that the items listed may not be relevant to the situation or purpose (figures 6.7 and 6.8). It may be more appropriate when using these methods to develop your own checklists and rating scales so they relate specifically to the situation. A further limitation with these methods is that they only require a tick in a box, and do not provide very much detail about the child.

In summary, through observations we are able to:

- get to know about individual children;
- study interactions in groups;
- find out about children's strengths;
- identify where children may be having difficulties; and
- evaluate the effectiveness of strategies used by adults.

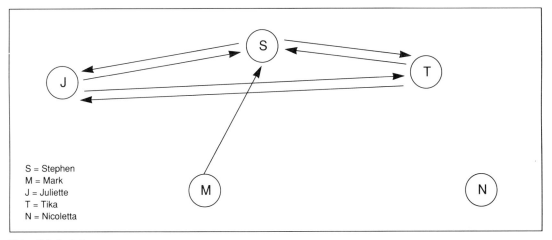

S = Stephen
M = Mark
J = Juliette
T = Tika
N = Nicoletta

Figure 6.6: Sociogram

CHECKLIST: GROSS MOTOR

CHILD'S NAME: D.O.B.:   DATE:

	YES	NO	COMMENT
Climbs ladder — 100 cm			
Runs easily			
Walks on tiptoe			
Balances on one foot — 5 secs			

Figure 6.7: Checklist

RATING SCALE: FINE MOTOR			
CHILD'S NAME:	D.O.B.	DATE:	
	ABOVE AVERAGE	SATISFACTORY	WITH DIFFICULTY
Uses scissors			
Holds pencil			
Writes name			
Threads five small beads			

Figure 6.8: Rating scale

When we collect information about children in early childhood settings it is important to take note of the following issues.

Confidentiality — Any information and interpretations of a child's development should only be shared with the family of that child and staff working with that child. Permission from the family should always be obtained if this information needs to be shared with resource workers or students on placement for practical experiences.

Unobtrusiveness — When undertaking observations of children try to be as unobtrusive as possible. While it is virtually impossible to be 'invisible', as children will want to interact with the observer, or often ask what you are writing, try not to be obvious by following the child around constantly, or by carrying a big folder and 'marking' off everything the child does. If the observer is obvious all the time, this will affect the child's behaviour and therefore alter the validity of the information.

Ongoing observations — Try to build up a comprehensive 'picture' of the child by using many different methods of observation in a variety of situations, and gathering information over a period of time rather than making assumptions based upon one observation.

INTERPRETATIONS

Once information has been gathered about a child across all developmental areas over a period of time, this information should be analysed or interpreted. We should ask what this tells us about the child to gain better insights into the child's development. Interpreting involves making inferences about the meaning of our descriptions of children's behaviour and interactions.

Lengthy interpretations are not always necessary, or even possible, for each observation. A number of observations may be collected and interpreted at the one time, to gain an overall picture of the child's development.

When interpreting observations it is essential to keep our minds open to all possible interpretations and to draw on a number of different observations in a variety of contexts before establishing areas of developmental concern. Working within a team approach and sharing observations and possible interpretations with other staff can help us to view a child's behaviour from different perspectives. Family members can also offer new insights into a child's behaviour. In this way we are better able to gain balanced and valid interpretations grounded on sufficient data. Figure 6.9 is an example of one method used to collect information about a child.

It is important to consider both the strengths and needs of each child. Strengths in areas of development or areas of learning that the child particularly enjoys can be identified, and interesting and stimulating experiences can then be planned to further consolidate or extend these skills. Any extensive delays in development or difficulties in certain situations must be identified based on an understanding of the child's growth and development. Planning may focus on providing a child with more opportunities to develop behaviours in particular areas.

POINTS TO REMEMBER ABOUT INTERPRETATION

- It is based upon an understanding of children's growth and development and of the individual child.
- The observer makes an inference based on observation, that is, interpretation follows observation.
- Try not to interpret based on insufficient evidence, that is, only one or two observations of a particular child.
- All conclusions are tentative and need to be continually revised and modified as children's behaviour is constantly changing and developing.
- Try to keep interpretations objective and unemotional. This is difficult due to interpreter bias — both from a theoretical and personal basis. It is difficult to not allow our personal feelings about a child, or our philosophical approach to education to affect our interpretations of situations. However, we need to be aware of these in order to be as objective as possible.

DEVELOPMENTAL SUMMARIES

Developmental summaries, or developmental records, are a way of organising information, including relevant background and family information, into a profile of each child. These records can be organised in a variety of ways to suit your needs and the needs of the service.

OBSERVATION

NAME: **D.O.B.:**

NOTE CHILD'S PERFORMANCE AS YOU SEE IT.

GROSS MOTOR (running, walking, free movement, use of equipment, climbing)

FINE MOTOR (cutting, art and craft, hand/eye coordination, drawing, threading, picking up etc.)

THINKING/REASONING (problem solving, puzzles, concentration, matching, attention span etc.)

SELF-HELP SKILLS (dressing, eating, food utensils, toiletting, care of own things, seeking help when needed etc.)

EMOTIONAL STABILITY (separation from parent, tantrums, coping with frustration, uncontrolled crying, reliance on adults etc.)

USE OF LANGUAGE (voice control, vocabulary, communicating to adults, communicating to children, clarity of speech etc.)

UNDERSTANDING LANGUAGE (following directions, understanding questions, listening skills, discrimination of words and sound etc.)

SOCIAL SKILLS (positive/negative behaviour, turn-taking/sharing, interactions with others)

PLAY (type of play, complexity of play, inventiveness, variety)

OTHER COMMENTS

OBJECTIVES

Figure 6.9: Collecting information about a child (Magic Pudding Child Care Centre, Sydney)

Each developmental summary should include the child's name and date of birth, as well as any relevant background information. This may include the date the child started attending the service, whether attendance is on a full-time or part-time basis, and information on medical history or allergies. Other information to be included may relate to the language/s spoken in the child's home (and who speaks these), the family's values and beliefs and their expectations for their child. Some families may not want to divulge this information and their right to not do so should be respected. All information recorded in a child's developmental summary should be treated as confidential and be available for discussion with the child's family at their request.

Information gathered from observations across all developmental areas should be summarised clearly and concisely, with each entry being dated. Positive statements of what the child can do provide more useful information on developing skills rather than statements of what she/he can't do — for example, 'J. skips with a galloping motion' rather than 'J. can't skip', or 'S. speaks Vietnamese fluently at home and is beginning to develop skills in the English language', rather than 'S. can't speak English'. Developmental records are usually organised so that information can be grouped into developmental areas. Different people will group areas of development in different ways, or use different terminology. What is important is that all areas of development are covered and that the information is organised in such a way that it can be easily followed and added to by those working in the setting.

Figures 6.10 to 6.12 are examples of developmental record formats developed by staff in early childhood settings.

Developmental summaries assist us in monitoring a child's growth and development over time. By dating and continually adding to developmental summaries we are able to look back and note the child's progress in different developmental areas. Children's progress is compared to their previous stage of development and their interests, rather than to other children and 'developmental norms'. Developmental summaries (figure 6.13) provide useful indicators of a child's progress to be shared with families, as well as information on which to base individual planning.

When summarising information for developmental summaries, it may become apparent that there are gaps in our information concerning a particular child's development, for example we may have no information relating to the child's strengths, needs and interests in the area of sensory development. This may indicate that we need to focus future observations on this area, or it may mean that we need to evaluate the existing program to ascertain if we are providing suitable opportunities for children to engage in sensory play. If the program does include ample opportunities for sensory play but the child we are observing does not become involved in these experiences, we may need to consider ways of integrating sensory experiences into the child's play, or assisting sensory development in some other way, such as at routine times. It would also be useful to discuss with the child's family the child's interests at home and their observations of his or her play, as well as family expectations.

Child's Name .... Date of Birth............./............./19 ......

Date	Cognitive	Language	Motor physical	Social emotional	Sensory

Figure 6.10: Developmental record format

Week beginning

Name:	Name:
Fine motor	Cognitive
Name:	**Name:**
Gross Motor	Social/personal
Name:	**Name:**
Self Help	Language

Figure 6.11: Developmental record format

Child profile

Name ....   **Date of Birth**.............../ ..../**19**........

Background Information	Physical Development	Language Development
(Siblings, medical history)	*Fine Motor:* *Gross Motor:*	*Receptive:* *Expressive:*
Social Development	Intellectual Development	Objectives
	Problem Solving: *Numeracy Skills:* *Jigsaw puzzles:* *Seriation and Classification:*	

Source: Walker, student UWS-Macarthur
Figure 6.12: Developmental record format

PLANNING IMPLICATIONS

Once a developmental summary has been compiled for a child, the next step is to consider the implications of this information for future planning. Planning implications are positive plans for action, or future directions for planning, based on strengths and needs as identified in the developmental summary and take into consideration the child's interests, and family background and expectations. Plans for the child in each developmental area, focusing on acknowledging and/or extending on existing skills, should be regularly monitored to account for new information.

Figure 6.13: Developmental summaries assist staff in monitoring a child's growth and development. Individual staff may choose to work on records for a particular group of children — but share this with other staff to assist in planning.

The next step in the planning process involves making decisions about which developmental area or areas as identified in the planning implications, will be focused on for an individual child in a particular planning period — that is, this week, or month or term. These decisions will be based on our understanding of the individual child's developmental strengths and needs as well as a knowledge of child growth and development. They may also reflect family wishes and aims for the child, as well as the impact that this area of strength or need may have on other aspects of development. The format in figure 6.14 is an example of how this information may be recorded.

COMPONENTS OF PLANNING

When planning for individual children we need to consider the following steps:

1. **Rationale** — Why are we doing this? That is, why are we deciding this area of development is important?
2. **Objective** — What do we hope the child will experience or have an opportunity to achieve? This may be broken down into long and short term.

Date	Planning implications	Objectives

Figure 6.14: Recording planning implications

3. Experience — What range of learning experiences can be utilised to help the child to meet the objective?

4. Strategies — What is the adult's role?

5. Evaluation — How did it all go? That is, do we need to change any of the above aspects for next time?

Even the most experienced early childhood educator needs to write specific plans which provide for a focus on individual children, however the amount of detail included on planning formats will vary according to staff skills and the needs of the setting. As staff develop experience in planning less writing may be required, however all of the components of the planning process need to be kept in mind and their appropriateness evaluated on an ongoing basis. The goals for individual children and the effectiveness of particular experiences and strategies in assisting the child to meet these goals may be discussed amongst staff at planning meetings or time may be set aside at staff meetings to focus on particular children.

The examples in figures 6.15 to 6.17 show that planning for individuals can be brief and simple and will depend upon staff skills and the needs of the setting.

Week 2:	Focus children sheet	Evaluation
Name: Objective:		
	Experience:	
Name: Objective:		
	Experience:	
Name: Objective:		
	Experience:	
Name: Objective:		
	Experience:	

Source: Ackerley, Gieske, Weber and Wilcomes, UWS-Macarthur Students, 1990
Figure 6.15: Focus children sheet

Focus children	Focus children's or small group objectives	Evaluation and follow-up

Source: Ackerley, Gieske, Weber and Wilcomes, UWS-Macarthur Students, 1990
Figure 6.16: Planning format for individual and small groups

Date: Caregiver:	Focus Children:	Reason: (Why did you choose this child?)	Aim/Goal/Objective: (What do you want the child to do?)	Evaluation: (Did it work?)

Source: Bonnyrigg C.C.C. 1990
Figure 6.17: Planning for individuals

RATIONALE

It is essential that we have a clear focus as to what we are planning for with respect to each child and why we are doing this. Considering the rationale for each goal encourages us to examine our beliefs as to what is important for a child to learn and why. For example, do we believe it is important for a child to learn shapes and colours when they have difficulties interacting with peers? We should be able to clearly articulate to others why we are focusing on a particular area and to link this to our knowledge of the individual child and to our understanding of child growth and development and developmentally appropriate practices.

OBJECTIVES

Taking a child-centred approach to planning means that we must focus on the child's opportunities or experience, rather than the adult's experience. This approach allows for effective evaluation regarding the child's development while an adult-centred objective allows for the adult to evaluate their strategies but not necessarily the child's development. Objectives that focus on the child assist us in evaluating the child's progress towards meeting the planned objective by clearly stating what we hope the child may have an opportunity to achieve or experience. Strategies that the adult may use to assist the child to meet the planned objective can then be indicated and evaluated separately.

WHAT ARE LONG TERM OBJECTIVES?

Long Term Objectives (L.T.O.s) are general outcomes for an individual child developed from observations/interpretations and planning implications, and over time should cover every aspect of the child's development. When formulating long term objectives, the time frame of the planning period (for example, a month or a term) should be considered so that objectives are not too long term. Long term objectives should be achievable, based on what you know about the child's present capabilities.

WHAT ARE SHORT TERM OBJECTIVES?

Short Term Objectives (S.T.O.s) are a way of achieving long term objectives through a series of steps. Each step, or short term objective, is a more specific statement of what we hope the child will experience or have an opportunity to achieve during a learning experience or series of plans. A series of S.T.O.s will generally be needed for the child to reach the L.T.O. and the steps will vary for each child according to their individual needs. For example, Ahmed may take six steps to reach a particular long term objective, while Daniel may reach the same objective in three steps.

HOW CAN WE WORK OUT THE SHORT TERM OBJECTIVES?

Short term objectives should be individualised for each child and should start from the child's present level of development. Each step towards the long term objective is building on what the child is already able to do or has experienced, and is 'upping the ante' (or expecting just a little bit more) in line with our observations of the child's development. However the short term objective may also relate to the same level of development but be extending or challenging the child to try something new, or think about problem solving in a different way, or in a different environment, or with a different group of children.

One way of developing short term objectives is to formulate each S.T.O. as you go along, based on observations and evaluation. As one S.T.O. is met the next S.T.O. is devised, and modifications can occur depending on what happened. It is also possible to work out a chain of S.T.O.s at the outset. This chain, or sequence of short term objectives, can be viewed as a possible plan for progress towards the long term objective, to be followed through and modified where necessary.

WHY DO WE SEQUENCE SHORT TERM OBJECTIVES?

By formulating a possible chain of S.T.O.s at the beginning of the planning process, we are able to get a clear picture of the steps that the child should take to reach the L.T.O. Each S.T.O. can be seen as a logical step towards the L.T.O., with each step sequenced in order of difficulty or challenge. Developing a sequence of S.T.O.s can help us to evaluate the appropriateness of the L.T.O. for the child's stage of development

— if we need a whole page of S.T.O.s to get to the L.T.O. then maybe it is too long term. Sequencing objectives can also help us to clarify our goals — it is difficult to develop a sequence of short term objectives when we have not clearly defined the long term objective.

When sequencing short term objectives it is important to remember that the sequence is only a *possible sequence*, and that it is necessary to continually evaluate the suitability of the sequence for the child in the light of information obtained from evaluations. It may be that the steps we planned for the child were too big and we need to break down the short term objectives into smaller steps, or to reevaluate the long term objective. On the other hand, we may have underestimated the child's capabilities and find that all of the steps that we outlined are not actually necessary — the child may meet more than one objective in a planned experience.

It is also important to consider the pace we planned for a child to move through the formulated objectives towards the long term objective. Each child will be different and require differing amounts of time and numbers of planned experiences to meet a specified short term objective. In some cases a child will need a number of experiences in a variety of contexts in order to meet a particular objective, while another child may meet the selected objective after only one or two planned experiences. Only a very specific objective would be perceived to be met after one or two possible experiences).

Ongoing evaluation of objectives is an essential part of the planning process as it helps to guide our future planning. We should ensure that our evaluations are used effectively by taking note of the information they provide and following through accordingly. This may mean that we move on to planning learning experiences that will help the child meet the next short term objective in the sequence, or it may mean modifying the existing short term objective to help make it more achievable for the child.

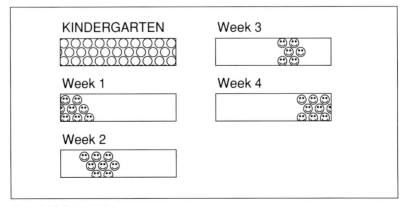

Figure 6.18: Focus children

Staff	Indoor focus children	Outdoor focus children
Week 1 20/4/90		
I: Manuella	Fabiola	Flavia
	Margarita	Fernando
	Andrezza	Enrico
O: Chung Sim	Paulo	Rodrigous
Week 2 27/4/90		
I: Cameron	Soneel	Paj
	Marissa	Emma
	Yasmin/Prashant	Anna
O: Jacqui	Sisomar	Emmanuel
Week 3		
I: Georgia	Joshua	Phul
	Phoebe	Vangmar
	Kesia	Mystery
O: Lynne	Yung Me	Chloe/Claire
Week 4		
I: Chung Sim	Tysook	Yesse
	Trung	Jun
	Lili	Jing
O: Manuella	Nhan	Arthur
Week 5		
I: Jacqui	Simon	Chaci
	Manik	Mirium
	Andrea	Victor
O: Cameron	Vanuska	Jay
Week 6		
I: Lynne	Millicent	Mary
	John	Rosa
	Pan	Victor
O: Georgia	Mari	Raffaella
I = Indoor O = Outdoor	After the 6 week period the indoor and outdoor focus children are planned for in the other environment	

Figure 6.19: Focus children rotational system

Source: Britton, Francesconi, Jones, Watson, UWS-Macarthur Students, 1990

Each cycle consists of 4 weeks	Week 1	Week 2	Week 3	Week 4
Team 1	Individual programming plans for focus children (B-groups)	Programming for whole centre (include B-group plans) Observe focus children (A-groupε)	Plans for focus children (A-groups)	Individual for whole centre (include A-group plans) Observe focus children (B group3)
Team 2	Programming for whole centre (include B group plans) Observe focus children (A-groups)	Individual plans Plans for focus (A-groups)	Programming for focus (include A group plans) Focus children (B-groups)	Individual whole centre children Children (B-groups) Observe

Figure 6.20: Timetable   *Source:* Denham, Dunn, Garck and Heyhoe, UWS-Macarthur Students, 1991

Indoor – Room 1	Indoor – Room 2	Outdoor	Night
Group 1	Group 3	Group 5	Group 7
1. _____ 2. _____ 3. _____ /____ 4. _____ /____ 5. _____ /____	1. _____ 2. _____ 3. _____ /____ 4. _____ /____ 5. _____ /____	1. _____ 2. _____ 3. _____ /____ 4. _____ /____ 5. _____ /____	1. _____ 2. _____ 3. _____ 4. _____ 5. _____ /____
Group 2	Group 4	Group 6	Group 8
1. _____ 2. _____ 3. _____ /____ 4. _____ /____ 5. _____ /____	1. _____ 2. _____ 3. _____ /____ 4. _____ /____ 5. _____ /____	1. _____ 2. _____ 3. _____ /____ 4. _____ /____ 5. _____ /____	1. _____ 2. _____ 3. _____ 4. _____ 5. _____ /____

Figure 6.21: Focus children

Source: Brookfield, Eden, Kirchner and Smith, UWS-Macarthur Students, 1990

LEARNING EXPERIENCES

How do we plan experiences to meet objectives?

Once we have developed long and short term objectives for an individual child, the next step is to consider the range of possible experiences that may help to meet those objectives. Whatever the focus of the objectives, it should be possible to meet these in virtually any curriculum or program area, at a variety of times and in different contexts. For example, consider the following children's objectives:

Allan:
For Allan to become actively involved in small group experiences.
Thom:
For Thom to further develop self-help skills.
Lillian:
For Lillian to further develop strength in pulling herself into a standing postion and in standing unaided.

Any of these children's objectives may be met in the indoor or the outdoor environment, at routine times such as morning tea as well as during self-selected 'free-play' or 'group time', within a range of curriculum areas such as art and craft, dramatic play or construction. When planning possible experience to meet each child's objective, we need to consider the whole day and the total environment. The experience that we select as being the most appropriate to implement for an individual child will depend on the interests of the child and the time of day. The objective need not specify the experience as we can use a range of experiences to meet the objective, and in that way be providing for individual children in several experiences on one day — without having to write lots of different plans.

The suitability of selected experiences needs to be evaluated on a regular basis. We need to consider whether the experience utilised was suitable in assisting the child to meet the objective and whether it was appropriate for the child's present stage of development. The child's interests and peer relationships also need to be considered when evaluating the appropriateness of selected learning experiences and in planning follow through experiences.

STRATEGIES

As well as thinking about what learning experience we are going to set up to meet a particular child's needs, we need to consider what the role of the adult will be in this experience. What teaching strategies should we adopt in helping the child to meet the planned objective? What are we going to do? What are we going to say? Do we need to do or say anything? How should we set up the environment?

As early childhood educators we need to be constantly evaluating the effectiveness of our strategies in line with the objectives for individual children. We need to ask ourselves if we were able to carry out what we had planned and whether, on reflection, these strategies were the most appropriate for meeting each child's needs. For example, were we able to give the child support when it was needed, to model appropriate language or behaviour if required and to stand back when appropriate?

HOW CAN WE CATER FOR INDIVIDUALS WITHIN A GROUP SETTING?

It may at first appear a daunting task to observe and plan for individual children when we have a group of 30 or 40 children in our centre or classroom. How do we make sure that we don't leave anyone out? How can we plan learning experiences that cater for all of the individual needs within the group? These concerns can be overcome by:

1. implementing a focus system approach;
2. planning to meet the objectives of a number of individual children in the one experience;
3. planning to meet objectives throughout the day, during routine times, transitions, self-selected play experiences and group experiences.

WHAT ARE FOCUS CHILDREN?

Adopting a 'focus child' approach is one way of ensuring that all children's needs are catered for over a period of time. A small number of children are focused on over a selected time frame and from current observations and developmental summaries objectives are formulated for these children. Learning experiences are then planned to meet these objectives throughout the day. By utilising a focus system, all children can be catered for within a fixed period of time and no child will be overlooked. The focus children approach allows you the time and space in your day to learn more about the individual child, to become more aware of each child's needs and interests and so plan or utilise relevant experiences.

When developing a focus system for a particular setting it is necesary to decide:

- the number of children to be catered for, *for example 5*;
- over what period of time, *for example a week*;
- in what parts of the program/day/week, *for example throughout the day*;
- who will plan and evaluate for these children, *for example all staff*.

Systems can be organised in a number of different ways depending on the setting. The number of children, the number of staff and the hours that the setting is open will determine the type of system that you adopt. For example, if the setting is a 40-place long day care centre where there are six staff, then each staff member may have a small group of children that they observe and plan for a set time period, such as three months, or the year.

Figure 6.22: Routine times, such as meal times can be utilised to meet objectives for a number of children. These times also allow for much adult–child interaction to occur.

If you are working in a school setting, you may have thirty children that you need to plan for on your own throughout the year. From a group of thirty children, six can be selected each week as focus children, so that over a ten week period each child has been focused on in detail for two weeks (figure 6.18).

Within the focus period, observation notes and developmental summaries can be added to, and objectives developed. Learning experiences designed to meet these objectives can then be planned, implemented and evaluated several examples of managing these systems are illustrated in figures 6.19–21.

In this way no child is left out or overemphasised, including the quieter child or the very interactive child. Each child is observed, planned for and plans evaluated over a set period in a systematic way.

While objectives for each child may be met in individual plans it is also possible to meet these same objectives in small group plans.

HOW CAN WE MEET A NUMBER OF OBJECTIVES IN ONE EXPERIENCE?

There are a number of ways that individual objectives for a group of children can be met in the one experience. These experiences may be initiated by the child or by the adult. When we are aware of the learning potential of experiences across developmental areas and the needs of individual children, we can plan experiences for self-selected play and small groups that will cater for the needs of a number of children at the one time.

CHILD-INITIATED EXPERIENCES

An experience may be planned with two or more focus children's objectives in mind and set up during 'free play' time, when children have a range of experiences to choose from. For example, the following children's objectives could be met in one experience in a range of curriculum areas.

Susanna

For Susanna to develop confidence in interacting with peers in small groups.

Carmen

For Carmen to develop finger manipulation skills.

Tam

For Tam to have the opportunity to hear and speak English in small group interactive situations.

For these children the early childhood educator may plan an experience involving play dough, because this is a shared interest of the children and would enable all objectives to be met. Particular strategies would then be planned to assist each child in meeting their objective. Each of the children is free to participate in this experience, or not, as they choose, although the adult may encourage them to become involved. However, they do not all need to be there at the same time, and other children may also choose to be involved and benefit from the experience.

On other occasions you may plan an experience to meet the objective for just one child, say Carmen. You may decide to set up a water play experience with a variety of accessories to further develop Carmen's manipulative skills. Other children may also become involved in this experience and their objectives may also be met. For example, Nina may become involved and meet her objective of developing descriptive language, along with Amadeu, whose objective is to further develop turn taking skills. These, and other children's objectives may all be met in this one experience, particularly if the adult is on hand to implement the appropriate strategies.

ADULT-INITIATED SMALL GROUP EXPERIENCES

If information collected from observations suggests that a number of children have similar or complementary long term objectives, they can be grouped together for a particular learning experience. In this case the adult selects the children to be included in the experience, hence it is adult-initiated. This may take place at a specified 'group time' or at any other time of the day, such as lunch time. The group experience will be planned with the needs of each individual child in mind, and include specific strategies to meet each child's objectives.

For example, there may be a number of children who need to further develop their divergent thinking skills and are at a similar stage in their development. A small group experience may be planned for these children to facilitate this development. Small group experiences may also be planned for children who have objectives in the same developmental area, but are at different stages of development. For instance, there may be a number of children with objectives in the area of gross motor development and an experience involving an obstacle course with varying degrees of difficulty may be designed so that each child is able to participate at their own level. As was indicated with child-initiated experiences, it is equally possible with adult-initiated experiences to plan small groups that cater for a range of objectives, across developmental levels. (Lambert et al. 1987)

HOW CAN WE MEET INDIVIDUAL OBJECTIVES THROUGHOUT THE DAY?

All activities during the day are learning experiences for children. Much of the day for young children, particularly for children under three, may be taken up with routines. These routine times can be utilised in ways that help children to meet individual objectives. Nappy changing, putting on children's shoes, or getting children ready for sleeptime provide an ideal situation where adults can interact with children on a one-to-one basis and promote development (figure 6.22).

Other routine times, such as meal times and morning and afternoon tea, can be utilised to meet the objectives for a number of children. For example, the objectives of all of the following children can be met at a morning tea group experience.

Danielle:
For Danielle to be able to share and take turns (Social Objective).
Francisco:
For Francisco to respond to verbal interactions from peers (Language Objective).
Katie:
For Katie to be able to make choices between a limited number of objects (Cognitive Objective).

Ricardo:
For Ricardo to become aware of a variety of smells (Sensory Objective).
Patrick:
For Patrick to develop eye-hand co-ordination in manipulating objects
(Fine Motor Objective).

Transition times, when children are moving from one area or experience to another, or waiting for lunch to be brought in from the kitchen, are also times when individual objectives can be met, for example, encouraging developing self-help skills (by setting the table, or self-service lunch) or creativity (working out creative ways they could move from one place to another, or what will be available at lunchtime).

As early childhood educators we also need to make the most of children's spontaneous play and the unplanned outcomes of planned experiences. This does not mean that we need to 'hover' over children all the time, or take over their play, but that we respond to children's interests and the cues that children give us. If we observe children's play and join in where it is appropriate, following the children's lead, then we may be able to extend a child's learning by offering suggestions for new directions or by providing further resources. If the adults in early childhood settings are 'tuned in' to children then many individual children's objectives can be met in this way.

Working with the strengths and needs of individual children is the central focus of early childhood programming. This is achievable where staff in settings design, develop and modify effective systems for planning and respond creatively to the influences on planning. Since time is one of the strongest constraints on children's chances to involve themselves in experiences, learning opportunities should be identified throughout the whole day, including arrivals and greetings, transitions, snacks, toileting and so on.

RECORDING PLANS

WHY WRITE IT DOWN?

Even the most experienced early childhood educator needs to write specific plans which provide for a focus on individual children. Writing things down helps us to clarify our goals and to be precise in stating our objectives, and ensures that all staff are informed as to what is happening. Written plans are also essential in terms of maintaining accountability to funding and licensing bodies and to families. Details of what happened each day can be communicated to families via a noticeboard or whiteboard, or in a newsletter.

Written plans help us to think clearly about what we are doing and why we are doing it. We are better able to articulate our aims and strategies to other members of staff, visitors and families when we have written them down. When plans are clearly written down we are better able to utilise resources. Staff are able to be consistent in the strategies that they adopt with individual children and to have input into deciding on how to set up resources to meet individual children's objectives.

Written plans also help us to evaluate effectively. Writing down individual children's objectives and our planned experiences, including strategies and resources, helps us to evaluate whether objectives were met and whether the experience was suitable, and if not why not. Written plans provide the opportunity for later reflection and are a basis for future planning. The depth of written planning will be dependent on staff skills and whether it will be undertaken by all members of the team or by individual members.

HOW CAN WE RECORD INDIVIDUAL PLANNING?

It is important to develop methods of planning that all staff can understand and use in order to reflect a team approach and to provide opportunities for everyone to participate in decision making. Formats for the recording of observations on individual children, developmental summaries and planning should be simple and to the point. For example, a planning format may ask:

- Why are you working on this area?
- What do you want the child/children to achieve?
- How will you help them to do this?
- How did it go?

All staff, regardless of levels of training or experience, will feel much more comfortable with these ideas, rather than jargonistic terms, and will feel confident in being able to record the necessary information. Staff with more early childhood training and experience can record in more depth, and may be able to assist other members of staff when planning as a team. As the team develop planning skills, gradual extensions and changes to the individual planning format can be made. Staff as a team should work out the most suitable method to use for recording individual planning. The overall planning format for the day, room or setting will indicate who the focus children are, but details about individual planning should be kept within the child's individual records for reasons of confidentiality. Depending upon how the focus children system operates, staff should be aware of what the focus child's objectives are and of possible strategies for working with the child, or know where to check this information in the child's file.

Writing down plans does not mean that they can't be changed.

Plans are *guides* for future action, not something set in concrete. It is important not to become 'locked into' following a predetermined plan, but to remain flexible. Changes to plans may be necessary due to an unexpected change in the daily routine or the weather, or due to the spontaneous interests of the children. Just because we have planned

something does not mean that it *has* to happen. We should be able to
'let go' of plans and follow the interests and lead of the children at times
— to be able to respond to the 'teachable moment'. The objectives that
we develop for each individual child are generally able to be met in any
number of experiences throughout the day and do not *have* to be met in
the experience that we planned. Rather than insisting that the child take
part in the planned experience or abandoning our plan altogether
because of unexpected changes or lack of interest, we should be flexible
enough to follow the interests of the child and to modify our plan
accordingly. The objective that we hoped the child would meet can still
be met, but in a different experience.

WHY EVALUATE INDIVIDUALS PLANS?

Evaluation is an integral part of the planning process. It is essential in
order to provide feedback on individual children's development and
progress towards objectives, as well as feedback on the overall program.
Evaluation allows us to determine the relevance of current objectives for
individual children and to modify these if necessary. Evaluation also
helps us to become aware of individual children's feelings, needs and
interests and to reflect on the suitability of selected experiences and
strategies in meeting each child's needs. Again these can be modified if
necessary, in the light of observations of each child's responses to
planned experiences. This evaluation actually becomes the ongoing basis
of our developmental records, that is, our evaluations are observations.

This then provides the necessary information to act as a basis for
future planning. If staff are able to evaluate as a team, then the process
of evaluation also contributes to staff development and the formulation
of shared goals. Planning formats should include an evaluation section to
ensure that this important aspect of the planning process is undertaken.
Team planning meetings should allocate sufficient time for the discussion
of the findings of evaluations and the implications of these findings for
future planning.

USEFUL RESOURCES

Lambert, B., Clyde, M., and Reeves, K. (1987) *Planning for Individual Needs in Early Childhood Settings*. ACT, Australian Early Childhood Association.

Veale, A. and Piscitelli, B. (1988) *Observation and Record Keeping in Early Childhood programs*. ACT, Australian Early Childhood Association.

7

GROUPING — LET ME COUNT THE WAYS

INTRODUCTION

Increasing numbers of young children are spending larger proportions of their time in group care outside the home. As children may be involved in a group setting from 6 weeks of age through their early childhood years and into school, many questions about grouping should be explored. This chapter focuses on the possible effects of different forms of grouping on young children's development, and how settings can use grouping methods to provide a high quality program.

WHY DO WE GROUP YOUNG CHILDREN?

Reid et al (1989) believe that learning is predominantly social and that it arises from our need to solve problems that involve other people, or to imitate the skills we see other people using, together with the guidance we receive from others.

The reasons we choose to use particular methods for grouping children in early childhood settings will be dependent on a wide range of issues. These may be related to the benefits for children, our personal and educational philosophies, recent research evidence, and the skills of staff within the setting. However, a recent study by Farmer (1990) has suggested that factors such as building design and organisation of physical environment, attitudes and expectations of staff and families, staff shortages as well as inadequacy of both pre-service training and practical experiences all have an impact on the understanding and choice of grouping methods used.

Irrespective of the form of grouping preferred within a setting, it is important to ensure that we understand the extent of benefits of a variety of forms and use these effectively within the program.

Within an early childhood setting we should look at maximising the potential of any form of grouping as increasing numbers of children are spending larger proportions of time in group care outside the home from a much younger age. They are therefore being placed in some form of group. There is a tendency for settings to focus on one form of grouping, without thinking about all the issues, or the range of grouping methods. This is sometimes a result of convenience or tradition within the setting. While a high proportion of settings utilise age grouping, this is only one way of organising groups, and there are many others that may be considered. As it is important for the child to be with others in a group situation to assist in learning, grouping becomes a major consideration in planning a program.

WHAT ARE THE DIFFERENT FORMS OF GROUPING?

What are the different forms of grouping? What impact do these have on young children's development? How can staff in early childhood settings use grouping more effectively? In exploring these questions, grouping can be defined as either homogeneous or heterogeneous as shown in figure 7.1.

Homogeneous groups are composed of children who are perceived to be *similar* in some way, for example, in age, ability or developmental level, skills, interests, culture or friendship. On the other hand, heterogeneous groups are based on *diversity*, for example, mixed ages, abilities, developmental levels, skills or cultures. The most prominent forms of grouping identified in early childhood settings are mixed age grouping (heterogeneous), same-age, and ability/developmental grouping (homogeneous).

However, there are some contradictions inherent in the concept of developmental grouping in the early childhood years. Due to the rapid development that occurs during the first years of life, children in early childhood groups are most likely to be of mixed developmental levels. For instance, the development that occurs between 6 weeks of age and 6 months of age is extensive, let alone the development that occurs between birth and 3, and between 3 to 5 years, which is typical of group structures in the Australian context in long day care settings. Because of rapid changes in development, it is suggested that in early childhood settings, ability or developmental groupings are difficult to judge and implement. In addition, children's development is not always even across all domains. Children may be advanced in their social skills, but less developed in their cognitive skills. A 2 year old and 4 year old may be at a similar level in some areas of development and therefore may need to be in the same group for certain experiences. This would lead to the notion of implementing a wide range of flexible grouping methods within an early childhood setting.

Historically, the focus of grouping has undergone several changes and has tended to reflect the educational philosophies of the era. The one room school was the norm until urbanisation and increasing enrolment

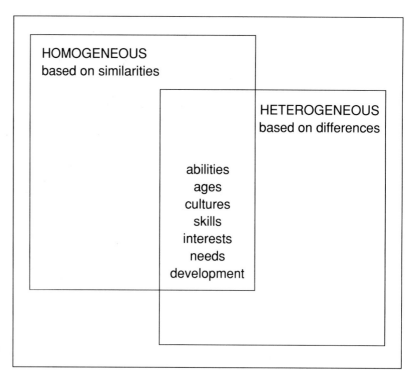

HOMOGENEOUS
based on similarities

HETEROGENEOUS
based on differences

abilities
ages
cultures
skills
interests
needs
development

Figure 7.1: Homogeneous and heterogeneous grouping

numbers in many geographical areas occurred and made separation into homogeneous groups possible. The one room school had children of differing ages, stages of development and skills in one group. While this school situation is still common in isolated, rural areas of Australia, teachers often see this form of grouping as a problem that needs to be overcome, rather than capitalising on and utilising the potential of the differences amongst children. Montessori settings have traditionally been made up of children of different ages and stages of development based on the rationale that this allows younger children to learn from older more developed ones. Paradoxically, peer interaction is not especially encouraged in this system, perhaps as the philosophy is based on children being independent and left to interact or not interact as they wish (Katz, et al 1990).

As knowledge of child development evolved with the work of Piaget, Erikson and Gesell, a view of children developing and learning in stages across all developmental domains grew. A principle evolved based on this knowledge that children of similar ages are developing at a similar rate, and therefore if placed together in a setting their needs can be better met. However, it can be argued that developmental theory specifies that while all children may go through similar developmental stages, this happens at an individual pace and a large variation in development can occur within a group of children irrespective of their age. Elkind (1987) argues that age grouping based on physical time denies the fact that children are 'organisms' and that they operate on variable biological and psychological time, not uniform physical time. A further argument could

---

Point-scoring over composite classes

TO THE debate raging about composite classes in NSW primary schools, can I please add the following comments.

1. Every class is a composite class in terms of ability. It is not unusual to have a reading age span of five years or more in any given class.

2. The success of any class, composite or otherwise, depends on the skill of the teacher and his/her ability to respond to children as individuals and provide challenges for the more able ones.

3. School is the only place where we are grouped strictly according to age. Such a grouping does not reflect the family or society and is not natural. It has grown out of a compartmentalised view of learning which is no longer popular.

4. There is no evidence that strictly age-graded classes provide the best learning environment or accelerate learning.

5. On the contrary, a child learns easily and quickly during its first five years in the home, interacting with its parents and siblings.

Many educators, recognising this, advocate composite classes across the grades, also known as "vertical streaming" or "family groupings", as the best environment for learning.

The present debate is another example of political point-scoring.

By all means address the issues of staff cuts and class sizes. However, denouncing composite classes as second-rate education is an untruth.

ROSEMARY HAMMERTON,
Kingsgrove

Figure 7.2: Letter to the editor

---

be made that developmental theorists intended to provide an understanding of children's development and learning. Their theories do not, and were never intended to provide a model for organising educational programs.

During the 1960s and 1970s the British model of informal, open education often utilised heterogeneous grouping as it matched the less rigid form of programming, and this continues today in so-called alternative or progressive schools. In the early 1980s, Neighbourhood Children's Centres, often renovated houses, utilised this form of grouping as it reflected a home-like environment. However, once these small centres were seen as uneconomical by the Federal Government, the 40 place model which separated children into 'under threes' and 'over threes' became the norm. Teachers in schools are currently going through the process of being 'forced' into the use of composite classes due to financial constraints. As identified by Rosemary Hammerton, in a letter to the Editor of the St George *Leader* (figure 7.2), there are many positive benefits to composite classes which will be lost on those who feel pressured into using this form of grouping for political reasons.

If forced to use a particular form of grouping, staff will find it difficult to use that form positively and effectively and to its full potential. Staff need to make choices on an informed basis, so that the full benefits of any form of grouping are utilised.

WHAT DOES RESEARCH TELL US ABOUT THE IMPACT ON CHILDREN'S DEVELOPMENT OF DIFFERENT GROUPING STRATEGIES?

Research has indicated that grouping strategies and the composition of groups affect the areas of social/emotional, cognitive and language development in young children. This research is summarised in table 7.1. While there is no research into the area of physical development, some assumptions based on practice and observation can be put forward.

SOCIAL/EMOTIONAL DEVELOPMENT

One of the many reasons for bringing groups of children together in the early years is to facilitate and enhance their social development. Social competence emerges mainly from experience in close relationships. Research on attachment has found that if children have problems in social/emotional development in early life it can affect their later development, particularly emotional stability and relationships with others. Hartup (1977) believes that peer interaction is also an essential component of the child's social development.

Evidence suggests that spontaneously formed peer groups are typically heterogeneous (or diverse) in composition. It is often assumed that social contacts for children in Western cultures are limited, to a large degree, to children of their own age. It is further suggested that the large populations characteristic of industrialised societies are necessary for age segregation to occur (Hartup 1976; Konner 1975, in Ellis et al 1981). Formal education systems in these societies also encourage age segregation with an entry age into school and a natural progression through the system according to age. However, Ellis et al (1981) found age segregation less common than cross-age interaction in spontaneously-formed groups. This study examined the composition of groups of children , aged 1 to 12 years, in a neighbourhood, urban setting. Results of this study suggest that children in the early childhood years prefer to interact spontaneously with a range of ages. The groups formed tended to be small, averaging about three members, and in the majority of observations the children were interacting with cross-age companions (figure 7.3).

Hartup (1989) believes that two types of relationships are necessary for optimum growth. These are, symmetrical interactions (that is horizontal relationships between children who have similar status and social power), and asymmetrical interactions (that is vertical relationships between individuals who differ in resources and may have a greater knowledge and social power than other individuals).

An example of the types of relationships and interactions that might occur in the early childhood years is shown in figure 7.4.

In respect to other aspects of social/emotional development, research indicates that children appear sensitive to the behaviour of their peers

Figure 7.3: Spontaneously formed groups tend to be diverse, ie children choose to become involved with children of different ages and development if the opportunity is available.

and are usually aware of different social roles (French 1984; Goldman 1981; Graziano et al 1976). Consequently, both older and younger children are able to adapt their behaviour in heterogeneous settings (Howes and Farver 1987). These settings elicit specific prosocial behaviours such as helping, nurturing, sharing and leadership skills (Melson and Fogel 1988; Roopnarine 1987; French et al 1986; Melson et al 1986; Berman et al 1977).

A question frequently asked by those involved with children in the early childhood years is 'Will older children hurt younger children?' Evidence seems to suggest that this is not the case.

Nurturing behaviour and empathy are considered important, perhaps essential, adult characteristics that involve fostering the development of another and being aware of their needs. Many early childhood settings which utilise heterogeneous forms of grouping with children from birth to 5 years of age, suggest that this form of grouping promotes nurturing behaviour in the children (figure 7.5). On the other hand, those settings that practice homogeneous grouping often indicate safety as a rationale, as it is anticipated that older children will hurt infants and toddlers. The limited amount of research investigating nurturant behaviour undertaken in group child care settings appears to support the former view, as do the results of studies which suggest that there are fewer negative interactions amongst children in heterogeneous grouping (Melson and Fogel 1988; Berman 1987; Melson et al 1986; Berman et al 1983; Berman et al 1977) .

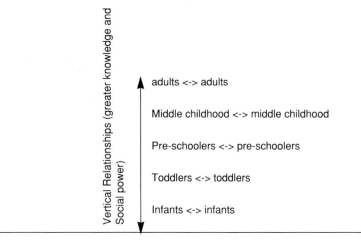

Figure 7.4: Relationships and interactions in early childhood years.

Figure 7.5: Even toddlers display caring, helping and nurturing behaviour in settings where this is encouraged and promoted.

Adding weight to the idea that heterogeneous forms of grouping support emotional development is the evidence that suggests that ability grouping (a homogeneous form) has been found to be detrimental to self-concept and self-esteem. This form of grouping both reinforces positive and negative concepts of each child's skills and becomes a 'self-fulfilling prophecy' — 'I'm not good at that'; 'I can't do that' ; 'Why should I try?, I'm in the poor reading group'; 'I need to keep up with the others'?.

Whether consciously or not, staff may react differently to children because of the way they are grouped, by either accepting that a child cannot 'do any better' or by having high expectations of another (Findlay and Bryan 1975; Hiebert 1983 in Unsworth 1985). Children may then begin to feel they have poor skills in certain areas. In summarising the affects of ability grouping on self-concept, Rosenbaum (1980) concluded that in most cases average and low ability students give lower self-evaluations if they are in ability groups than if they are not. (Heibert 1983: p.243 in Unsworth 1985)

COGNITIVE DEVELOPMENT

The influence of grouping upon the child's cognitive development appears to be related to two main issues — cognitive conflict and cooperative problem solving. Research suggests that 'cognitive conflict' is more likely to occur in situations where some children are operating at a higher cognitive levels than others (Lambert 1988).

Cognitive conflict arises from interaction amongst children of different levels of cognitive development. Children gradually develop their abilities to construct and problem-solve skills as they meet discrepancies and conflicts in relation to the ideas and perspectives of other children (Azmitia 1988; Lambert 1988). As little of this research focuses on cognitive conflict in children under 5 years, Azmitia (1988) implies that this may be a result of the general acceptance of Piaget's claim regarding preschoolers egocentrism.

More recent research implies that preschoolers are less egocentric than Piaget had considered (Azmitia 1988; Lambert 1988). Other researchers have identified empathy and nurturing behaviours (Melson and Fogel 1988; Berman 1987; Melson et al 1986; Berman et al 1977), and role asymmetry (Hartup 1989; French 1984; Graziano et al 1976) which demonstrate how preschool children are able to take the perspective of other children. In order to clarify this situation further research is essential. This may mean investigating a range of issues such as the child's level of social skills ; the way in which tasks are presented to very young children; children's interactions during play in small groups; and, the adult's role in assisting young children to resolve conflict. Since children are able to alter their behaviour and interactions in response to their peers' developmental levels, (Hartup 1989; French 1984) it is possible cognitive conflict would be promoted more often in heterogeneous groups.

Cooperative problem solving is likely to be effective when children share a goal but each child has different perspectives on the best way to reach that goal (Tudge and Caruso 1988). Consequently, in situations where young children have a wide range of developmental differences, they have the potential to learn from each other. Azmitia (1988) identified alternative methods of preschoolers' problem solving where they learnt to solve problems by observing and being guided by a child with more highly developed skills (an expert).

Given this situation the child needs to participate in all experiences at their own level of competence. Brown and Reeve (1985) suggest that education aimed at a wide range of abilities encourages the child with less developed skills (the novice) to learn at his/her own rate as well as meet some of the challenges offered by the child with more developed skills (the expert). This suggests the adult's role is significant in planning for learning and interacting within a learning environment, which assists children to participate at their own level, thus individualising children's learning opportunities. As a result, individual children are expected to gain different concepts, skills and attitudes from the same situation.

Ability grouping through labelling of children has been seen to harden designated catagories — that is to identify children in a positive or negative way. This situation has reinforced failure and competition. It has not encouraged children to learn from each other and the adult to recognise the diversity of skills children do develop (Findlay and Bryan 1975; Hiebert 1983 in Unsworth 1985; Mycock 1966). As we regard children as individuals, we should be able to assist and extend their learning as needed, rather than group them according to their current level of skills.

Children's learning best enhances their development when their experiences are socially directed by more capable individuals. These individuals with more developed skills can provide prompts towards increasingly complex solutions, ask leading questions, and cause the child with less developed skills to defend or modify his/her views (Vygotsky 1978 in Katz et al 1990). As a result it seems that both children and adults can provide these challenges and offer varying degrees of cognitive support. Children with recent experience in mastering concepts and skills may in fact be better able to help the child still developing the skill as their language, understandings and perspectives may be much closer to that of the child in comparison to that of the adult.

The issues related to cognitive conflict and cooperative problem solving, as well as the difficulty in identifying the child's specific levels of development across a range of dynamic domains according to chronological age, provides support for the notion of heterogeneous grouping.

LANGUAGE AND COMMUNICATION

As communication is social by nature, grouping plays a large part in its development. Through interaction with others, children develop understandings of the social conventions of language, or their communicative competence. In addition, 'communicative competence', or language interaction skills, has been found to make a significant contribution to cognitive development. Research has suggested that children as young as 2 are able to adapt their verbal communications to the age of the listener in heterogeneous groups, for example, using shorter words, rising intonation and repetition when talking with babies (Howes and Farver 1987; Shatz and Gelman 1973). It has also been suggested that if very young children are placed only with peers of similar language development they will tend to have 'collective monologues', that is limited verbal communication with little vocabulary, infrequent verbal exchanges, and dependence on adults for language expansion (Hamilton and Stewart

1977). Hence the role of the adult, or the older child, in interacting with and responding to infants and toddlers, individually and in small groups, is essential (as discussed in chapter 10 Infants and Toddlers).

As children learn language over time, they learn to use language for various functions — to get picked up, to make meaning as they make sense of the world, and to develop competence with language structures. All these aspects of language development arise from the child using language in active and interactive situations, that is small groups (Wells 1985). The smaller the group, the more opportunities the child is likely to have to talk and listen actively with others.

Since language is above all social, particular types of groups would seem to offer more reasons to the child to talk. Friendship, interest and culture groups in particular are situations where children immediately have shared backgrounds and experiences that support and foster further talk and meaning making. Since children of different stages of development vary in their language development, it is probable that heterogeneous groups offer more diversity of language development and hence more opportunities to the young child for language learning.

PHYSICAL DEVELOPMENT

As previously stated, there is limited research which investigates the effect of grouping on the physical/motor development of children. Assumptions based on observations however, can provide some insights into different aspects of grouping and physical development.

Within heterogeneous groups children are at differing levels of development in their physical skills. As with other areas of development, this would then allow children to imitate and model the skills being demonstrated by more capable children, thus giving them impetus to try new skills. In addition to this, the environment is likely to be affected by this form of grouping as adults are more likely to set up a wider range of experiences and equipment for the broad span of development they are catering for, thus providing a more challenging environment for children to explore. Staff will not get locked into only providing certain experiences aimed at particular stages of physical development. This is not only a positive step in providing a challenging environment which will help children to try new things, but it also allows children to practice skills and gain confidence if there is a variety of levels catered for, without feeling they must try new things all the time. Children gain a perspective of where they have come from as they see children trying to walk or coordinate equipment, and where they are going as they see others using equipment in ways they have not yet thought of.

Safety, particularly where there is a wide span of ages, is often a concern for staff. Children are often aware of their own limitations and will decide how best they might use the equipment or environment. Different children will climb in different ways, and so it is once again up to the adult to adapt their expectations of children and what they do, or how they might use equipment. It is also up to the adult to adapt

Figure 7.6: A challenging environment

Figure 7.7: A challenging environment will help children try new things, practice skills and gain confidence. Very young children will often work out their own way of using equipment that may not have been provided in a situation catering to a particular level of development only.

their level of involvement, that is, to be aware of children with less developed skills and assist when necessary. There may also be other opportunities where small groups could be used at different times of the day to allow children with differing levels of development to have time to themselves.

LARGE OR SMALL — WHAT ABOUT GROUP SIZE?

Another consideration in relation to grouping in early childhood settings is that of group size. Evidence that small group sizes are more conducive to positive developmental outcomes for children has been found in many research studies(Clarke-Stewart and Gruber 1984; Cummings and Beagles-Ross 1983; Howes 1983; Smith and Connelly 1981; Bruner 1980). Small group sizes encourage positive social interactions amongst

Table 7.1: Provides a summary of the impact of grouping on young children's development with relevant research for further reading.

Developmental area	Issues	Related research
Social/emotional development	While formal education encourages age segregation research indicates that spontaneously formed groups are heterogeneous in nature	Ellis, Rogoff and Cromer, 1981
	Symmetrical interactions (horizontal and vertical) interactions are necessary for positive social development	Hartup, 1989
	Children enter cross age interactions with an understanding of the roles played by others, i.e., friendship, providing help, receiving help, providing sympathy, receiving sympathy, leadership	French, 1984 Brody, Stonemen and MacKinnon, 1982; Graziano, French, Brownell and Hartup, 1976
	Positive interactions more common within heterogeneous groups. Pro-social behaviours... turn-taking, sharing, help-giving, empathy and nurturing, positive interactions more common. Children engage in less teacher-directed play, younger children engage in more complex and interactive play, less negative interactions and lack of aggression, older children master important social skill, spend more time with peers than adults.	Goldman, 1981; Clarke-Stewart, 1987, Howes and Farver, 1987; Roopnarine, 1987
	Within heterogeneous groups – nurturant behaviour and empathy – older children interact positively with babies, particularly if with them over a period of time, less sex differences in nurturing behaviour with under fives reasonably equal in reactions, to babies older children go to infants when distressed and try to calm infants, leadership behaviour not dominating particularly when with infants for longer periods, infant's behaviour contributes to situation.	Melson and Fogel, 1988; Berman, Monda and Myerscough, 1977; Melson, Fogel and Mistry, 1986; Berman, 1987; Berman, Smith and Goodman, 1983.
	Within homogeneous groups ability grouping tends be detrimental to self-concept and self-esteem, reinforces positive and negative concepts of self, reinforce failure.	Easthope, Maclean and Easthope, 1986; Hiebert, 1983 in Unsworth, 1985; Findlay and Bryan, 1975; Mycock, 1966.
Cognitive development	Cognitive conflict arises out of interaction with children of different levels of cognitive maturity, children develop a variety of ways to solve problems, cooperative problem-solving is developed with a shared goal and different ways of attaining it, peer tutoring effective as children closer in ability than adult, allows older children to consolidate skills.	Azmitia, 1988; Lambert, 1988; Brown and Paliscar, 1986; Vygotsky, 1978; Tudge and Caruso, 1988
	Same ability grouping tends to harden designated categories, produces learned behaviour.	Easthope, Maclean and Easthope, 1986; Hiebert, 1983 in Unsworth, 1985; Findlay and Bryan, 1975; Mycock, 1966.
Language development	In heterogeneous groups, older children adapt verbal communication to the age of listener, young children's linguistic maturity improves, children are more appropriate models than adults as are a closer language model, older children extend their language skills through adaptations. In homogeneous groups tend towards 'collective monologues' with not enough diversity in language models.	Shatz & Gelman, 1973; Howes and Farver, 1987; Lougee, Greunich and Hartup, 1977; Hamilton and Stewart, 1977; Bates, 1975.
Overall development	Small group sizes are more conducive to positive developmental outcomes, encourage positive social interaction, lead to less restrictive behaviour from adults. Large groups lead to less adult-child interaction, less child-child interaction, less social stimulation, less active involvement in experiences.	Howes, 1983; Cummings and Beagles-Ross, 1983; Clarke-Stewart and Gruber, 1984; Bruner, 1980; Smith and Conelly, 1981.

children and lead to less restrictive behaviour from adult caregivers. When young children are placed in larger groups there is less adult-child interaction, less social stimulation, and less active involvement in experiences. While there is a great deal of evidence to support using small groups, many settings continue to utilise large groups throughout the day. Perhaps the constraints of staff-child ratios, building design and time lead staff to use this form of grouping. Another possibility exists, that staff may be unsure of how to implement small groups within these constraints. With a greater undertanding of different forms of grouping and their implications, early childhood educators should be able to more effectively implement many of these ideas.

WHAT FORM OF GROUPING REFLECTS A DEVELOPMENTALLY APPROPRIATE PROGRAM?

Freedman (1982: p.197) suggests that grouping reflects the goals, even the national goals, of a program.

> Where the primary goal is to produce open, sociable children who are able to accept and give help, heterogeneous grouping is preferred. Where the goal is to teach a set body of material and to formalise the relationship between dependants and caregivers, homogeneous grouping is favoured.

While different programs stress different ideas and beliefs, and therefore use different approaches, issues of high quality care and developmentally appropriate practices would suggest that heterogeneous forms of grouping may be more reflective of the goals of early childhood programs in Australia. If one of the major features of early childhood education is to meet the needs of individual children, then attempting to group children based on similarities may be inappropriate.

Unsworth (1985 p 32) indicates that:

> No matter what criteria are used for allocating children to classes or groups, the result will always be a collection of individuals who are more different than they are alike. Approaches to grouping must emphasise these differences and capitalise on them to promote effective learning.

Perhaps then, it is time to use these differences and capitalise on the learning that can occur amongst a diverse group of children. As Unsworth (1985) has implied, the teacher's attitude is the key in terms of making appropriate decisions about grouping that benefit children's learning and development.

A distinction should be made between grouping and programming as these terms are often confused leading to decisions being made about a particular form of grouping based on its perceived connection to another aspect of the program. Grouping refers to the way in which

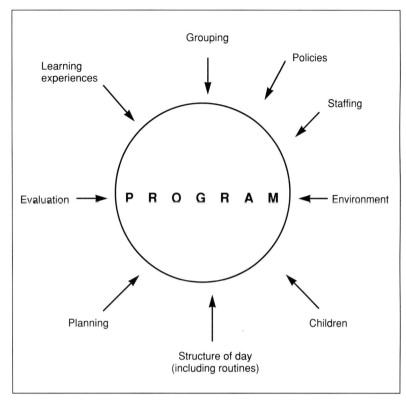

Figure 7.8: An outline of the various aspects of programming, including grouping.

children are brought together or the type of grouping techniques utilised in a setting. Programming incorporates a wide range of factors including curriculum organisation and the structure of the day, as well as grouping techniques (figure 7.8). For, example, a common belief is that mixed age grouping is only possible when all the children are together for the whole day in a completely open, unstructured program. A decision may then be made not to utilise this form of grouping because staff may want a more structured program, rather than on the issue of composition of the group. It is important to be clear about all the different aspects of programming, including grouping, so we can make valid decisions and evaluate the different aspects, rather than make sweeping changes to the whole program.

HOW CAN WE USE GROUPING TO THE BEST ADVANTAGE AND FOR THE BENEFIT OF THE CHILDREN CONCERNED?

Many settings use an 'overall' form of grouping, that is, a way of grouping children for the major focus of the day. In settings for children under 5, children might be age-grouped, developmentally-grouped, or mixed age-grouped for freeplay times. Within a school setting classes are usually formed on age or mixed age (composite) criteria. Sometimes the single class and teacher are together, in other cases teachers team

TIMETABLE – MONDAY, TUESDAY, WEDNESDAY, THURSDAY, FRIDAY		
6 am	Children Arrive Free Play Indoors (Quiet Activities) Children have breakfast if needed As more children arrive, more experiences are set up.	Mixed Age Interest/friendships Needs based
8.30 am	Outdoor area set up Indoor/outdoor play (small room only)	Mixed Age Interest/friendships
9.45	Morning tea plates/drinks taken inside and outside for children to take as they want it. Adults assist young children.	Needs based
10.30	Children-staff set up environment for developmental play.	
10.45	Developmental play — environment set up to cater for particular needs. Groups in – Big room – Small Room – Outdoor	Developmental levels Infants, toddlers, pre-schoolers
	Indoor areas packed away while children help rostered staff set lunch tables and put beds out.	Needs based
	Children wash hands for lunch (toilet if needed)	
12.00	Lunch	Focus groups (small)
12.45	Relaxation time — story, music	
	Infants — cot room 1 Sleepers — small room Resters/non-sleepers — big room/with quiet activites	Needs based
2.30	Children and staff put beds away Children have afternoon tea	Needs based
3.00	Indoor/outdoor play (big room only)	Mixed- Interest/friendship
5.00	Children help pack away outdoors and go indoors (dependent on weather). Free play — quiet activities. Late snack.	Mixed- Interest/friendship Needs
6.00	Children go home.	

Figure 7.9: Example for LDC of different forms of grouping that may be used throughout the day.

teach with more than one class. Within a classroom, sometimes children are taught as a 'whole class' for most of the day, while sometimes there is a short time for 'whole class' focus, with the possibility of children learning individually or in small groups for a major part of the day.

These *smaller* groups may be based on needs, developmental skills, project interests or many other bases.

An example of a daily schedule within an early childhood setting illustrates the different forms of grouping that may be used in one setting (figure 7.9).

What are some other factors that are important to implementation of grouping methods?

WHEN IS IT APPROPRIATE TO USE A LARGE OR SMALL GROUP?

Group size should:
- vary according to purpose;
- be small enough to encourage active participation for all children;
- be large enough to encourage diversity and differing ideas; and
- be considered with reference to time factors.

Large groups are most beneficial when children:
- will benefit from a shared experience;
- are together for short periods of time; and
- are grouped for a defined purpose.

Large groups are least beneficial when children:
- are likely to be frustrated or bored by not being able to work at their own level or speed;
- are locked into routines due to the convenience of the grouping;
- are together for long periods of time; and
- are grouped for general purposes that should be met in small groups.

Smaller group sizes are most beneficial when they:
- enable adults to work with individuals within the group;
- allow for a greater amount of individual participation;
- allow children to work at own pace/developmental level;
- provide greater opportunity for development of language skills;
- allow children to have responsibility for own work/learning;
- help cooperation;
- allow for a variety of learning experiences and activities within the overall setting; and
- allow for a variety of materials (if there are a range of small groups occurring) from which children can choose.

Smaller groups are least beneficial:
- for emergencies such as fire evacuation; and
- for consistency when explaining a safety/emergency issue, such as where children may not be able to play during renovation.

Figure 7.10: Larger groups can be positive when children will benefit from a shared experience for a short period of time

Figure 7.11: Smaller groups can be positive in allowing for a greater amount of individual participation and enabling adults to interact with individual children

Small groups may be part of the overall grouping strategy, for example, learning centres within the classroom, or spontaneous grouping in freeplay, where children choose to go to a particular experience.

WHAT SORT OF GROUPS SHOULD BE USED?

Rather than restrict differences, use a variety of flexible groupings to deal with a wide range of children's responses, and a variety of different situations.

In the past, many settings have tended to have a fixed 'grouptime' which has usually focused on the areas of music and language. That is, a large group for 'storytime' or circle time. While this type of experience can be very enjoyable, it is not the only possible focus for group experiences. On the other hand, we must ensure that this 'grouptime' is not the only time we read a story to children, or share language and music experiences. We should do this throughout the day with individuals and small groups.

If we think about our aims we may discover there are many different ways to achieve these throughout the program, not just at a specific time.

For example, some of the aims for a 'grouptime' may be:

- to introduce new ideas;
- to encourage interaction between children;
- to encourage children to use group skills; and
- to meet individual needs.

There is no reason why these aims can not be met in small groups, for example at lunchtime, or in a spontaneous situation for example, at the water trough.

When making decisions about what type of small groups might be used in the setting, the following aspects might be considered:

- The focus of the group — Why are we having this group?
- Who will be involved in the group, which children?
- How will we implement this group? How will we fulfil our focus?
- Where will this group take place within the setting?
- When will this group take place?
- Will the group be spontaneous, compulsory or free choice?

Small group work can be undertaken by each member of staff working on a method that utilises their individual skills. For example, a bilingual staff member can take a language group with different small groups, on different days. Other members of staff may have drama, cooking or music skills to share with small groups. The list is endless! It only requires creative thinking and encouragement of the existing skills of staff members.

These methods can be used in any setting. In a school setting staff may take groups across different classes. In a preschool setting there may be four staff members in a double-unit preschool with forty children; four small groups with ten children each can take place, rather than two large groups. By rotating the groups of children around the different staff members during the week, all the children benefit from the variety. Staff also benefit as they see a different group each day so do not need to develop different daily plans, but can modify the weekly plan to suit each group, if appropriate. In this way, staff are better able to focus on planning to suit the needs of particular children.

One basis for small groups could be developmental areas. An example is shown below.

Grouptime **Grouptime** *Grouptime* **Grouptime** Grouptime
Grouptime had enough?

Why do we have group times? answer than one eh!

We need to consider each group time that we have during the
day: young toddlers, toddlers, older children, afternoon, pre
lunch.
It may be helpful to analyse each time separately. We should
use this format:

Reason: Why do you think we should do a group time with this
particular group of children?

Long term aim: What do we hope to achieve with these kids
by having a group time?

Short term aim: What can we achieve from day to day?

Description:
Planning — How do you tie in with your planning what you have
observed, read in the developmental records or discussed with
other staff or parents?

Time — What time of day and what length of time is best?

Activity — What prompts you to use that particular activity to
achieve the aim?

How should we gather the children for the activity?

How should we settle them? Who should we not bother with
on that day?

How will we present the activity?

How will we end it and get ready for the next group?

How to clean up?

Evaluation: How can we keep learning from our experience in
presenting the groups? How do we record those evaluations of
individual activities and individual children's responses to
them?

Figure 7.12: This was developed
by one setting to assist staff to
think about the issues related to
group experiences with children.

Source: Magic Pudding Child Care Centre: 1989

WHAT AND WHO?

Focus	*Staff member*
Cognitive Development	Mary
Social/Emotional Development	Sue
Language Development	Abdul
Physical development	Nicky
Rotation (different development area each week to allow staff planning time)	Bill

For a three month period each staff member plans small group experiences related to an area of development. These groups can be with different children each day, and take into account the needs of individual children (perhaps based upon a focus system approach as outlined in chapter 6 Planning for Individuals).

HOW, WHEN AND WHERE?

As these groups are planned around developmental areas and individual children, the range of possible experiences is endless. Many learning experiences across different curriculum areas could be used, so staff would experience variety. Staff could use any part of the environment for the experience if it were spontaneous, or have rostered times for groups if a planned experience and specific space or area was necessary. The timing of groups would relate to whether a particular space was required. Or again, if it were to be spontaneous, timing would be less important.

Rotating staff members allows for one staff member to rotate on a weekly basis around the different developmental areas. That is, one week on social/emotional development, one week on cognitive development, and so on. As a staff member is not required to implement small groups for one week, time is available to plan for the next cycle. Whoever participates as the rotating member must feel confident in this role. At first the most experienced staff member can rotate until others feel comfortable with the role. The rotating staff member may choose to not always implement experiences, but use the time to observe children's development in the focus developmental area for use in future planning.

A further example of how a range of grouping forms might be used in a 'workshop session' in the first years of school is outlined below.

A TYPICAL WORKSHOP (APPROXIMATELY 2 HOURS)

- Uninterrupted sustained silent reading
- Whole group — as individuals (including adults) read for 10 minutes.

- Demonstration writing
- Whole group — as adult demonstrates her shopping list

- Friendship experiences
- Small groups — interest and needs based as children go to learning centres, or select particular experiences.

- Sharing discussion
- Whole group — as pairs (children) share their experiences and learnings

The adult is likely to be the teacher, but this approach could work well in a team teaching situation, and also with family involvement. These are just two examples of ways of sharing skills and workload, while meeting the needs of individuals and small groups.

PRACTICAL CONSIDERATIONS — HOW CAN WE ORGANISE GROUPING?

COMPOSITION OF GROUPS

- Allow for flexibility by trying not to change groups regularly.
- Periodically create, modify or disband in order to meet new needs as they arise.
- Allow for child-initiated groups, as an alternative to adult-initiated groups.
- Vary group size according to purpose.

ORGANISATION

- Allow for choice with a variety of experiences; for example, individuals and groups can decide where to participate in the experience.
- Have clear strategies about how you will implement any grouping method, what you want to achieve with this form of grouping, and how staff will be utilised.
- Monitor the groups and grouping methods in order to evaluate any need for change.

WHAT SHOULD ADULTS PREPARE FOR?

- children's understanding of the composition of the group where applicable, for example, if kindergarten or year one children are to work on a project;
- children's past experiences with grouping and their group skills;
- movement around the environment and use of the room or total setting;
- movement from whole group ——> small group ——> individual if necessary;
- any limits that need to be set in place for effective implementation;
- the role the adult will play in any grouping strategy and interactions;
- organisation of physical space and materials;
- the most appropriate type of grouping to suit objectives whether for the child and/or experience.

WHAT SHOULD CHILDREN BE ABLE TO DO?

- have access to and use resources and materials freely;
- develop problem solving skills, or be assisted to do so initially, and begin to use these;
- develop interaction/negotiation skills with other children;
- be aware of any limits and the needs of others;
- be able to ask for help.

ARE WE USING GROUPING EFFECTIVELY?

As each setting is unique, with different needs, it is important for staff and families at each setting to work through the following ideas as a team so that all involved will feel comfortable and confident with the forms of grouping being used. In this way each setting will be able to meet the needs of the children concerned, and at the same time enable staff to provide and use grouping methods that suit each member's skills and interests. The following ideas, strategies and examples are only guidelines to be used to assist each setting to develop relevant and workable methods.

When making decisions about grouping, the following aspects can be worked through. Figure 7.13 shows an example of the following process in action.

WHAT ARE SOME OF THE ALTERNATIVES?

The team needs to brainstorm all the possible types of grouping they can think of — mixed age, same age, cultural, first language, interest, friendship, developmental, ability, skill and so on. Most groups can be formed on a homogeneous basis (similarities) or heterogenous basis (differences) within these methods. These groups can also be large or small.

WHAT ARE THE BENEFITS?

In the next stage, the team should share their ideas on what they believe the benefits are of each form of grouping. This allows each member of the group to participate and either face their fears about particular forms, or to draw out all the possible myths and realities, and any concerns of each form of grouping. At this stage, these ideas could also be built upon by using relevant resources such as videos, references and articles, and networking with other settings about their ideas and implementation.

WHAT PARTS OF THE PROGRAM MIGHT BENEFIT FROM THESE TYPES OF GROUPING?

After finding out lots of ideas and information about different grouping methods and their benefits, it is possible to investigate parts of your daily program that might benefit from a particular type of grouping. For example, if we look at what you hope to achieve or develop in young children during lunch times, we can then match this with the type of grouping that will help you achieve these goals. It may be important to look at the daily schedule to see what possibilities exist.

HOW COULD STAFF BE UTILISED TO IMPLEMENT DIFFERENT GROUPING STRATEGIES?

Once the team has decided on the range of possibilities they would like to implement, the use of staff within these various forms of grouping can be developed. For example, if primary caregiving is decided upon as a grouping method for developmental records and planning, then initial groups of children and adults could be established.

WHAT CONSTRAINTS SHOULD BE OVERCOME TO IMPLEMENT THESE STRATEGIES?

At this stage, any possible constraints that may affect the implementation need to be addressed so that this will progress as smoothly as possible. For example, does the use of the building have to be addressed with some possible rearrangement of equipment or space suggested? Do staff feel that, although they would like to try the suggested strategies, they would like some in-service first? Considerations of staffs' skills and interests? Once these issues have been faced and worked through, the transition to any changes will be smoother and more effective.

WHAT IS OUR PLAN OF ACTION?

The group may like to devise a series of steps or a six month plan of action, rather than starting everything next week! Strategies should be developed to help the group get started and ensure that their ideas are put into practice. A starting point may be to say 'What can we do to move towards these ideas in the next week?' then move through a series of steps towards the goal.

HOW AND WHAT WILL WE EVALUATE IN RELATION TO GROUPING?

Once these changes have started to be implemented in any setting it is important to evaluate the effectiveness of what is happening. For example, if the team is using a particular method of grouping to promote an area of development or goal of the program, is the method achieving this? Is the implementation running smoothly or are modifications necessary? Decide on what will need to be evaluated and how the group will evaluate before you start any implementation. These aspects, along with when to evaluate (preferably at regular intervals), will assist the team in ensuring that evaluation actually takes place and that modifications to improve the situation are carried out.

Remember, the most important thing to do is to think about grouping, rather than accept the status quo...look at why a particular method is being used and how the setting might be more effective in its use of grouping.

ARE WE USING GROUPING EFFECTIVELY?
An example of the process in practice

The following process is an example, and as such only provides basic guidelines and ideas for each area. The depth each setting will go into will vary — but there are lots more ideas each setting can address than those outlined in this section.

The process can take place in staff/parent meetings where all ideas are shared. This process may take anywhere between 3 months to a year, depending on changes that may need to be put in place.

SETTING:

40 place Long Day Care Centre with children from birth to 5 years.

20 children under 3 years/20 children between 3–5 years.

The building is standard design for N.S.W. under the Federal Government program.

WHAT ARE SOME OF THE ALTERNATIVES?
WHAT ARE THE BENEFITS?
BRAINSTORMING

DEVELOPMENTAL GROUPS

Children of similar developmental level e.g. infants, toddlers, preschoolers, are grouped together.
— assists in "skill" building
— allows "younger" and "older" children to have an environment planned for special developmental needs.

BUT

— may miss out on opportunities to learn from other children
— may be a lack of diversity from which children might benefit.

CULTURE GROUPS

May be based on the same culture
— provided sense of security
— can develop appreciation of own culture first language
— use bilingual/bicultural staff skills

BUT

— other children and staff may not benefit from being involved or "exposed" to diversity.

INTEREST GROUPS

Either groups formed by staff or children based on interests.
— can vary in size
— encourage teamwork and social interaction
— committment to experience if formed by children
— learning enhanced as children are interested

BUT

if always formed/directed by adult, children's interests may not really be followed through — but adults.

SOCIAL GROUPS

Social or friendship groups formed based on social ties.
— stable group with children in the first years of school
— greater commitment and thus learning is encouraged
— enhances social development

BUT

— shy children may have little interaction with other children.

Figure 7.13: Making decisions about effective grouping strategies.

SAME AGE GROUPS

**Children of the same age are grouped together —
1 yr, 2 yr olds etc...**
— can expect a "similar" reaction to equipment use
— may make planning easier for staff with less
   experience/training
BUT
— limits social interaction with various children of
   different developmental levels even though same
   age
— children may be at different developmental levels
   but tied to group due to age rather than needs.

MIXED AGE GROUPS

Children of mixed ages are grouped together.
— easing transitions/more "home like"
— children can interact with a wide range of
   ages/levels of development
— children interact with children in caring, nuturing
   manner
— competition lessoned as children at a wide range
   of development levels
— staff develop a wide range of skills across
   different ages
— younger children model older children
— older children practice/master skills as they work
   with younger children
— children can mix with groups as they feel
   comfortable
— less stress on staff as ages/needs of children are
   diversified e.g. not overpowered by physical
   demands of very young children
BUT
— need to be aware of safety needs with respect to
   equipment/environment
— staff need to feel "comfortable" with a wide range
   of development
— strategies for meeting individual needs are
   important

PRIMARY CARE GROUPS

One staff member "attached" to small group of
   children.
— ensures individual needs of children are met
— can be based on any criteria (culture, mixed
   age...)
— older children could also be "responsible" for
   younger children.
BUT
need to ensure staff are aware of other children not
   just group.

NEEDS BASED GROUPS

Children are grouped together based on needs
— children with similar needs can have these met
— assists staff in looking at needs such as sleep and
   other physical needs
— enhances social development
BUT
if used all the time may have a negative approach to
planning i.e. Staff may not look at strengths.

Figure 7.13: (continued)

WHAT PARTS OF THE PROGRAM MIGHT BENEFIT FROM THESE TYPES OF GROUPING?

After investigating a range of forms of grouping, these ideas are formulated:

OUR TYPICAL DAY

Arrival — parents, children and staff	**MIXED AGE** enables children to make transition from home more secure and comfortable.
	NEEDS BASED for those children requiring breakfast and meeting other physical needs.
Free play	
— Morning tea — Physical needs/routines — Small groups	**MIXED AGE** incorporating smaller, spontaneous groups based on *interests, friendship and needs*.
	This allows children to follow through their own interests while allowing for needs, including physical, to be met individually or in small groups.
Developmental play	**DEVELOPMENTAL GROUPS** To allow for children's (infants, toddlers, pre-schoolers) particular needs/strengths to be planned for within the environment. Three areas to be planned for — but children may still choose to move to another area if interested.
Lunch	**MIXED AGES** to reflect a more secure environment and allowing older children to help younger children to feed themselves. **Primary caregiving** may also be used to assist in small groups for lunch — but this will be based on children's attachments also and may change.
Rest/quiet time	**NEEDS BASED** — with "long sleep area", "short sleep/rest area" and "quiet play". Infants can also utilise cot room.
Free play — Afternoon tea — Small groups	**MIXED AGE** — incorporating smaller, spontaneous groups based on *friendship and interests* (as with morning). *Needs* for physical and other aspects of development.
Home time	

—	Transitions throughout the day will occur in small groups.
—	Specific small groups initiated by staff based upon a variety of forms such as culture, developmental areas etc., will be carried out during free play. Staff will use skills as appropriate and will work as a team. Children may choose to participate or continue with free play.

Figure 7.13: (*continued*)

	HOW COULD STAFF BE UTILISED TO IMPLEMENT DIFFERENT GROUPING STRATEGIES?			

FOCUS CHILDREN SYSTEM/PRIMARY CARE GROUPS

Staff will use a focus children system where *all staff* plan with approximately 4–5 children in mind each week (see chapter 6). However, the concept of primary care groups will also be taken into account at mealtimes and rest if applicable.

MIXED AGE/DEVELOPMENTAL GROUPS

Planning will be based on rosters, that is, indoor/outdoor free play will be planned and implemented for program based on shifts for staff.

For example:

WEEK	STAFF	AREA	SHIFT
Week 1	Mary Bob	Indoor	7.30–3.30
	Nhan Jane	Outdoor (small groups if desired)	8.30–4.30/ 9.00–5.00
	Richard Ursla	Focus Groups (developmental)	9.30–5.30
Week 2	Bob Richard	Indoor	7.30–3.30
	Mary Jane	Outdoor (small groups if desired)	8.30–4.30/ 9.00–5.00
	Nhan Ursla	Focus Groups (development)	9.30–5.30

This roster encourages all staff to work and plan with others on a continuing basis and rotates through a 6 week cycle.

Teams of 2 staff plan each week and focus on a particular aspect of the program, and thus a different aspect of grouping. All staff have an opportunity to plan with a different form of grouping in mind — taking individuals into account through the focus children system and developmental groups. The focus of groups will be different depending on staff skills and children's needs and interests.

	WHAT CONSTRAINTS SHOULD BE OVERCOME TO IMPLEMENT THESE STRATEGIES?	

BUILDING DESIGN	— mixed age grouping will be carried out by allowing for children to free "flow" from indoor -> outdoor rather than 2 smaller (20/20) groups of mixed ages due to the building design focus on 2 large play rooms with nappy change at one end OF building.
CHILDREN'S NEEDS	— Developmental groups will allow children to have time to be with children of similar developmental levels if they choose. Planning can focus on these developmental areas.
	— Physical requirements such as sleep to be based on needs.
INDIVIDUAL NEEDS	— To be met through focus children system.
	Inservice to be organised regarding this aspect.

Figure 7.13: (*continued*)

WHAT IS OUR PLAN OF ACTION?	
Six Month Implementation Phase as decided by Staff and Families	
1. Inservice to be organised to assist in developing Focus Children system. Appropriate system to be developed.	Approx. 2 months.
2. Needs Based groups.	Immediately.
3. Mixed Age.	First 2 months — morning/afternoon/lunchtimes.
	Implementation during free play after initial trialling of above. Process to take approximately 6 months.
4. Developmental Groups — to be organised re planning and environment.	After 1 month establishing organisation, to be implemented during free play — but decreasing in time as Mixed Age and focus children strategies are developed.
5. Ideas for focus after of small groups. Staff discuss needs of children and staff interests and skills.	4 months development and sharing ideas re organisation and possible implementation.\n\nStaff to develop possible formats for planning and implementation (see attached).
— Trial	2 months.
6. Evaluate.	At end of 6 months with discussion re modifications. Modifications may occur to the different aspects outlined above as necessary throughout 6 months period.

HOW AND WHAT WILL WE EVALUATE?
The following areas may be looked at:\n\nIs the implementation running smoothly?\nWhat modifications are necessary?\nHow are children reacting to change?\nHow are staff reacting to change?\nHow are families reacting to change?\nAre grouping forms integrating effectively?\nAre the grouping forms meeting desired aims?\n\nA possible evaluation may be developed for use in following 6 months to assess final question more effectively.

Figure 7.13: (continued)

USEFUL RESOURCES

Dalton, J. (1984) *Adventures in Thinking*. Melbourne, Nelson.

Farmer, S. Grouping — Its Role in Programming, in *Working Smarter...not just Harder*, Papers presented at State Conference of Australian Early Childhood Association, NSW Branch, 1990.

Jones, J. Grouping — Let me count the ways, in *Rattler*, 12, Summer 1989/90, Sydney, Community Child Care Cooperative.

Reid, J., Forrestal, P., and Cook, J. (1989) *Small Group Learning in the Classroom*. Western Australia, Chalkface Press.

Van der Veer. Mixed Ability Teaching in *School Education Journal* Number 1, September, 1991. NSW Department of School Education.

8

MAKING THE MOST OF RESOURCES

INTRODUCTION

Effective use of resources, both human and material, is an important indicator of a high quality program for young children. The way that we organise resources can either result in environments that help us to meet our goals for the program and for individual children, or in environments that work against us achieving these goals. Environments can enable the adults in the setting to fulfil our roles with as little stress as possible or they can add to our stress. From the child's perspective, environments can be places where they are able to explore and develop at their own pace and engage in interactions with people and objects; or places where they are rushed, or in Elkind's term 'hurried' (1981), from one routine or experience to the next, and from one developmental stage to the next.

Environments include more than the physical space. *The Macquarie Pocket Dictionary* (1982) defines environment as:

— surroundings or conditions which influence the life and work of a person or community of people; and

— all of the conditions amongst which an organism lives and which influence its behaviour.

As well as the physical aspects, and the organisation of time, environments include objects and people and the ways that they interact. It is necessary to look at all of these parts, and how they function as a whole, when considering environments.

EMOTIONAL CLIMATE

Environments convey messages as to how we are valued as people and the way that we are expected to behave. They are 'regulators of our experience' (Prescott 1979: p.1), influencing the way we see ourselves and the way we interact with others. Different environments may be welcoming or intimidating, 'warm' or 'cold', 'hard' or 'soft'. We all feel comfortable and 'at home' in some environments and insecure or uncomfortable in others. Environments influence the way that we see ourselves and the way we feel about ourselves, as well as the way we behave. As Greenman (1988) states, the environment 'dramatically affects the quality of our lives'. Early childhood settings, particularly long day care centres, are places where children and early childhood educators spend a large part of their day (figure 8.1) and 'we need to view these settings as places where children and adults live together — places for children and adult lives' (Greenman 1988: p.5).

It is important to recognise the impact that the environment has on our lives and the way that it influences our behaviour. Adults and children all behave differently according to the type of setting they are in. The environments that we create in settings for young children should therefore be designed to promote the types of behaviour that the community, families and staff consider important. The philosophy and goals of the setting should be reflected in the way that the environment is organised. For example, if we believe in promoting independence and self-help skills in children, then this should be reflected in an environment that provides a range of equipment that is easily accessible to children, as well as sufficient time for children to complete routine tasks at their own pace.

What is seen, heard, felt, smelt (and tasted!) will vary for each participant in the setting. We tend to only see the environment through our own eyes, but we need to also think about how it might appear through others' eyes. How does it appear to babies from floor level? What opportunities will toddlers find for exploring? How will families feel when walking through the door for the first time? How will a child feel walking through the school gate on their first day? How will a new member of staff feel in the setting?

Adults in early childhood settings often focus on the functional aspects and are concerned that the environment is orderly, clean and safe. While these are extremely important factors in environments for young children, we also need to consider how the space responds to children's need to be active learners and to their need for comfort and security.

Although children need to be presented with a variety of new experiences, they also need to be in an environment where things are predictable and familiar. Environments for young children should be stable places where there are familiar objects and people, and where at least some things remain constant. There needs to be a continuity between the early childhood setting and the home, so that children are surrounded by familiar objects, languages, songs and foods.

Figure 8.1: Provision for adults, as well as children, is important.

Children also need familiar staff members. This does not necessarily mean that each child should be attached to one primary care giver only, but that there is a group of staff that each child and their family can comfortably relate to. High staff turnover and constantly rotating shifts, which are often the reality in long day care settings, can make this difficult to achieve at times, however thought can be given to organising staff rosters to ensure that there is a familiar face to greet the child and their family each morning.

Consistency, in terms of a stable group of staff that children feel comfortable with, is important, but consistency in the physical environment is equally important. A consistent physical environment is, as Dimond (1979: p.27) states, 'an identifiable space whose parameters are regular, dependable and comfortable'.

The need for a familiar and safe environment should be balanced with the need to provide appropriate challenges and opportunities for children to assert their independence. Environments should be carefully designed to ensure children's safety. When this is the case, adults can devote more time to engaging in meaningful interactions with children rather than 'rescuing' them from potential disasters. Within this indoor and outdoor environment there should be familiar experiences that children can revisit as well as new and stimulating experiences that challenge children's developing skills. If the environment never changes children may become bored and frustrated, but if they are presented with too many new experiences at once, or if every day when they walk in the room has been totally rearranged, they may feel disoriented and insecure.

USE OF PHYSICAL SPACE

When planning environments, thought should be given to creating a variety of play spaces and learning areas with the use of furniture, shelving and room dividers and clear pathways between these areas. Gonzalez-Mena (1989: p.175) suggests that the room need only be divided from the adults' waists down, so that there are a variety of interesting spaces for children, but the adult has a clear view of everything that is happening. Within each learning area equipment should be available on open shelves so that children have ready access to materials, while equipment not in use can be stored at adult height, although still available to children on request.

Temporary spaces can be created by the use of curtains or fabric, plants and boxes, or by hanging blankets from the wall, furniture, trees and so on. Areas can also be defined with the use of rugs, blankets and cushions, and hoops or tyres on the floor or grass. These can easily be rearranged by adults and children to create a variety of spaces. Learning centres, such as dramatic play, reading/language or investigating can be located in these spaces. Small spaces can be used to create cosy spaces or to provide different materials for children to explore, such as musical instruments or mobiles. More permanent spaces can be created by the use of lofts, platforms or forts. Interesting entrances can also be created to lead children into these spaces. For further ideas on creating spaces see Greenman (1988).

Although each space is planned with a particular learning experience in mind, it is necessary to keep boundaries flexible and not to confine experiences only to a specified area, by for example insisting that books stay in the library area. Learning cannot be compartmentalised into disciplines such as Science, Art and Literature. Learning centres often make use of a variety of resources and materials, such as cassette players with picture books; or paints, paper and brushes with computers. Each learning area has the potential to incorporate a variety of curriculum and developmental areas, and children will constantly find new ways to integrate materials. Toddlers in particular need the freedom to be able to carry things around in their arms or in bags, to push them in trolleys and to 'dump' them in unpredictable places.

Within a school setting learning centres are also an effective means of organising physical space whilst catering for individual children's needs.

Learning centres are one way to build on children's interests and to plan integrated experiences that provide for child choice and child initiated learning within an effective learning environment. The degree of choice and independence is closely related to the experience and skills the children currently enjoy. Often learning centres will form part of the developmental play program at school, or part of a workshop approach either in relation to the integrated curriculum or major curriculum areas. Whether in the first, second or third years of school, and indeed later in primary schooling, learning centres provide the ideal means to make the most of children's styles of active learning within a child initiated approach. Learning centres provide a very social means of learning, as through the interaction, much peer learning takes place.

Basically learning centres are a collection of resources with particular experiences in mind which children may engage in at their own pace and interest. This usually occurs without direct adult interaction. However sometimes the adult may focus on interaction with a particular child or small group during this time. The learning centre needs to be located in a suitable corner in the classroom and as it is organised with a particular interest and in an attractive and appealing manner, it draws children's attention.

In order to cater for the diversity of children's development, the experiences in the learning centre need to be openended and provide a range from which children can choose.

For example in developmental play sessions, the whole environment may be set up with many learning centres both inside and outside the classroom. Learning centres may focus on blocks combined with travel agency ie large dramatic play centre, waterplay with complex accessories, modelling with playdough, painting with a variety of implements, box construction, books and cushions on the verandah, lego construction sets. With the allocation of resources, the child will be able to select her/his own aspect of play as well as the other children that she/he interacts with. The adult is also then able to interact with selected children in small groups as they engage in their learning centre. There is also the opportunity for team teaching where other adults interact with individuals or small groups of children within the learning centres. This team teaching situation ideally may extend to co-operative planning and evaluation with regard to the children's learning outcomes as well as the provision of the learning centres.

Within a Year 1 or Year 2, learning centres are still most appropriate ways to facilitate children's learning. Through involvement with concrete materials in a social context, children are able to explore individually as well as in groups, the particular experience offered. There may be more explicit connections to major curriculum areas, through more sophisticated and detailed resources, but the basic principles of active engagement, peer interaction, and openended experiences do not vary. Aspects of major curriculum areas are likely to be integrated bearing in mind that children tend to strongly ignore curriculum/subject boundaries and usually learn in an wholistic manner.

Learning centres can run all day everyday or they can operate for nominated sessions throughout the day. They may have an integrated focus or incorporate a curriculum emphasis. Adults may present one learning centre within a workshop approach or several learning centres at the same time. The manner of implementation depends on the children's past experiences of independent learning.

To operate successfully, learning centres need to be introduced and designed with input from the children. Since children in the centre will be engaged in experiences independently, they need a clear idea of the possible experiences. Some adults discuss and create direction charts with the children to ensure they know the experiences on offer. Some adults stress the interaction and small group aspects by designing experiences to be done in pairs and hence promote cooperative learning. The nature of the experiences offered by the learning centre strongly reflect the adult's philosophy and the children's development.

Since children are engaged in experiences without direct adult interaction, record keeping needs to be well developed and constantly monitored. Children can keep contracts where they indicate which experiences they engaged in and how they felt about them. This can be done on a class chart or on an individual basis. Evaluation needs to be also done by the teacher as to the potential of learning experiences achieved, unexpected learning outcomes, usefulness and availability of resources, interests of the children, children's responses to the experience, development of skills, concepts and processes etc. It is essential to evaluate closely in the early stages of each learning centre in the classroom, especially in relation to implementation, so that refinements and adjustments can be made.

Where provision is made for children to share experiences from the learning centre with the whole group, they have the opportunity to demonstrate their learning as well as their developing independence and decisionmaking skills. Within the workshop approach, there is ample opportunity for a small group to share with others their learnings from the learning centre as children sharing in pairs within the whole group.

Effective use of physical resources enables a number of different groupings to occur throughout the day and caters to children's social and emotional needs. Whatever the setting, it is important that we consider children's needs in all developmental areas.

Spaces, both indoors and out, can be designed to encourage a child to: engage in solitary play as well as small group experiences; to enable a child to find a quiet secluded place to sit as well as to move around freely; and to provide opportunities for real life experiences and fantasy play. Thought should be given to grouping similar types of experiences together, for example quiet experiences near each other and active or noisy experiences in an area where they will not disturb others. The flow of traffic should also be considered when grouping experiences (see figure 8.2).

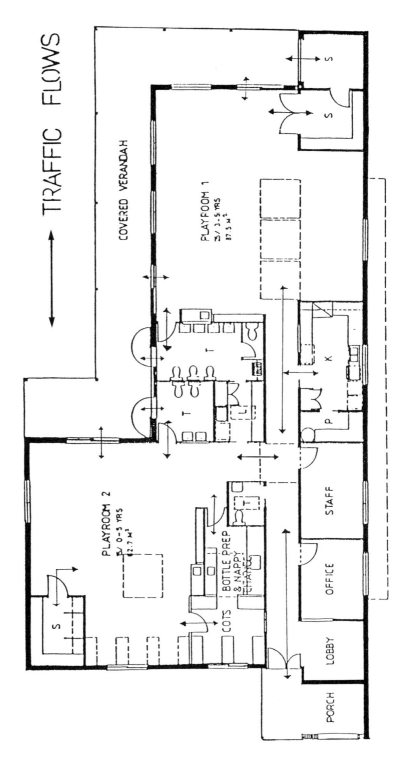

Figure 8.2: Traffic flows

Reproduced courtesy of Denham, Dowe, McParland, Mitchell and Wilde UWS-Macarthur Students 1991

MATERIAL RESOURCES

EQUIPMENT

Children prefer equipment that does something, that responds to their actions — equipment that they can have an impact on (Irvine 1986), such as dirt, which turns to mud when you add water. Equipment that children can use in a variety of new and creative ways, either alone or with others, and that has multiple uses, enables children to develop their imagination and to gain a feeling of competence. Equipment that children can use in different ways at different stages of their development does not need constant changing. 'Basic', open-ended materials such as blocks, clay, water and sand should be provided on an ongoing basis, rather than changing 'gimmicky' toys and experiences.

When planning focuses on 'basic' materials and experiences that are initiated and directed by the child rather than the adult, the adult has more time to be with individual children. That is, experiences that do not require constant adult direction and supervision, free adults to become involved in more meaningful exchanges than the 'how to do it' variety. An environment prepared with a set number of experiences from which children can choose, means that the adult can be free to interact with individual children, rather than needing to 'roam' the room supervising all areas. When adults are sitting still in one place for a period of time, children are more likely to approach them to share in their experiences.

Greenman (1989: p.24) also suggests 'building learning into the setting', by attaching equipment to surfaces such as walls, fences, doors and the backs of cupboards where it is easily accessible to children. Bead frames, steering wheels, doors with latches and locks, telephones and fabric with zippers and velcro are some examples of learning materials that can be attached to a variety of surfaces. Large pieces of paper with crayons or felt pens on strings, large chalkboards and chalk or sheets of contact, sticky side out, can be attached to surfaces such as walls or fences to provide ongoing art and craft experiences. This reduces the amount of time staff spend taking out and putting away equipment and again means more time with children. Routines and blocks of time can be organised so that some equipment can be left out for the whole day.

WHAT ARE THE NEEDS OF CHILDREN AND ADULTS IN EARLY CHILDHOOD SETTINGS AND HOW CAN THESE NEEDS BE MET?

CHILDREN'S NEEDS

Observations of individual children and participation in their play help us to evaluate each child's needs and to arrange the environment in ways to meet these needs. Environments for young children need to be flexible and adapt to the changing needs of children as they grow and develop. In each setting there will be children at varying stages of development, so the environment should cater for a wide range of developmental levels.

Children need the time, space and freedom to develop creativity and problem solving skills, which at times may mean that the environment appears chaotic rather than orderly. Particularly for children under 5, early childhood settings should be places where they are able to explore using all their senses and their whole bodies to move about the environment. This means that the environment needs to be rich in sensory experiences and to have a variety of spaces for children to move in and through.

Children should also have a sense of control over what happens in their lives, which means that they need opportunities to make meaningful choices throughout the day. Experiences that each child can succeed at, in their own way and at their own pace, are vital for children's developing sense of competence and self-esteem. Each child should feel that they are accepted and respected as a wothwhile human being, that their skills, interests and ideas are valued within the setting.

ADULTS' NEEDS

In providing effective environments for young children it is essential to consider the needs of adults as well as children. As Gonzalez-Mena (1989: p.189) points out, adults have the same range of needs that children have and early childhood settings should consider adults' social and emotional as well as their physical and intellectual needs. Staff and parents need to feel valued for the role they play in children's lives and staff need regular, honest feedback about the job they are doing. 'Children need to be around adults who see themselves as worthy' (Gonzalez-Mena 1989: p.189) and who have high self-esteem, as adults are important models for children's own developing self-esteem.

While settings designed for young children accommodate the needs of young children with child-sized furniture, it is also necessary to provide adult-sized furniture and spaces designed for adults. By providing these the setting conveys the message that adults are respected. Environments that cater to adults needs, for example with adult-sized furniture, can also make it easier for both staff and family members to engage in individual and small group experiences such as sharing children's literature. Consideration of health and safety issues, such as procedures that reduce the amount of heavy lifting that adults are required to do, can help reduce stress as well as injuries.

Opportunities for staff to interact socially with each other and with family members are important in terms of meeting staff's social needs. Staff rosters can be organised in ways that provide staff with opportunities for shared lunch and morning tea breaks, as well as times to exchange information with parents. Planning in teams also gives staff members time to interact with each other and share ideas. When staff support each other and work together cooperatively there is a greater sense of job satisfaction and self-fulfilment. One measure of effective early childhood programs is the extent to which staff feel comfortable interacting with each other and exhibit a sense of team spirit (Jorde-Bloom 1988: p.3).

Staff also need opportunities for intellectual growth and professional development. Time to keep up to date with new developments in early childhood education, as well as the opportunity to extend on skills, are vital in maintaining a high quality program as well as meeting staff needs. As each individual staff member's needs and interests will vary, professional development programs that are designed to cater for personal growth will be of most benefit to staff and children. Jorde-Bloom (1988: p.36) suggests that those early childhood settings that value professional development provide release time for staff to attend workshops and conferences and to visit other early childhood settings, as well as provide a range of professional journals, resource books and video tapes in the staff library.

If the environment supports adults, needs and eases the performing of everyday routine tasks, then this will improve the quality of life for all concerned.

The physical setting and the way that space is organised can have a powerful effect on staff morale and hence their disposition and ability to carry out program objectives (Jorde-Bloom 1988: p.13). Poorly organised environments can become frustrating and stressful for both adults and children and have a negative effect on the behaviour and attitudes of both. It is important to pay attention to aspects such as lighting, noise, ventilation, furniture, storage and resources so that the physical environment functions smoothly.

A well organised environment results in staff having more time to spend interacting with children, rather than in searching for equipment. Planning for large blocks of time and providing open-shelving for children to select their own equipment for play means that adults can spend time focusing on children rather than constantly setting up and packing away equipment. Clearly organised environments also mean that parents, volunteers, grandparents and other visitors are more able to find their way around and to take a more active role in the program if they desire.

The needs of families should also be considered when planning the physical environment. The setting should welcome families on their arrival, provide spaces that encourage family members to spend time in the setting and provide clear information and communication systems (figure 8.3).

Some of the issues to be considered in creating a supportive environment for staff and families are:

- clear goals and policies that are communicated effectively;
- well established routines, without being overstructured and inflexible;
- efficient, clearly labelled storage systems;

Figure 8.3: An area for adult and child to spend time together.

- well organised room arrangements with easy access to materials;
- easy access to necessary information and appropriate people and resources;
- effective means of communicating between staff and between staff and families about each child and the program;
- adult-sized furniture;
- space for relaxation and privacy away from children;
- own space for personal belongings.

General information about what is happening within the setting can be communicated to families via noticeboards, newsletters, or whiteboards, while individual and confidential information between families and staff can be conveyed with the use of communication books or pockets for each child. Families can also provide information for staff in these pockets or communication books. A variety of communication systems should be utilised, including spoken, written and pictorial, so that varying degrees of literacy skills are catered for. Wherever possible

Name:
MEALS: TIME:
If applicable:
Independent   Served self
Required help   Poured own drink
TOILETING:
REST/SLEEP:
Quiet activities
Rest — no sleep
Sleep   Time:
Other interesting facts about your child's day: (new experiences, songs, stories, development)
Source: Forbes, French, Stacey and Wade, UWS-Macarthur 1991

Figure 8.4: Information sheet

notices should be translated into the relevant community languages of the families involved.

Communicating information to families on a daily basis does not need to be a time consuming process. Figure 8.4 is an example of an information sheet for families. Forms like these could be filled out and placed in each child's communication pocket (figure 8.5) at the end of the day. Other communication devices are shown in figure 8.6.

Adults in early childhood settings need to constantly plan, organise and evaluate the environment in order to meet the needs of children, families and staff. Greenman (1988: p.42) suggests that the role of the adult is one of: environmental planner, participant and evaluator. Effective evaluation and planning enable the adult to spend more time participating in day-to-day activities and interactions with children.

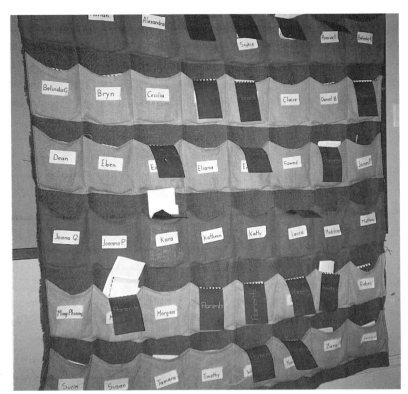

Figure 8.5: An example of communication pockets.

Figure 8.6: Easels as communication boards can be easily moved around.

Interactions between adults and children are one of the key indicators of high quality early childhood programs (Phillips, 1989). Caregivers who are responsive to children's needs and are able to engage in positive interactions with children on a one-to-one basis are essential for a high quality program.

Gonzalez-Mena (1989: p.12) stresses the importance of investing in quality time with young children. One example of quality time is paying full attention to and interacting with children at routine times such as nappy changing. Another type of quality time is being available (by just sitting on the floor or nearby children's play) and being responsive rather than directive. Equally important is becoming involved in children's play as a shared experience. In group settings the environment can be planned in ways that free adults to give each child this type of time on a daily basis.

HOW CAN WE ORGANISE EFFECTIVE LEARNING ENVIRONMENTS?

Children are learning from everything that happens throughout the day, from interactions with objects in the environment, with other children and with adults. When planning and evaluating environments for young children we must consider whether opportunities are provided for active, 'hands-on' learning, both individually and in small groups, soft responsive areas or what Schurch (1988) calls 'comfort zones', and time for one-to-one interactions between children and adults.

Some aspects to be considered in planning learning environments are:

VARIETY OF SPACES

- Are there spaces for children to be quiet and reflect on their day?
- Are there spaces for children to be active and noisy?
- Can children view the environment from different perspectives, such as through the leaves of a tree or from different heights?
- Are there a variety of textures for children to feel with their feet and hands?
- Do cosy, 'secret' places exist where children can find spaces to be alone , such as under a blanket, behind the lounge, or in the garden?

OPPORTUNITIES FOR A VARIETY OF GROUPINGS

- Is there the time and space for children to engage in solitary play (figure 8.7)?
- Are there opportunities for children to initiate their own small groups around experiences that interest them (figure 8.8)?
- Do adults interact with children on a one-to-one basis and in small groups?

Figure 8.7: Engaging in solitary play.

Figure 8.8: Small group engaged in similar interests.

- Do children have opportunities to interact with small groups that represent diverse stages of development?

FLEXIBILITY

- Is there a variety of equipment that caters for different developmental stages (figure 8.9)?
- Are children able to choose their own play equipment?
- Is equipment accessible to children?
- Are children encouraged to use equipment in new and creative ways and challenged to solve problems?
- Is there equipment both indoors and outdoors that children can move to create their own play spaces?
- Do adults move large outdoor equipment to provide appropriate challenges for children?

AESTHETICS

- Is there a warm, friendly feeling that makes this an enjoyable place to be?
- Is the natural environment reflected in the use of light, colour, and decorations?
- Are there paintings, sculptures, wallhangings, and other works of art that children can explore using all their senses?
- Are there soft areas both indoors and out with blankets and cushions for sitting on and relaxing?
- Are there different textured surfaces for children to interact with and on?
- Are there interesting patterns and colours in the fabrics and decorations used and in the plants, both indoors and outdoors (figure 8.10)?
- Are there things to swing and be rocked in such as hammocks, chair swings and rocking chairs?
- Is there a variety of music, musical instruments and wind chimes for children to enjoy?
- Are there culturally familiar artefacts for children to respond to?

There are many formal and informal ways of assessing the environment. Some commercially available materials, such as the Early Childhood Environment Rating Scale (Harms and Clifford 1980) and the Infant/Toddler Environment Rating Scale (Harms, Cryer and Clifford 1990) outline means of looking at many areas of the environment and rating these. Areas covered include:

- meals;
- sleep/rest time;
- furnishings;
- room arrangements;
- language interactions;

Figure 8.9: Providing opportunities for children of mixed stages to interact.

- space and time for gross and fine motor experiences;
- health and safety policies and practices;
- groupings; and
- play and choice.

Often different staff may have different experiences and expectations that they bring to the setting, or different perceptions as to how the environment is working. Completing a rating scale such as this can help staff to identify areas of concern, and even conflicting expectations, which can then be discussed more openly. Participating in self-evaluation as part of an accreditation process is also a very effective way of assessing the existing situation and as a team formulating goals for particular areas.

Other means of evaluating either materials or the total environment can be found in commercial programs or can be developed by the staff. The Alerta program (Williams and DeGaetano 1985), for example, provides guidelines for assessing the learning areas available in the environ-

Figure 8.10: A variety of colours, patterns and textures.

ment, with a strong cross-cultural focus, as well as a number of questions that can be asked regarding stereotyping of learning materials, such as puzzles, books and posters. Some of these include:

- Are illustrations of the physical characteristics of characters in the materials unreal or unnatural (for example Asians portrayed as yellow, Blacks having white facial features, Native Americans having red skin)?
- Are high status occupations (such as being a doctor or holding a decision-making position) associated only with men in the story? (Williams and DeGaetano 1985: p.257)

Staff can create their own brief checklist or questionnaire for learning materials that is relevant to the particular context that they are in. Evaluation formats can also be devised to provide feedback on the extent to which learning areas, such as the dramatic play, library or art areas reflect an anti-bias approach, cater for creativity and problem solving and so on.

SOME QUESTIONS RELATING TO THE LIBRARY AREA

- Is the library area in a quiet spot?
- Are there a range of comfortable furnishings?
- Do children have easy access to the books?
- Are there enough books for the number of children using the area?
- Are there a variety of books written in the languages that are spoken by the children in the setting and community members?
- Do some of the books' contents and illustrations represent the diversity of backgrounds within the setting and local community?
- Do the books contain positive images of male and female roles, differing lifestyles and cultural practices, and sexual preference? Are people of different ages and abilities depicted positively?
- Are the images and information contained in the books accurate and representative of everyday experiences and events? (Adapted from Hopson 1990: p.26)

MAKING THE MOST OF HUMAN RESOURCES

Research and practice indicates that team work and collegiality leads to job satisfaction and self-fulfilment for all members of the team. Team work characterises effective, high achieving settings, and leads to a program where all concerned are heading in the same direction and working towards the same goals. Where staff work as a team, and there is a high degree of collegiality, individuals feel free to express opinions openly, and are supportive of one another (Jorde-Bloom 1988).

If a setting is to work with a team approach, then this should be reflected throughout the entire program, that is in the philosophy, goals, planning strategies, and the implementation and evaluation of the program. If team work is considered to be an important aspect of the setting, then this should be reflected in the philosophy and goals from the start.

For example, the philosophy may state that a team approach, where all staff are respected as individuals as well as valuable members of a team, is seen as important within the setting. This may be reflected in goals that include:

- to ensure that staff needs are catered for within the program;
- to ensure that staff are respected and treated as individuals with worthwhile contributions;
- to have regular staff communication; and
- to encourage a team approach where all staff do most jobs,

except where expertise is needed e.g. first aid
(Magic Pudding Child Care Centre, Sydney, 1991)

While we often think of team work as involving all the staff in the setting, we sometimes forget that families, children, the community and the
management group are also part of the team. Effective team work needs
to consider ways of involving all of these groups in the program, from
the development of a philosophy to evaluation of the program. In this
section we will concentrate on the role of staff in a team approach, but
we should not lose sight of the other members of the team and the roles
that they have to play.

Effective teams have a clear purpose and work together to meet common goals, where the needs and development of the children and a
developmentally appropriate program are more important than the individual aims of each member. The key to a successful team is that each
member and their contribution to the team is valued and that all have
input in the decision making process. This means that the individual
skills and needs of staff members are not overlooked. These aspects
should be addressed when considering staff development needs in the
setting.

To build a good team you need to:

■ Create an atmosphere of open communication and honesty, where
  opinions and questions are valued.
■ Accept that people make mistakes.
■ Understand that each member has a role to fill and appreciate that
  role.
■ Evaluate your own performance and how you fit into the team regularly.
■ Help others to succeed.
■ Cooperate with each other on daily tasks and share responsibilities.
■ Use the individual skills of team members and share your skills and
  resources.
■ Develop yourself professionally, as that will help the team to grow.
■ Accept criticism without becoming personally affronted.

WHERE CAN WE START?

Research by Johnson and Johnson (1991) has shown that groups working together over an extended period of time go through various stages.
During the *forming* stage, members are polite, avoid conflict and are clarifying their task. The next stage is one called *storming*, where as members
come to feel more comfortable with each other they engage in conflict.
While this is an important stage, it is hopefully moved through to the
next stage of *norming*. During this stage greater group cohesion develops
and team members exhibit more willingness to share ideas and
resources. The next stage is one of *performing*, where a cooperative group
climate with effective problem solving and task accomplishment can

occur. The final stage of *mourning* occurs when people leave the group or the group is coming to an end. In addition to these stages outlined by Johnson and Johnson, it could be said that if the group is a long term one a *'renewal'* stage may occur, where members renew their ideas and need different motivation.

It is important to realise that all of these stages are to be expected, and more importantly, to work out where your team fits into these stages. Once the group has done this, it can work on ways to consolidate the activities of the group or move on to the next stage if appropriate.

When working as a group, it is essential to formulate clear goals in order to provide direction. Goals should be clearly defined so that we know what we are trying to achieve and also so that we can evaluate 'how we are going' towards achieving each goal. When formulating goals and developing strategies to meet them, it is important that everyone in the group has input into making decisions. When making group decisions encourage innovative ideas and provide everyone with the opportunity to share their ideas with the group. It is often a useful strategy to write down all ideas on a whiteboard or butcher's paper and to then weigh up the potential benefits and disadvantages of each solution generated. In this way all ideas are acknowledged and examined. By following these strategies, all members of the team are encouraged to offer ideas and participate in the decision making process. When all members of the team are involved they are more likely to be happy with the decision, and committed to making it work. Once a decision has been made a plan of action can be formulated, again with input from all members of staff (for further information on goal setting see chapter 5).

Effective communication is the first step in team work. Staff should listen to each other, and to families, children and community members, and be responsive to concerns and new ideas. Channels of communication should be open at all times, so that information flows between staff members and between management and staff, and families and staff. Clearly defined job descriptions, policies and procedures, and the effective communication of these, are also essential to a well-functioning team. 'Only when definitions and implementation are orderly can employees understand how the nature and scope of their jobs meshes with the expectations of others' (Jorde-Bloom 1988: p.8).

All staff should know the expectations of their roles and how these are to be fulfilled within the setting. In many cases staff roles and responsibilities may be similar and roles can be clarified by coming together as a group and discussing them. Staff may individually interpret their role and what responsibilities it entails and then come together as a group. By considering the similarities in roles, staff may as a group develop a core job description that applies to all staff. Any items from the individual lists not within the core job description, may then become additional responsibilities for those individual positions, for example the nurse or the director, or it may be decided that only the director takes on additional responsibilities. Whatever the group decides, the process of looking at what we all do allows members to realise that we are all working towards the same goals and share many of the same skills, but that we also bring particular expertise to the group.

The group may decide to share some roles in order to alleviate staff stress. Rotating roles, shifts and tasks provides variety for staff and allows each staff member time away from children on a regular basis. Staff may decide, for instance, that on one day a week a different member of staff cooks and the cook spends time with the children, or that all staff undertake some administrative tasks. Rosters for various tasks provide staff with the opportunity to develop a range of skills and at the same time ensure that all of the 'jobs' get done and that the load is shared.

One aspect of working as a team is the delegation of tasks to different members of the team. When delegating, it is necessary to recognise and accept that individuals will all approach tasks differently. Pressure for staff to complete tasks in a set way can lead to resentment and a reluctance to participate at all. The issue of members of staff receiving differential pay based on the extent of their qualifications and experience should also be dealt with sensitively. Staff may feel that they do not want to take on extra responsibilities when their rate of pay does not reflect this. These feelings must be taken into account and accepted by the group. It may mean that some members of staff need to receive support and resourcing from staff with more experience and training. For example, one member of staff with more background in planning may act as resource person for other members of staff and rotate from one small planning group to another providing support and assistance.

Team work is particularly important in planning and programming. All aspects of planning benefit from a team approach and staff members and families can be included in a range of ways. Some aspects of programming in which different team members can have input include individual records for children, planning for individuals and grouping. Members of the team may be involved in discussing and devising systems, such as methods of record keeping, planning formats, ways of grouping children, and systems for catering for individual children. Staff as a team may be involved in discussing individual children's progress and in planning and evaluation.

HOW CAN WE PLAN AS A TEAM?

If staff are to plan as a team, time must be set aside on a regular basis to allow this. If planning is based on different teams planning for different parts of the program, time should be allocated for groups of two or three staff to plan together or, alternatively, staff may need time to plan together as a whole group. While time may be available at either end of the day in school and preschool settings, rosters should be developed in long day care centres that enable staff to have time away from children to plan as a team.

When developing rosters, staff must be aware of licensing regulations for their setting and ensure that adequate staff–child ratios are maintained at all times. Licensing regulations must also be considered when allocating staff to different areas of the program.

If the setting follows a focus system approach (see chapter 6), where each staff member has a number of children that they focus on for planning, the staff as well as the children can benefit. By each staff member collecting information on focus children and developing records, staff are all able to use and further develop their skills. Information can be shared with a planning team or at a staff meeting, where staff can gain increased understanding from the interpretations and perceptions of others. Staff with a greater amount of experience and/or training, as well as suitable resources, may bring new insights to the planning team and support the development of staff skills.

Each individual team member will bring strengths to the program, whether their skills are in a community language, art and craft, music, management, or any other area. These individual skills should be respected and encouraged, both in working with children and sharing with other members of staff. Staff skills can be utilised when implementing small group experiences with children. For example, one member of staff may be interested in environmental experiences and organise small group experiences in this area, while another staff member may be interested in involving small groups of children in cooking experiences. Professional development programs should be devised that provide each staff member with opportunities to build on their strengths, either through inservice programs or further training, and share their skills with others. If individuals grow, then the team will also grow.

USEFUL RESOURCES

Gonzalez-Mena, J. and Eyer, D. (1989) *Infants, Toddlers, and Caregivers*, Mountain View, California: Mayfield Publishing Company.

Greenman, J. (1988) *Caring Spaces, Learning Places: Children's Environments That Work*, Redmond, WA, U.S.A.: Exchange Press.

9

EVALUATION — PURPOSES AND PROCESSES

INTRODUCTION

The Macquarie Pocket Dictionary (1982) defines evaluation as the process of 'appraising carefully' or 'ascertaining the value of' something. Within early childhood settings, educators are constantly appraising and assessing the value of a wide range of things, from the suitability or effectiveness of a planned experience, to the best time to hold a family meeting or the most beneficial way to organise staff rosters.

Evaluation is something we do every day. However, to be effective and to form the basis for explaining what happens and why, the process, focus, purpose and methods of evaluation need to be clarified and documented.

WHAT IS EVALUATION?

Evaluation is a decision making process that involves staff, management and families in the following steps:

- deciding why we are evaluating;
- deciding what is to be evaluated;
- deciding on appropriate techniques, time frame and staff, management and family roles;
- gathering the relevant information;
- interpreting and sharing the information; and
- using the information and interpreting in future planning and action.

WHY IS EVALUATION IMPORTANT?

Within this approach, evaluation is seen as part of the ongoing planning process. The evaluation process can be applied to all aspects of the early childhood setting: the children, the staff, one's self as well as to the overall program and management. Evaluation is such an integral part of all planning, that it is present in almost everything we do — for example the evaluation sections on daily and weekly planning formats as well as regular overall program and management evaluation. Evaluation enables early childhood educators, management and families to make valid decisions and judgments about what has happened and what they believe will be best in the future. Whilst on one hand evaluation is looking back on what has happened, evaluation can also be the starting point for planning. For example, staff, management and families may describe and assess the current needs of those involved before designing and implementing a particular program or making changes to an existing plan. In sum, evaluation offers continuous opportunities and means by which early childhood educators, management and families can be more effective within their setting. Throughout several chapters in this book, evaluation is considered in relation to particular aspects of programming and planning. In this chapter, the general principles of evaluation are discussed.

WHAT INFLUENCES EVALUATION?

Clear understandings of the nature of the setting is essential, as there are many influences which affect our decision making, planning and hence evaluation. As discussed in chapter 4, the complexities and details of philosophy/ideology and the setting provide many influences for our planning. These influences can appear as both positive and negative as they impede or facilitate our decision making (figure 9.1).

Much of what we decide to evaluate depends on our changing knowledge, values and assumptions about children, about ourselves, about the adult's role and about the environment. We all have ideas about children and learning which derive from a number of sources, such as our own experiences, the experiences of others and our own education and professional development. In deciding what to evaluate, we need to be aware of these ideas and how these may influence what and how we evaluate. For example, if we think that children learn through taking in lots of information that the early childhood educator has decided is important, then we will probably evaluate how well the child can recall that information. In this case we are evaluating teacher-selected products of learning.

If, on the other hand, we think that children learn as they actively try to make sense of their world around them by thinking and acting upon the environment, then there will not always be a product to evaluate. Rather, the focus of evaluation will be on the processes which the child has used to develop understanding.

In a similar fashion, if we believe that the format of the written program is an indicator of how appropriate that program is for children, then we may evaluate programs in terms of the formats used. If we believe that

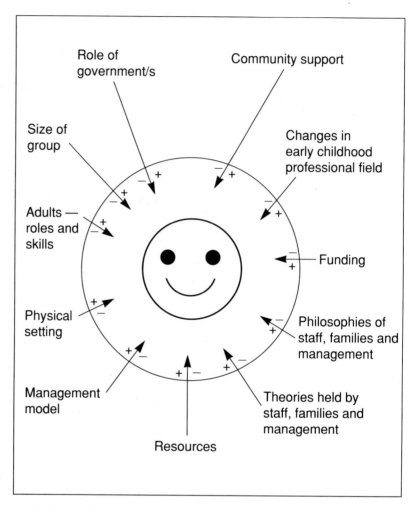

one indicator of the effectiveness of the early childhood program is reflected in the quality of the interactions between children and adults then we will be evaluating the program in terms of features which are widely recognised as important to children's development and learning.

The knowledge, values and assumptions we hold form part of our philosophy. This personal ideology, as well as that held by the other members in the early childhood setting, will influence the ways we evaluate. It will influence the ways we observe and gather information, as well as how we interpret and implement evaluation. In many instances the philosophy of early childhood settings will contain statements inferring evaluation. They may be similar to the one listed below:

> To provide a caring supportive environment which reflects individual and cultural diversity for everyone at the centre.

As early childhood educators we need to be aware of the philosophy of the setting and to adopt evaluation techniques that are consistent with that philosophy. The kinds of evaluation used in a particular setting, in a general sense, are natural extensions of the philosophy of that setting.

Within each setting, the decision makers need to respond in new and creative ways to make the most of those things that influence our decision making. This strongly relates to having a positive and creative mindset to meet contradictions and conflicts, or perceived conflicts, and in implementing, interpreting or integrating evaluation into daily practices. One of these issues in decision making relates to balancing long and short term evaluation. The decision makers need to set clear priorities in regard to short and long term evaluation. One example of short term evaluation would be for an early childhood educator to evaluate a new child's transition into the setting in order to meet the immediate needs of the child. An example of a long term evaluation could be planning for continuing staff development. Balancing the influences that impinge on our decision making is a significant aspect of our role as evaluators and educators.

HOW MIGHT WE DESIGN OUR EVALUATION?

Evaluation needs to commence from an informed and well considered base. We need to consider the following aspects so that we make the best decisions (as seen in figure 9.2.)

If we consider these aspects of evaluation as a team effort, we can refine the focus, purpose and nature of alternative evaluation methods in order that time and energy can be spent finding out what we do want to find out: in other words, working smarter not harder.

The evaluation process begins with clarifying the focus and the immediate purpose, selecting only the most appropriate methods to meet the stated focus and purpose, interpreting, sharing and reflecting upon the collected information and then implementing decisions in future planning. In this way the evaluation process is constant and ongoing. It requires us to be sensitive and flexibile in order to make decisions that contribute to merit and worth at every stage of the evaluation. In this way the process of evaluation seeks to be responsive to the nature of our early childhood setting in order to provide us with relevant and informative feedback (figure 9.3).

Within the diagram, attention is paid to why we want to evaluate: *the purpose;* what we actually want to do — *the focus*; how we are going to do it (techniques), the people involved (staff, management, families, advisers) and time — *the method* and what will we do now — *the integration* into the daily program, as well as the basic processes of information collecting, interpreting and implementing. Each of these parts is considered below.

1 WHY? — THE PURPOSE

What is the purpose of the evaluation?

Within early childhood settings, the overall purpose of evaluation

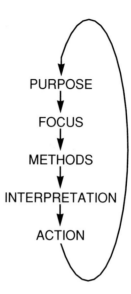

Figure 9.2: Designing evaluation

generally can be best described as to 'contribute to the improvement of teaching and learning' (Johnson 1989: p.509).

As well as this overall aim, any evaluation needs to have a sharper intention, that is the particular aspect we wish to evaluate. For example:

> Purpose: to establish developmental records to use in continuous evaluation of children's development *to immediately inform staff* for individual planning

> Purpose: *to inform staff for future planning* in relation to the setting environment in terms of its reflection of families' diversity

As part of the purpose, it is important to identify for whom and what our evaluation is aimed. In respect to the first example this may mean evaluation is for staff information to plan to meet the needs of individual children, as well as family information to convey how their child is developing. Clearly the foundations of our focus and purpose are linked to our ideology as discussed in the chapter 4 'Getting Started'.

2 WHAT? — THE FOCUS

What will evaluation focus on in the early childhood setting?

All aspects of the setting can be evaluated, including:

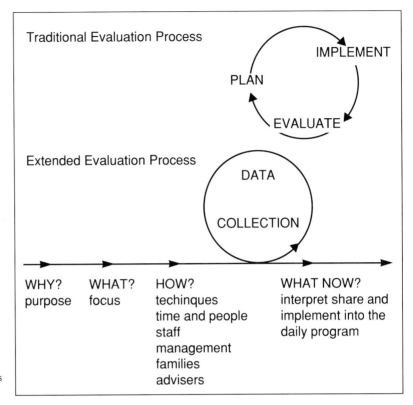

Traditional Evaluation Process

IMPLEMENT

PLAN

EVALUATE

Extended Evaluation Process

DATA

COLLECTION

WHY?
purpose

WHAT?
focus

HOW?
techinques
time and people
staff
management
families
advisers

WHAT NOW?
interpret share and
implement into the
daily program

Figure 9.3: Evaluation process cycles

- children
- role of staff, adults, families and management in the setting
- resources
- environment
- overall program.

These aspects can form the broad focus of particular evaluations and are explored further in various chapters throughout this book. In chapter 7 'Planning For Individuals' evaluation is considered as one part of the planning cycle for individuals and small groups. Evaluation of staff, adults, environment and resources is discussed in terms of the planning process in chapter 5 'Approaches to Planning' and chapter 8 'Making the Most of Resources'. Evaluation in regard to the overall program will be explored later in this chapter.

The specific focus of the evaluation will vary with each evaluation undertaken. The focus may be all the children in the setting; it may be program design and implementation, such as approaches to investigating or language and literature ; it may be staff appraisal for future professional development or even the effectiveness of our own role within the setting. The nature of the focus is often clearly linked to the purpose for which you are evaluating and your overall philosophy.

The focus must then be clearly stated before starting:

Focus — to *continually evaluate children's* development to inform individual planning in the centre or classroom.

Focus — to *evaluate the centre/classroom environment* in terms of approaches to *diversity* in relation to informing staff for future planning.

Focus — to *evaluate the effectiveness of staff/family communication* to inform proposed staff development.

3 HOW? — THE METHOD

What techniques, people — staff, management, advisers, families — and times will we use? Once we have clarified the focus and purpose for our evaluation, all possible techniques, people and time should be considered. There is a wide range of techniques available. Critical decisions must be made about each technique as they vary widely, in the nature and quality of information gathered and importantly, in the amount of time and energy expended. Throughout this book, in the various chapters previously mentioned, examples of techniques are included. The quality and relevance of information gained from various techniques should be predicted so we can make informed decisions. Sometimes information collected is sketchy, lacking sufficient detail for any valid interpretation. Other times there is so much information that analysing is an overwhelming task.

All people can take important roles in the evaluation. There are several benefits for individuals as involvement in evaluation can be a powerful form of professional development and informed staff are often the best implementers of evaluation decisions. Where the individuals take a teamwork approach to evaluation, the workload is considerably reduced for all concerned and interpreting and sharing becomes an interactive learning process.

It is useful to write down this kind of decision making information and predict some outcomes from the use of each technique as seen in the following matrix. By exploring the available options on paper, considering who is involved, how and when the information is gathered and thinking about likely outcomes, mistakes can be made on paper, rather than with people. Thus time and energy is spent on effective evaluations. Decisionmaking of this nature is seen in the matrix in figure 9.4.

By going through this process we can pinpoint some of the opportunities as well as any constraints and difficulties associated with the focus, purpose and selected methods we have chosen for evaluation. Taking time to fill in a matrix such as this in the beginning, may well save lots of time and energy down the track.

By considering the information in the matrix we can refine on paper important decisions about the design of the evaluation and make the best of features, for example the skills and expertise of people involved in the setting in which we are working.

PURPOSE: To inform staff for future planning in relation to the setting environment in terms of its reflection of families diversity.

FOCUS: To evaluate the centre/classroom environment in terms of approaches to diversity.

SELECTED TECHNIQUES: 2,3,4,5.

TECHNIQUE	WHOM	WHEN	FOCUS	LIKELY OUTCOMES	DECISION
1. Written survey	— all staff — 6 — each staff member to contact 10 families each to share the load	over two weeks	all families	— some families will respond in detail — some families won't feel comfortable writing about their reactions — several families will find writing in English or their first language difficult	— insufficient information — may be misinterpreted — can't be anonymous **NOT SUITABLE**
2. Personal interview	— all staff — 6 — each staff member to interview 10 families each	over four weeks	all interested families	— more families likely to respond to personal contact — issues can be explored and handled sensitively	— enhance staff/families knowledge and communication — families likely to share perceptions **SUITABLE**
3. Observations of children and incidental interactions with children	— focus children — groups	over two weeks	— each staff member's focus children group	— children's perceptions are vital to investigate — children's interactions with the environment	— enhance staff/child knowledge and interactions **SUITABLE**
4. Observations of environment	— all staff	over two weeks	— indoor/outdoor experiences — equipment — resources eg books, music, songs, instruments — languages/dialects used by staff	— menu	— emphasis within the daily program can be described
5. Staff observations and strategies	— all staff	over two weeks	— all staff	— awareness of own interactions — effectiveness of strategies	— informative description of staff interactions and strategies — leads to staff development **SUITABLE**

Figure 9.4: Choosing evaluation techniques

4 WHAT TO DO WITH THE INFORMATION? — INTERPRETING AND SHARING AND TAKING ACTION

Once information has been gathered, we need to interpret it and to share it in order to make sense of the findings. Evaluation with a child focus may mean looking at a range of anecdotal records for a child and making interpretations based on knowledge of child growth and development together with an understanding of this particular child. Evaluation with a broader focus may mean looking carefully and identifying consistent and/or paradoxical patterns and events within the gathered information regarding how the setting reflects the diversity of the setting's familes.

Once interpretations or patterns have been established, we need to decide how to act on this information and how to implement our new insights into daily practices and programs.

WHY EVALUATE THE TOTAL PROGRAM?

Initially it may seem unnecessary and redundant to evaluate the total program since evaluation is part and parcel of daily planning and evaluation formats. However, unless we periodically stop, investigate and reflect on what makes up the total program, we may get caught up in focusing on our special interests and get sidetracked into some of the many tasks that constitute the busy day's program.

As discussed in chapter 1, there are various accreditation programs being currently trialled in Australia. The importance of accreditation was recently acknowledged and given creditibility by the federal government with the allocation of $1 million towards the development of a national system of accreditation. The focus of these total program evaluations is comprehensive and considers many important features including staff, children and families as well as the physical environment.

Features relating to staff include staff–child interactions, curriculum, staff–family interactions, administration, staffing levels and education, physical environment, health and safety, nutrition and food service, and evaluation within the setting for example, are part of the accreditation system in the National Asociation for the Education of Young Children model. An evaluation of this coverage and complexity must be coherent and valid. This evaluation is carried out by the staff, director and families as a self-study. This description is then confirmed by a validator and an external committee. The process takes into account the observations of staff and families as well as the outside validators.

Evaluating on such a wide, but focused framework offers us the opportunity to identify strong consistencies, and paradoxes in our setting. It provides a representation of and constructive feedback about the program that acknowledges and encourages the extension of what we are doing well and assists us in what we need to improve. This kind of feedback process should enhance our competence as choice makers and problem solvers: skills, abilities and attitudes which are necessary for living in a changing modern world (Jones 1991).

A further benefit of this approach to accreditation, is the opportunity for staff to observe, record and reflect on the experience. This is a valuable alternative to the traditional inservice, because shared evaluation is occurring on site, within a familiar context and by the staff and families of the setting, and in terms of their common goals.

WHY REFLECT ON DAILY PRACTICES?

Early this century Dewey proclaimed the virtues of reflecting on practice and making active choices in future action. He wondered whether much of what happened in schools was the outcome of

> 'routines, traditions, accident and transitory accidental influences' and whether this was due to the lack of 'systematic methods of inquiry which were brought to bear on a range of facts, [which] enable us to understand them better and to control them more intelligently, less haphazardly and with less routine' (Amidon and Hunter 1966: p.8).

Although Dewey was referring specifically to schools, the situation has relevance to all early childhood settings today.

Current researchers believe that reflecting both upon our practices and 'reflecting upon our reflections' (Schon 1983, 1987) is an imperative practice for all professionals. If we are to grow and develop as individuals and contribute to significant issues in the field of early childhood, we must think back on what we do and *why* we do it. Whilst preservice and inservice education is constantly improving and increasing, early childhood educators are finding themselves in situations that their education has not prepared them for. New issues are constantly surfacing and within these issues there are many shifting grounds, values and practices.

Other educators have emphasised the importance of adults reflecting on their practices, sharing with others and encouraging others to do the same in order to find their own ways in meeting the issues in the field. (North 1987 in Newman 1990)

Mayher sees the role of professional educators as

> To become part of the conversation. To write our own chapters, based on our experimentation, and reflection and to urge students and colleagues to write theirs. To recognise that the greatest support we can expect from others is not the surety of answers but the excitement and rewards of becoming part of a wider profession that takes our journey seriously and recognises the need for mutual respect along the way. (Mayher in Newman 1990 p.xvi)

In other words, the ability to be flexible, to share with others and to be responsive to meet changing needs and potentials is essential in order to go forward.

There are many benefits to reflection as adults are empowered within their setting.

> Their teaching is transformed in important ways: they become theorists, articulating their intentions and finding connections with practice. (Stillman and Goswami 1987, preface)

Although these researchers were referring to whole language teachers, the implications of reflection upon practice remain valid for all professional educators. Empowerment of early childhood educators is vital as they reflect critically and consider the nature of the policies and practices on programs of high quality in early childhood services.

HOW DOES EVALUATION RELATE TO RESEARCH?

Monighan-Nourot (1990) stresses the importance of combining reflection with research. Research and reflection enables us to understand why we do what we do and to tell others about this. She suggests that research and reflection will enable us to avoid situations where

> teachers of young children have adapted traditional practices without questioning their origin and meaning in the lives of the children they teach.... many teachers are unable to articulate a defense of play in the curriculum and are vulnerable to pressures to conform to the behaviouristic standards of the elementary school... (1990 p.80)

If we critically evaluate our practices on a regular basis and actively reflect on what we are doing and why, we are engaged in our own research. By 'REsearching' (Berthoff 1981) in our own setting, looking for the 'patterns that connect' as well as those that don't, we can make sense of our practices and take them further.

Being aware of research readings we can call upon, assists us to articulate the bases behind our practices and be constantly linking theory and practice.

Thus research can be a natural extension of our daily program within the setting. It need not always take the form of our reading about research happening 'elsewhere' with outside researchers entering a setting and 'doing research'. As informed educators, there are many kinds of evaluation available to us in our setting — action research, collaborative research, teacher research etc. It is important to view ourselves as part of this endeavour as we are engaged in closely examining what we do.

USEFUL RESOURCES

Bredekamp, S. (ed) (1991) (revised Edition) *Accreditation Criteria and procedures of the National Academy of Early Childhood Programs*. National Association for the Education of Young Children. Washington, D.C.

Connelly, F.M. and Clandinin, D.C. *Teachers as Curriculum Planners*. (1988) Teachers College Press. New York/Ontario.

Jorde-Bloom, P. (1988) *A Great Place to Work: Improving Conditions for Staff in Young Children's Programs*. National Association for the Education of Young Children. Washington, D.C.

Phillips, D.A. (ed) (1987) *Quality Child Care: What Does Research Tell Us?* National Association for the Education of Young Children. Washington, D.C.

Williams, L.R. and De Gaetano, Y. (1985) ALERTA. *A Multicultural, Bilingual Approach to Teaching of Young Children*. Addison Welsey Publishing Company. Menlo Park.

Part 3
DEVELOPMENTALLY APPROPRIATE PRACTICE

INTRODUCTION

One vital aspect of developmentally appropriate programs for all children involves being able to match observed actions and behaviours with expected stages of growth and development. To achieve this, we should have a good understanding of the nature of growth and development for young children. Knowing what to reasonably expect from a young child and relating this to our observations, provides the basis of a developmentally appropriate program.

Planning for the young child must reflect an acceptance of the uniqueness of each individual and their family, who they are and the experiences that they bring with them to the early childhood service. This means having an awareness of general trends in growth and development, but not expecting each and every child to do the same things in the same way at the same time. Having respect for children and their experiences is the basis of a set of principles discussed by Gonzalez-Mena (in Gerber 1979; Gonzalez-Mena and Eyers 1989). The onus is on the early childhood educator to show this respect for the individual by actively involving the child in meaningful experiences; allowing privacy and space; responding to the various forms of communication used by the child; recognising feelings — both of the child and the adult; encouraging children to develop their potential; building trust; modeling suitable behaviour and allowing the child the freedom to learn through exploration.

While all children are unique, there are some general trends in growth and development that need to be taken into account when planning a program. In the next three chapters, some of the special features relating to infants and toddlers, preschoolers, and children in the first year of school will be considered, as well as some general implications for planning which arise from an awareness of these issues.

10

INFANTS AND TODDLERS

PLANNING FOR INFANTS AND TODDLERS

Developing an infant–toddler program involves much more than understanding growth an development — it also involves knowing the individual child and their family, respecting differences among children and families and planning appropriate experiences based on this knowledge.

What do we know about the growth and development of young children? To emphasise the significance of the infant–toddler years, growth and development is described in several areas. However, it should be noted that, while these divisions can be identified, much of what happens in growth and development involves several or even all areas. This means that though it is easy to describe growth and development in areas, what is often observed by early childhood educators relates to more than one area.

SENSORY DEVELOPMENT

Infants and toddlers are often described as relying on 'sensorimotor' understandings of the world. While this is not the only way infants and toddlers come to know and understand the world in which they live, sensory and motor experiences play a significant role in the child's growth and development.

The infant's senses are operating, with different levels of efficiency, from the time of birth. Young babies can hear, and soon recognise familiar voices. They can also see, though initially their vision is fuzzy and blurred. For the young infant the things that can be most clearly seen are those that are about 25–30 centimetres away, which is about the distance between an infant and adult during feeding. Some things are also more interesting to look at than others, such as areas of contrast, curves or angles, things that move as well as faces that talk.

We can use this information in planning by providing plenty of opportunity for interactions that involve talking with infants, looking at infants and providing things for them to look at. Mobiles and other interesting things, such as chimes that move or make a sound in the wind, can be hung around the infant. While those that are some distance away may not be clearly seen, they do provide experiences in locating sound and tracking movements. When creating an environment it is a good idea to look at things from an infant's perspective: does the environment look interesting from a prone position, or is it only interesting at an adult level?

As well as being able to respond to things, infants have some ability to 'switch off' when they are surrounded by too much stimulation. They can close their eyes, or even turn away from people and things. Just as older children and adults need to have some relatively peaceful times, infants need the same. Sometimes an upset infant may be reacting to too much, rather than too little, stimulation.

Adults need to be sensitive to the cues of infants. At times of awareness, the infant may happily engage in and respond to their surroundings. An observant early childhood educator can 'tune-in' to an infant's changing state, and can respond to the changed tone of a cry, or the drooping of eyelids in an appropriate way.

The other senses are also operating from birth, with infants responding to differences in tastes and smells. Infants can both touch and respond to touch, though some parts of the body are more sensitive than others. As well as infants varying in their sensitivity to touch, there are significant cultural and family differences in the appropriateness of certain types of touching. These need to be considered in the interactions of the early childhood educator and the child.

Because the mouth is so sensitive, it is an area that provides a great deal of information about the world of people and things. Most things are put in the mouth at some point (figure 10.1). In planning an environment for young children that allows them the opportunity to explore and find out about their world, we should also be conscious of the safety of that environment, and ensure that anything that is likely to go in the mouth does not present a danger to the child.

As infants grow and develop, their ability to physically explore their environment increases. Toddlers can call on a wider range of means to explore their surroundings, and most actively do so: they are constantly expanding their horizons by feeling, tasting, looking at, hearing and smelling as much as they possibly can. Children at this time are keen explorers, eager to investigate as much as possible. Sometimes this eagerness is regarded as setting out to be 'naughty', when more realistically it reflects a great inquisitiveness and curiosity. Part of the challenge of working with toddlers relates to planning and providing environments that allow children to use their eagerness to do things; to climb, reach, manipulate and discover.

We all learn through our senses, whatever our age or stage of development. For infants and toddlers, though, the use of the senses is perhaps

Figure 10.1: One way of exploring objects is to mouth them. Most things are put into the mouth at some time.

Figure 10.2: A learning environment for infants and toddlers can include a variety of sensory experiences, such as this trail of different textures.

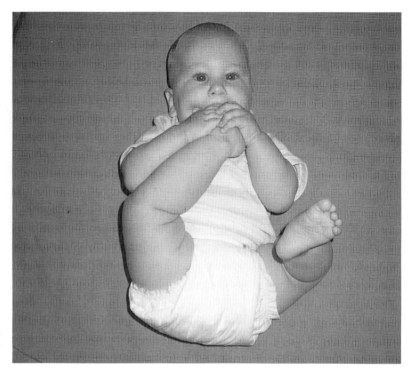

Figure 10.3: Many sensory experiences involve the child's own body.

Figure 10.4: Large muscle movements can be encouraged through experiences such as soap painting.

the major mode of interaction with their world (figure 10.2). It is therefore of vital importance that their environment is one that is safe and that provides ready access to the myriad of sensory experiences that surround them.

Equipment should be safe for mouthing (as well as chewing, sucking, biting and so on), safe for inquisitive fingers (and/or toes), as well as durable enough to stand up to rigorous exploration. We all need to remember that children are really curious about all aspects of equipment and toys, including how things come apart, and that this, in turn, means that close supervision of infants and toddlers is essential. The most unlikely objects can become dangerous in certain circumstances.

Infants and toddlers engage in a lot of sensory experiences (figure 10.3) that involve their own bodies; for infants the discovery of their own hands and feet can be a source of stimulation, enjoyment and concentration that lasts for a lengthy period. We need to ensure that the time, opportunity and encouragement needed to partake of these experiences is provided.

There is no need to 'swamp' infants and toddlers with an overabundance of 'equipment'. Leaving an infant in a cot full of toys does not necessarily provide the optimal sensory environment. The touching, feeling, talking adult is one of the most interesting and stimulating 'toys' a young child can have. We need to ensure that we regularly interact with young children, as well as providing equipment for them.

The environment we provide needs to be accessible to young children. Shelves that are packed with interesting things that are visible, but out of reach, are frustrating and a potential cause of conflict. On the other hand, open, easily reached shelves can aid in the young child's selection of materials. The hard to reach cupboards can be kept for dangerous or inappropriate items.

MOTOR DEVELOPMENT

Most of the very young child's movements are not consciously controlled; rather they relate to a range of reflexes. As the child grows and develops, more and more movements and actions can be controlled and coordinated. The development of complex actions, like walking, is a gradual process. Even after the child has taken their first steps, much practice is needed to become competent and to develop further skills such as running or skipping.

Generally, the infant develops control over muscles and movements of the head and shoulders before those of the legs and lower body. Once the child can support their head, they are able to look around at interesting things, follow objects and locate sounds. Gaining control over the head and shoulders is a significant part of developing the ability to crawl and walk; both of which would be very difficult if the head was wobbling from side to side.

Walking and grasping and other motor skills are not ones that we have to 'teach'. As children mature, the ability to control motor skills,

Figure 10.5: Finger rhymes can encourage small muscle movement, and can be lots of fun.

and to combine them in more complex ways, increases. In planning an environment, we can encourage this progression by providing opportunities to practice already acquired skills and to experiment with newly emerging skills. Placing infants and toddlers in positions where they cannot move freely, or manoeuvre themselves into various positions, such as swaddling a child, or placing them in a swing or seat for prolonged periods, will not encourage a range of motor movements. Young children need to try out different muscle combinations and movements through practice, if they are to develop motor skills.

By placing infants on different surfaces, such as grass, carpet, tiles, we can provide a valuable opportunity for both sensory and motor skills. The toddler also needs lots of opportunity to practice and experiment. Once mobile, the toddler is continually refining the skills of stepping, balancing, walking and climbing. Toddlers may appear clumsy as they try to balance, move in a particular direction and reach for a toy at the same time. It is understandable that, with all this going on, the child is somewhat oblivious of other children or objects that happen to be in the way.

It is necessary for early childhood educators to display confidence in the child's abilities while they are practising a particular action. For example, we need to resist the urge to constantly 'help' or 'protect' the early walker. If we have provided a safe environment, our moral support, in the form of verbal encouragement and physical proximity, will be more beneficial to the child than a continual hovering. Calling to a

Figure 10.6: The size and accessibility of equipment needs to be considered when planning for infants and toddlers.

toddler 'you'll fall!' may have that exact effect; perhaps 'hold on tightly' or 'you're climbing well' would be a safer and more positive approach.

When planning for infants and toddlers, we need to constantly remind ourselves that the general trend for motor development is to progress from large or gross muscle control, to fine or small motor control. This awareness would mean that we provide experiences that encourage full arm movements such as soap or finger painting (figure 10.4), before expecting the same child to manipulate a fine pencil.

Infants and toddlers do not separate movements into particular areas and do not associate gross motor movement only with outdoor times, and fine motor activity with indoor times. In planning an environment, a variety of experiences should be encouraged (figure 10.5), both indoors and out, where large and small muscles can be used and developed.

The amount of space infants and toddlers require is an important consideration. Space is needed to successfully push trolleys without too many frustrating obstacles; to use large muscles to jump and run; to lie quietly on soft furnishings. When setting up an environment, we need to ensure that we provide sufficient space — some private and some open space — as well as the time to use this space. A balance is needed for all children, so that the child who is not keen to run and jump is able to have some space in which to sit or relax without being run over or jumped on, and without impeding those that are running and jumping.

The amount, size and suitability of the equipment provided needs to be considered (figure 10.6). An infant who has mastered the difficult task of raising their head and chest off the ground and who then tries reaching out for interesting objects only to have those objects roll out of reach, may well become frustrated. The rolling toy may be more suited to a toddler, who can crawl or chase after it as it rolls away, and a toy, such as an activity centre that responds to actions, but does not roll away may be more suitable for the infant.

Boys and girls need also to be encouraged to participate in a variety of motor experiences. Too often, boys are praised for their active running or jumping, while girls are encouraged to participate in more fine motor experiences such as painting or drawing.

Cultural and family expectations are also important and need to be taken into account when planning. It may well be that what the early childhood educator believes to be important does not coincide with the expectations of all families. We should be able to communicate and negotiate with families about our expectations of the children and the bases for these. Above all, we need to show an acceptance and an understanding of family concerns.

SOCIAL-EMOTIONAL DEVELOPMENT

The infant is born into a social world, a world of interactions and relationships. From birth, the infant plays an active role in both initiating and responding to social interactions. As well as actively engaging in interactions with adults, some studies of very young children have described a pattern of interaction and pauses that closely resembles a conversation. Interactions among children and among children and adults are important features of early childhood services that are implementing developmentally appropriate programs.

One of the major features of social development for young children is the development of attachment. Attachment is a two-way process, usually between parent and infant. Having strong emotional ties to one or two people enables the infant to feel secure and confident in the environment. The feelings of security and comfort that are part of attachment allow the young child to explore and interact, knowing that a secure base is always close by. Infants that do not have secure attachments, such as those reported in some large orphanages, do not grow and develop in the same way as infants that do have such ties.

While strong attachment seems to happen automatically for many parents and infants, this is not always the case. Some infants may not be responsive to the adult, and some adults may have difficulty feeling close to infants who do not respond in commonly accepted ways. The infant's temperament, as well as their physical well-being, can partly determine their 'cuddliness' and responsiveness. Not all babies snuggle or like to be held; some become quite tense and agitated at physical contact.

The infant who has developed secure attachments is likely to more easily develop other relationships and social skills. Other relationships can include a type of attachment to the early childhood educator. Though important, these are secondary attachments, formed after and not as strong as those formed with the parents.

As adults, we have many special relationships; young children can and do benefit from the same. Relationships with parents, siblings, grandparents, neighbours and the like can be a source of great pleasure to the young child. While having relationships with a number of special people can actually broaden the range of people who care about the young child, problems may arise when there are so many new faces and relationships that the infant becomes overwhelmed and confused. Such a situation could arise in a child care setting where, because of staff turnover, or illness, the child may not be able to recognise a familiar face on arrival. It is important in services, whenever possible, to have at least one familiar face to greet a young child in the morning and to farewell them at the end of the day.

From very early in life, children are developing a sense of self and of self-esteem. They begin to see themselves more and more as a separate person with ever increasing abilities to influence their physical and human environments. How others respond to them plays a major role in determining how children actually view themselves: some will view themselves in a positive light, knowing that they are worthwhile individuals with a valuable contribution to make. Others will have a much more negative image, perhaps feeling that they have little of value to share and that they are always getting things wrong.

During the first year or so of life, the infant who feels secure and valued will develop what Erikson describes as a sense of basic trust. This is the feeling that their needs and wants will be consistently met. The child who is unsure about whether or not such needs will be met, or who is uncertain of the type of response to expect, may well develop a sense of mistrust.

This is not to suggest that an early childhood educator should automatically drop everything when an infant signals a need, but rather that the adult needs to know the individual child, know what is needed, and even how urgent that need is. Knowing what the child needs is clearly seen in situations such as separation times, when a parent is leaving. A responsive early childhood educator can make the process much less traumatic for the child and the parent by being sensitive to the needs of the individual child.

An important feature of helping the child to cope with such situations is to openly recognise the feelings that exist. By verbalising an understanding of the child's feelings and accepting them as real, the early childhood educator can help the child to recognise that it is perfectly acceptable to feel a particular way, as well as helping the child to deal with the situation. This is important for all children, not just infants and toddlers, and certainly for boys as well as girls.

Erikson's next stage is one where the child is faced with a growing sense of autonomy, or alternatively, with a sense of shame and doubt. Developing autonomy is seen in the toddler's push for independence — the desire to do things themselves, by themselves. It is also seen in the example of toilet training. To become toilet trained, toddlers have to master a complex set of actions. Not only do they need to have the necessary physical control, but also the ability to understand what is going on and the willingness to proceed. A child who is encouraged, but not forced, to coordinate these actions, will be likely to become independent in toilet training and feel a satisfactory sense of mastery. A child who is pushed, and even punished for accidents, is more likely to feel a sense of shame and doubt about their own worth and ability. It is also important to remember that while the toddler may display a surprising level of independence and confidence, they will also experience times when this independence and confidence fails them. The toddler who seems to be fully toilet trained will still have accidents. This is not usually a source of concern and does not necessitate 'punishment'; rather the support of a consistent and caring adult is more likely to help the young child deal with the situation.

The toddler whose favourite words are 'no' and 'mine' is not deliberately setting out to be difficult, rather this represents an exploration of a growing independence in the world (figure 10.7). The early childhood educator should be supportive of this desire for independence, and provide realistic, if limited, choices and alternatives, allowing the toddler to make some decisions within their everyday environment.

Planning for toddlers showing such independence requires patience and lots of opportunities for active involvement in doing things for themselves. By believing in their abilities, refraining from solving problems for them and helping them cope when things don't quite work out, the early childhood educator is providing a positive base from which the young child can experiment. This is often easier said than done, and it should be remembered that it is often the attempt to undertake a task, rather than the eventual outcome, that is important.

Toddlers can also become very frustrated when things don't go according to plan, and a patient and comforting caregiver can often help before things become too frustrating. We can plan the environment, both human and physical, to minimise these frustrations by things like providing easels that can be reached or construction sets that take into account the toddler's height and manual dexterity. Equipment can be placed within reach, and made readily available, rather than having it sitting enticingly on a shelf above reach.

The third of the eight stages described by Erikson is one of initiative versus guilt. The toddler at this stage is a keen explorer, inventor and creator, whose initiative can be striking. While still not totally in control of their own body, the toddler within this stage is keen to try out all sorts of new experiences, from climbing the tallest tree, to finding a way to hold water in the bathroom sink. The role of the early childhood educator is to plan an environment that is exciting and challenging and that allows and encourages this initiative, but one that also sets some limits, so that the safety of all children is considered.

We need to provide avenues for exploration that are challenging, yet safe. The young child's ability to learn from experience and from active involvement is important and should be encouraged. Being inquisitive

Figure 10.7: Conflicts can arise when toddlers are not able to consider another's point of view.

and curious are important aspects of learning, yet they can be devalued when a child constantly hears 'get down', 'come away from there', or 'you can't do that'.

The infant and toddler can engage in many social interactions, but should not be expected to display the range of social skills exhibited by older children. These skills are constantly developing through practice and observation, but do develop gradually. The toddler is likely to seek out the company of other children, but not necessarily to share toys or equipment, or even to always engage in a meaningful conversation. At times, they will astound us with their willingness to share, and should be encouraged in doing so, however, situations where toddlers are forced to share are likely to lead to frustration.

Playing alone, or alongside others, are common actions among toddlers. The lack of interaction is not necessarily because the children are asocial; it is more likely to be because they are concentrating on different things. If we observe the play of toddlers, we can see that there is sometimes a preference for playing alone, and at other times, there is a desire to play with other children (figure 10.8). We should make sure that the opportunities for both types of play exist.

Although often described as essentially egocentric in outlook, toddlers do have some ability to interact or share or to be concerned about others. When such egocentric interaction does not occur, however, it is often because the toddler is entwined in their own approach or concern and is not aware that somebody else may have a different view of things.

Infants and toddlers experience many of the same emotions as adults,

but often do not have the necessary language skills to share these. The result is that we often have to rely on physical reactions or expressions as indicators of emotions or feelings. It is essential that early childhood educators accept and respect the feelings of young children: they are real and they are important. Educators can also help children develop ways to cope with those feelings. Infants and toddlers show fears, perhaps as a response to a loud noise, a new person, a large dog, or even to something that is unfamiliar. Older toddlers may add fears of imaginary things like monsters, or of the unknown, like the dark, to the fears above. These fears are real, and telling a child that they are not real, or that there is nothing to worry about, probably won't help a great deal. Supporting the child, and where possible, discussing the fear, is a preferable alternative.

This involves strategies such as 'active listening' where the child is assured that the adult is paying attention by their closeness, their appropriate comments and their genuine empathy. By talking to the child about the fear, we acknowledge its existence and can begin to address it. Each individual child requires a different approach in situations such as these, and once again, knowing and understanding the child is vital.

Young children worry about a wide range of things; things that may never occur to adults. Fears or concerns can result from the child making connections between things that may have happened around the same time, but that have no other connection. The young child who believes that her 'Mummy left home because I was naughty' is one example, where the two events occurred at around the same time, and so became connected for the child. Knowing the individual child, and remaining a secure and predictable person in their life can help uncover some of these connections and help the child to understand and overcome some of the concerns.

Often toddlers, in particular, are scared by their own feelings. Toddlers who become very worked up by a problem or a situation and who find themselves in the middle of a tantrum, can be quite scared. Accepting and respecting the toddler's feelings are important, as is offering some options as to how those feelings might be handled. The early childhood educator shouldn't expect the toddler to become a logical rational being whilst in the middle of a tantrum, but when things have calmed down, the message that the child is still valued and loved is important.

Young children get angry, and again, may not know how to control the feelings involved. The important thing for the educator is to ensure that other children, as well as the angry child, do not hurt or get hurt. By seeing the anger as real, and by discussing it and even modeling appropriate reactions to their own anger, the adult can introduce ways of dealing with anger that are acceptable. In planning an environment we can often plan to avoid anger and frustration, for example, by having more than one of each piece of equipment; by planning to meet physical needs whenever necessary, so that a hungry child is not kept waiting for lunch until everyone else is ready; and by allowing sufficient space and room to move (figure 10.9).

Planning will not avoid all frustration and anger, and neither should it. Such situations do provide opportunities for children to practice problem solving skills, to engage in cooperative actions and to practice strategies for coping with anger or frustration. Helping children deal with these feelings is a more realistic approach than trying to totally avoid them.

COGNITIVE DEVELOPMENT

The young child is actively learning about the world through interactions and explorations. Much of what is understood about the world and the people and things in it comes in the early years, from sensory and motor experiences. Experiences that encourage children to see, hear, smell, touch and taste things, to put things together in different ways, and to see what happens next when certain actions are performed, all help the child build up ideas and concepts about the things around them. The infant sucking a thumb may be engaged in a process of active learning and exploration, as is the toddler who is participating in finger painting.

Very young children will often focus on exploring their own body as well as exploring the toys and objects around them. One common feature of the young child's exploration is that, sooner or later, most things are put in the mouth, or sucked upon. While this is often a valuable learning experience, part of the responsibility of the early childhood educator is to ensure that objects mouthed are safe and suitable for

Figure 10.9: There are times when the play of young children shows anger and frustration.

mouthing. The educator should also be prepared for things to be spat out, and probably, picked up by another infant or toddler. Once again, safety issues are important, particularly in relation to swallowing items, dangerous items that are likely to be put in the mouth, and the transmission of infectious diseases.

One of the significant features of cognitive development within the first year is the development of object permanence, where infants become aware that things out of sight still exist, even though they cannot be seen. It is significant because it involves the child being able to make and refer to a mental image of whatever cannot be seen. The young child who realises that something still exists even when out of sight is likely to search for it. This can mean that the young child can become very upset at the realisation that a parent or special person has left, yet still exists somewhere...somewhere where the child cannot find them. The early childhood educator needs to be aware of the child's need for comfort and reassurance on these occasions. A primary caregiving approach to grouping children can help in situations like this — a familiar caregiver often can offer comfort and security until the other person returns.

An awareness of object permanence also means that games such as 'peek-a-boo' attain a new level of importance. There are lots of similar games that can be played, all promoting the idea that things can disappear and reappear.

Within the toddler period, children enter what Piaget has termed the 'pre-operational' stage of cognitive development. Probably the most important feature of this period is the young child's increasing use of symbols; a process that began with the ability to mentally represent things as seen in object permanence. The child's increasing use of language and their involvement with pretend and dramatic play are particularly noticeable.

Also noticeable is the toddler's curiosity and initiative which is displayed in the exploration of the environment. By about the second year of life, the child is learning about causes and effects — about what is likely to happen if this happens first. This is related to the young child's developing understanding of spatial relationships, that is, of how things move, where they are, the sorts of space they take up and the like. While the display of curiosity and initiative is important to developing an understanding of the world, it also stresses the importance, for the early childhood educator, of maintaining a safe environment. A balance needs to be established so that an environment is neither so 'safe' that it is barren and boring, nor so challenging that it is dangerous or overwhelming.

Infants and toddlers are typically most concerned with concrete or direct hands-on experiences. Specifically, they are most interested in what is happening to them. Piaget and others have called this 'egocentrism'. While more recent research has indicated that young children are not as totally egocentric, nor egocentric for the length of time, as previously indicated, there are many instances of young children being unaware that the experiences or perspectives of others are different to their own. The toddler talking to his grandmother on the phone, and holding up his sore finger to the mouthpiece for her to see and kiss it better, is but one example.

A young child's egocentricity should not be confused with the term 'egocentric' as applied to adults behaving selfishly. The young child, who will on occasion display egocentricity is unaware that things could be seen or interpreted differently, whereas this does not often apply to the 'egocentric' adult. Though we can find several instances of young children behaving in an egocentric manner, we should not assume that this is always the case. The young child who comforts another, or who offers to 'share' something valuable, may be demonstrating the move away from egocentrism. While we shouldn't expect all young children to share, we can offer support and encouragement when situations like this do occur. Perhaps the strongest encouragement for sharing and other nonegocentric behaviour occurs when we model these things. All children are individual; some will be obviously egocentric for longer than others. Perhaps, even as adults, we are all a bit egocentric in some ways at some times.

The planned environment can be instrumental in supporting and encouraging the areas of language and play. One way that play can be enhanced is through the provisions of props. The provision of realistic props is important for young children, as one of the early forms of pretending involves children using objects to represent other things, such as when the cup from the teaset can be used to represent a real cup and real tea. This also relates to the young child's need to use concrete materials, rather than the abstract. While realistic props are important, it is equally important that children have the time, space and freedom to experiment with and use the equipment in a variety of ways.

Promoting play as an active learning experience is one of the most effective strategies for encouraging social and cognitive development. Play experiences are significant in children's developing understandings of the people and things around them; of how people interact and how people see things differently to themselves. Play provides opportunities for exploration and self-initiated activity, for discovery and for trying things without having to worry about the consequences. In this way, play enables the child to continually build up and add to, their understanding of the world around them.

In planning for play, we need to provide an environment that encourages and values play as a powerful learning experience. This means having supportive humans as well as physical resources. An encouraging adult can act as an extender or enricher of the play, but the ownership and control of the play must rest with the child.

To encourage and enrich play experiences, educators can help children make the play more complex by introducing new equipment, resources or perspectives. While adding new things to a play experience can be very worthwhile, we need to remember that some of the most intense and complex play involves some of the oldest and most used equipment. Children need to be able to return to familiar and comfortable experiences, such as family corner or blocks, and to feel competent in their use of materials, or in the roles they adopt. However at other times, the introduction of something new can spark a whole new interest in the possible play and encourage that play to develop in new directions. An adult who is aware of this can promote play by providing a mixture of old and new play resources and environments.

One of the many real advantages of play is that a wide range of children can engage in the experience, at whatever level is appropriate for them. This can clearly be seen in play experiences that involve a mixed age range. The involvement of older children in play can often lead to an enrichment or extension of that play and the related learning experiences. While the older children often direct the play, the younger children can certainly make valuable and innovative contributions.

Young children are developing the ability to use symbols and this is seen in the increasing use of language as well as in pretend and dramatic play. A program based on play enables young children to interact with others at a level appropriate to them, and to take away from the experience things that are important and meaningful to them. Through play, the incredible creativity of the young child can be encouraged. Infants and toddlers are certainly able to put things together in novel ways, and to experiment with materials and equipment as well as ideas and sounds. Whether they are making the important discovery of how the paste brush glides along a box, or placing blocks in a novel arrangement, there is an element of creativity present. To encourage creativity, and exploration and experimentation, early childhood educators need to be wary of relying

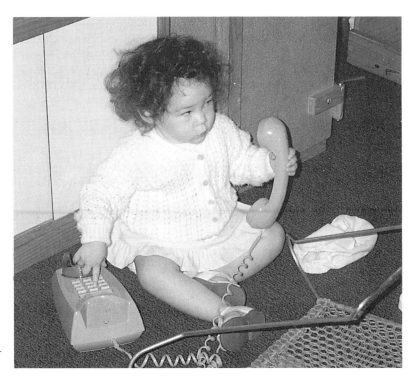

Figure 10.10: The play of toddlers can be based on imitation.

on teacher-directed or end product experiences. Allowing young children the time and space and support to experiment (figure 10.10) and discover often means that we do not have to 'teach' the child how to participate.

LANGUAGE DEVELOPMENT

Infants experiment with making sounds almost from the moment of their birth. Though not being able to form words they have powerful and effective ways of communicating. Infants constantly strive to make sense of their environment and their experiences as they respond to the pitch and tone of the voices from the faces that talk to them. Infants are inherently socially active as they respond to these faces.

This social interaction begins as babies and carers in the family and the early childhood setting interact with wordless communication. As the carers attend closely to sounds which may have meaning in their culture, they respond immediately to the baby's sounds, smiles, squeals, gestures and body movements. It is believed that the experience of turn taking, as in conversation, begins in such encounters. The carers are assisting the beginning of the infant's interaction development and hence communication skills. Although the child does not respond in conventional language ways, it is likely that infants are making sense of the environment around them and can probably understand much more than they can indicate.

As well as communicating with smiles and gestures, the infant coos and babbles to make a marvellous string of sounds. The infant constantly explores and practises with all sounds that their mouth and hands can make, and later reduces their focus to the sounds, intonations and the rhythms of the language around them, whether it be English or another language.

Later as the child becomes aware of objects in the environment, these objects enter the adult–child interactions. The child seeks to name objects like the bottle, food, teddy and to play peek a boo games with people and things. Both these kinds of experiences are highly interactive and assist the child to further explore their environment. Though at this stage, the child cannot speak in recognisable words, it is important that adults interact with and involve the child in conversations. When we talk to infants and toddlers about what we are doing, what will happen next, what we are using and so on, then we are providing demonstrations for the functions or purposes, the meanings, the sounds, as well as the structure of the language. All these experiences help the child to develop understandings about language, how it works and most importantly what people use it for.

For some children the language that the adult uses may not be the one the child hears at home. By using key words, phrases, rhymes and songs of the child's first language the carer may present familar language experiences and build bridges between home and the setting. In doing so, the educator displays value and recognition for the child's first language. This can best be achieved through consulting with families and resource centres which often have publications and tapes of 'survival' phrases, as well as songs and rhymes in various languages.

Responding to a young child's language is important. Things like imitating the 'sounds' of the language they make, for example the blowing of raspberries, answering what could be a child's question, singing to the child, chanting finger plays and many other similar experiences, all help to give the child the message that using language is an enjoyable social experience. As well the child learns that language is a means of making meaning with other people. The role of the adult demonstrating language needs to be stressed; not only are adults demonstrating sounds and words, they are demonstrating some of the purposes for which language is used as well as the features of interactions. This can be clearly seen when we answer a child, wait for their reply and then make another comment or response.

By the end of their first year, the infant may begin their earliest language utterances which relate to their own functions and purposes. The child may be gesturing and vocalising without using conventional words, but it may be quite clear in the situation that they have a purpose in mind for their sounds and movements. They may be making sounds to gain the attention of others, to direct attention to something or to indicate something that they want. Over time and with lots of practice and interactions, these vocalisations and gestures for particular purposes will develop into more conventional language forms. As well as developing understandings of the purpose for which language can be used, children's language development occurs on two other fronts — the development of meaning and the development of language structures.

Part of the meaning making occurs during adult–child interactions where objects are labelled and naming games are played with things in the child's immediate environment. Here the child has much opportunity to explore and make sense of their world as well as to practice and refine their language as they babble and make sounds. When the child does start to use their own invented words like *maa* — *mum, and ikk* — *egg*, they are more able to use, experiment and practice with language in their own social context to satisfy their own needs.

Part of the development of language structures starts with the child naming things with single word utterances for example, *more!, yummy, milk*. Often these words will begin sounding like part of the intended words or phrases like in *eeyoulata* — *see you later*. Children may then go on to use two word utterances like *Da gone* and *me up*. After an initial constant use of a limited number of words, toddlers rapidly expand their use of words to about 200. Other language structures that begin to develop towards the end of the toddler stage relate to the use of simple direct questions like *where ow?* (cat) and *where Grandpa?*

Many toddlers talk to themselves, continuing the practising and refining of their language. You can often hear a toddler chanting or repeating some sound, word or phrase over and over again. This occurs as the toddler selects her/his own aspect of language to rehearse and develop. As a consequence of this, a group of toddlers are often involved in 'collective monologues' and hence do not provide a great deal of interaction for each other.

By far the best way to encourage the language development of the infant and toddler, is to provide an environment that surrounds the child with meaningful and interactive language. Having the radio and television on all day may provide the sounds of language, but not the social interaction that is so much a part of language development. Meaningful language experiences for young children include lots of talking and listening; conversations about people and things visible to and of interest to the child, reading and telling stories, singing, chanting nursery rhymes and the like. These can occur throughout the day, adapted to suit the child, the adult, the time of the day and any other relevant aspects of the situation. For example, lullabies or quiet songs may be appropriate for rest time; singing games, chants and rhymes for nappy changes. The adult who interacts with young children individually and in small groups in this way, and who can engage the child in interaction and experimentation with language, is providing the child with important demonstrations and opportunities for language learning. As well as presenting the functions/purposes, sounds, rhymes and words of language, the adult is also demonstrating language structures.

Young children need many opportunities to practise the pronunciation of sounds and words in order to get their approximations closer and closer to the conventional pronunciations within their family. We shouldn't expect perfect pronunciations or articulation when the child is

Figure 10.11: Being an effective listener in not always easy.

learning to say sounds and words, nor should we expect the 'adult' form of words and structures and 'correct' the invented words like 'ow' (cat). Rather, we should focus on responding naturally to the child's intended meaning and expanding on the child's language, providing appropriate feedback through conversational language.

There are lots of language games that can be played with young children that encourage the use of both receptive and expressive language skills, but that do not place pressure on the child. Games such as *'round and round the garden'*, *'touch your nose'* (or any other body part) and *'what's this?'* can be lots of fun for all concerned. When the adult shares books and stories, songs and rhymes, they provide great opportunities for the child to be immersed in the rhythm, and patterns and flow of language. There are many occasions for adults to use and encourage children's use of language. The experiences can easily be integrated throughout the day and they don't require lots of equipment.

When the adult interacts with the young child, it is important that the experience is a shared one so that the adult has a similar interpretation of the event to the child. The adult may need to modify or shorten slightly their language without resorting to baby language, that is, using simple phrases and sentences like *round and round*. The adult may slightly exaggerate their intonation to stress key words within the phrases and sentences as they accept and respond meaningfully to the child's attempts to communicate.

The other important aspect of the adult's role is to be an effective listener. This is more easily said than done as many young children's

Figure 10.12: Each child partici-pates differently in language experiences.

developing language is at times difficult for us to understand (figure 10.11). While the young child may not be able to produce many words, we shouldn't underestimate their ability to understand, or to enjoy experimenting with sounds and sound combinations. However, through the use of contextual clues and knowledge of the child, the adult can predict what the child may have meant. It is important to check that this prediction was the meaning intended by the child so the adult can respond appropriately, rather than with a neutral and numbing *mmmmm-mm*. The task of extending and prolonging the meaning making in the language of the infant or the toddler during this interaction is an essen-tial role for the early childhood educator, since peer interaction at these stages are rather limited.

As with all areas of development, there are vast individual differences in the development of language. The use of language experiences throughout the day that encourage participartion and interaction for real purposes, rather than perfect language production, enables all children to listen, to join in, and to practice the language they are developing, whenever and however they feel comfortable. Not all young children will sing a song right through, but they may just listen, or join in for some parts; not all will engage in an indepth conversation, but they will usually engage in a questioning and answering manner at some time; not all children will want an adult to read a whole book, some will turn to favourite pages and stories. We need to allow for this individual varia-tion in our planning (figure 10.12), and to remember that providing an encouraging and interesting language environment involves all staff interacting with the individual infant and toddler in a variety of ways throughout the day.

CONCLUSION

The world of the infant and toddler is expanding all the time. The young child is developing a greater knowledge and understanding of themselves and the people and things in the world around them, and the ability to use this understanding in their interactions. Areas of growth and development are closely linked and intertwined: developments in one area are likely to influence developments in other areas. For example, the child's increasing mobility and motor development enables them to reach out and to grasp things as well as to crawl or walk and so to explore more things around them.

An awareness of the expected patterns of growth and development will enable us to consider what will be developmentally appropriate for children in the early years. This understanding though, must be tempered and balanced with a detailed knowledge of the individual child. When we are able to match what we know about the child and what we expect from suitable stages of growth and development, we have the starting points for putting into practice a program that is based on the individual and that is directly relevant to them, their needs and their interests.

USEFUL RESOURCES

Berk, L.E. (1991). *Child development* (second edition). Boston: Allyn and Bacon.

Gonzalez-Mena, J. and Eyers, D.W. (1989). *Infants, toddlers and caregivers.* Mountain View, CA: Mayfield Publishing Co.

Rogers, C.S. and Sawyers, J.K. (1988). *Play in the lives of children.* Washington, DC: NAEYC.

Wells, C.G. (1986). *The meaning makers: children learning language and using language to learn.* Portsmouth, New Hampshire. Heinemann Educational Books.

11

FOCUSING ON PRESCHOOLERS

INTRODUCTION

Focusing on 'preschoolers' within a program involves the same fundamental aspects as focusing on infants and toddlers, or focusing on children in the first year of school. That is, planning appropriate experiences is based on the understanding of fundamental growth and development, combined with a knowledge of and respect for each individual child and their family. In the following context, the preschool child is a term generally used to cover the period of about three to five years.

We can focus on children in many ways. In the following discussion, the general patterns of growth and development, and ways in which these can be catered for in a program, are considered. It needs to be stressed though, that while we can speak of certain areas of growth and development, in reality these areas all overlap and influence each other.

PHYSICAL AND MOTOR DEVELOPMENT

In the preschool years we see a slowing of the overall growth rate compared to that of the infant/toddler period. This obviously has implications for motor development, but also for nutrition; Gething and Hatchard (1989: p.154) note that

> because their energy requirements per kilogram of bodyweight decline, it is normal for children between three and six to eat less in proportion to their size than infants do.

The preschooler is steadily growing and changing proportions, resulting in the loss of the 'rounded baby-like contours', and the lengthening of their limbs, trunk and lower body. In other words, the shape of the body undergoes noticeable changes. With this comes greater fluency of movement and an increase in the number of motor tasks the preschooler can attempt and attain. The 3 year old, for example, is much steadier in terms of balance than the younger child (figure 11.1), and is much more likely to swing his or her arms around rather than having to use them as an aid to balancing.

With developing expertise, the child in the preschool period experiments with movements such as running, jumping and galloping. It is also not unusual to see children putting together a range of movements in novel and interesting ways, followed by fits of laughter.

The preschooler's gross motor skills are improving rapidly, but should not be 'neglected' in favour of the promotion of fine motor and cognitive skills, as tends to occur in 'academically' oriented programs. All areas of growth and development should be focused on within this period. Preschoolers need the opportunity to consolidate their gross motor skills through exercising their whole body. In turn, this will enhance their overall physical development as well as gross and fine motor development.

Programs aimed at children within the preschool years have generally recognised

> the importance of exercise and physical activity...[and] have included a diversity of movement programs in their curriculum planning. Such programs appear to enhance not only physical development, but also creative expression, confidence and self awareness. (Helms and Turner 1986: p.218)

DIFFERENCES IN DEVELOPMENT

The development and use of motor skills is influenced by a range of factors. Genetic factors, such as body shape and size, as well as strength are important, as are the child's personality and temperament. The child who is persistent or the child who has a positive attitude towards themselves and their ability, is more likely to feel successful in the use and mastery of motor skills.

Some researchers such as Ames et al (1979 cited in Anselmo 1988) have reported gender differences in physical and motor development. These researchers suggest that 'in the early childhood years, girls tend to develop more rapidly and to be more advanced than boys in exhibiting certain behaviours' (p.241). It must be stressed however, that it is hard to separate biological differences from those that are caused by the opportunity to practice particular skills and the encouragement given to children to participate in certain experiences. It is often the case that some boys may be encouraged to be more boisterous in their play, whereas girls may be more often rewarded for quieter, less active interactions. Early childhood educators must be very aware of the opportunities

Figure 11.1: The preschooler's developing balance and coordination is a feature of motor development.

and encouragement provided for all children. This awareness can form the basis of a program where both girls and boys are encouraged to participate in a wide range of experiences that will promote their whole development.

There will almost certainly be wide differences in the physical and motor development of children within the preschool years. All children are growing and developing at different rates, as well as having different experiences and different opportunities to practice certain skills and actions. It should not then be surprising to observe one preschool aged child having difficulty manipulating a pair of scissors, while another preschooler very adeptly manoeuvres a similar pair of scissors. The role of the early childhood educator is to encourage each child's development, through acceptance of their prior experiences and through guiding experiences that build upon and extend the understandings gained from those experiences. The educator may then, for the first child, plan experiences designed to help the child become familiar with scissors; with how they can be held, how they feel and what they can do. For the second child, the planned experiences could involve a variety of material to cut as well as some real purposes for cutting, such as making and cutting out a sign. In each instance, the child can succeed at their own level, without fear of being compared to someone else and found to be lacking.

Clearly, the young child's physical growth and development will significantly influence their motor development. Physical growth and development can not only effect the child's ability to engage in experiences, but also their self-concept. Children within the preschool period have a growing awareness of how others perceive them, and this influences how they see themselves. The child who is tall is often regarded, by both children and adults, as 'big', and therefore more capable than the smaller child. Early childhood educators need to avoid falling into the trap of assuming that the child who is growing and developing in physical areas will have attained the same level in all other areas.

In reality, many preschool children seem 'clumsy' as they experiment with their body and the way it moves. Practise in a range of skills and situations can help develop proficiency. Practise can involve having access to equipment, such as balls, ladders, jumping boards and balancing beams, bicycles or tricycles and the like, as well as having the space, time and the encouragement to facilitate participation.

As mentioned in the discussion of infants and toddlers, the general trend for motor development is to progress from gross to fine motor control. However

> it does not always follow that good gross motor control will automatically lead to good fine motor ability and vice versa. Therefore, both these areas require attention during periods of growth and development. (O'Brien and Zwiani 1984 p.vii)

The preschool years are characterised by an amazingly high energy level and the desire to practise basic developing motor skills anywhere and everywhere. Confining children indoors for compulsory 'academic' programs will inevitably lead to what we may consider 'inappropriate' use of gross motor skills. A flexible program that provides opportunities for continued release of energy and practice of motor skills takes the preschooler's motor requirements into consideration. Planning for the preschooler that takes this into account could involve experiences that encourage large movements programmed both indoors and outdoors, with children free to move in or out as they desire.

Motor skills can develop as rapidly as maturation and body size allow, through practice and contact with other children. 'Organising' children's motor play into games often negates the child's willingness to participate or keenness to 'imagine' and 'invent' ways to use their motor skills. The vital factor is preparation of a relatively safe, but challenging motor environment with constant, but not overbearing adult supervision.

The early childhood educator needs to observe constantly to be aware of each individual child's developing motor skills and then provide an environment that allows realisable challenges. It is important that support be positive, and that each child is encouraged to approach equipment and experiences at their own pace. By lining children up to hop or skip or gallop on cue so that we can assess their motor development we inadvertently give the message that if they are unable to do so, that they have 'failed'. Unobtrusive observation and appropriate verbal or physical support however, encourages the individual child to continue on their own path of physical skill development. It also encourages the early childhood educator to consider positive aspects of development, such as what the child can do, rather than what they cannot.

An amazing increase in skills occurs during the preschool years concurrent with rapid muscular development. The preschooler has generally mastered numerous isolated motor tasks and now has the increased ability both cognitively and physically to combine these into new patterns of movement and skill mastery. The inventiveness children employ to move their bodies from one point to another is just one example of this. Gething and Hatchard (1989: p.154) note that:

> With stronger bones and muscles, greater lung power and improved co-ordination between senses, limbs and central nervous system, they can do more of the things they want to do.

Preschoolers, as all children, need to be developmentally ready and willing to learn new skills. Our role as early childhood educators, therefore, is to provide a challenging motor environment that takes into account the various levels of development within a group of children, and also one that acknowledges the children's interests, not purely what we feel like presenting or are interested in.

Helms and Turner (1986: p.226) highlight several ways in which we can assist the motor development of preschoolers:
■ With patience, allowing the individual child the time and effort they require for skill development, while avoiding 'pushing' children to perform at 'expected' levels. Children are the best judges of their own capabilities and we need to learn from them.
■ Avoiding comparison. No purpose is served by comparing one individual to another, due to the vast differences in how children develop motor skills and the levels of proficiency they will reach;
■ Providing an appropriate environment which has a balance of space and equipment that is able to be utilised at different levels and with a relative degree of success for each child;
■ Accepting individual accomplishment. Proficiency in one motor skill doesn't always mean proficiency in another area. A lot of motor skills develop individually and require the combination of different skills.

These suggestions apply equally to experiences designed to promote gross and fine motor skills. The coordination of fine motor skills is also developing rapidly within the preschool years. Though a lot is happening, few preschool children will have developed full control over a range of fine motor skills, such as writing and cutting, in this period. Instead, this is a time where practise and experimentation are to be encouraged.

The preschooler will usually move from holding a pencil, crayon or paintbrush in a full fist grip, to a more adult like 'pencil' grip, making writing and drawing somewhat easier to control. A range of experiences contribute to strengthening the hand and to coordinating the movements of the fine muscles within the hand. These include using manipulative equipment (figure 11.2), threading, cutting, puzzles, dress-ups that

Figure 11.2: The preschoolers develop fine motor skills and the opportunity to practise these mean that many are able to use a pencil with a great deal of control.

involve buttons or zips, and experimentation with a range of writing and drawing materials.

Manipulating scissors can be a very rewarding, and a very frustrating, experience for many children. Once again, the opportunity to practise is important in the development of this skill. Educators need to consider opportunities provided for practise, as well as the materials available. During this time, young children usually express a preference for using a particular hand and the provision of scissors that can be readily used by both left and right handed children will be important.

By the time the child has reached the end of the preschool period, at about age 5 years, dramatic changes will have occurred in both the competence and confidence with which motor experiences are undertaken. Most children will appear more coordinated, and even confident in tasks such as throwing, running and kicking, and catching. Some children will be confident in writing their name and cutting out, and others will be quite able to tie shoelaces. The array of individual differences is remarkable. What is important to realise is that such differences do not necessarily mean that a child has a 'deficit' or inability to undertake such skills. The differences indicate different rates of growth and development, different experiences and different interests. Given this diversity, each child's attempts and efforts should be acknowledged and respected.

Figure 11.3: The availability of props often encourages quite complex episodes of play.

SOCIAL AND EMOTIONAL DEVELOPMENT

If asked why they send their children to preschool, many parents would reply that it is vital for their social development. Many early childhood educators also emphasise the importance of social development and the preschool child. There are many aspects of social and emotional development that relate to the child within the preschool years. Several of these issues are considered in this section. While these issues are important in the young child's social and emotional development, they are also integral parts of other areas of development. Developments in children's play, for example, also reflect and influence many of the developments occurring in cognitive as well as social and emotional areas.

During the preschool years, children's interactions with each other and adults take on some new dimensions. This can be clearly seen in play situations: where there is a move from solitary or onlooker play towards parallel play; where children are near others as they play; and to cooperative play, where much of the play is decided through interaction and negotiation. While aware of this typical progression of play, we should recall that the preschool child will move among these different types of play, according to the circumstances prevailing (figure 11.3). It is important that preschoolers have opportunities for solitary, as well as cooperative play.

While various levels of play can be identified (Rogers and Sawyers 1988) we need to be wary of identifying certain types of play with particular aged children. Young children will, at different times, be involved in onlooker, solitary, parallel, associative and cooperative play. The preschool child may be capable of playing cooperatively with peers, in sociodramatic play, however they may also be happy to engage in constructive solitary play for great lengths of time. Each of these types of play is valuable, and resources that facilitate a wide range of play experiences should be provided.

Sociodramatic play (where children are involved in shared pretend play) becomes a great deal more complex during the preschool period. At times, the imagination of the preschooler and the complexity of the play situations that develop are quite incredible. Dramatic play, initially, centres on things that are familiar to the child, such as routines like mealtimes, bathtime, getting ready for school or preschool and the like. This play often includes very accurate imitations of people, such as parents or educators. The accuracy with which children can recreate one's habits and foibles is at times, very disconcerting.

There are many ways and means of drawing upon and extending the complexity of young children's play. Play can be made more complex by the addition of props, changing the environment, asking questions, suggesting directions and enacting favourite or made up stories. As important as these ideas are, without the time, space and freedom to develop their play, the intricacy and detail of children's play can be extremely curtailed. There are many ways in which dramatic play can become an integral part of the program, rather than something that is limited to family corner.

There are some types of dramatic play that arouse concern among some parents and early childhood educators. Usually, these are the rough and tumble types of play, often expressed in superhero play such as Teenage Mutant Ninja Turtles. Adults are often concerned that superhero play can become aggressive, and try to ban it altogether. Often though, banning the play makes it more attractive to children, whereas focusing on the positive aspects of such play and encouraging the children to incorporate or build upon these, may be more effective.

Preschoolers seem to quickly develop a distinction between 'play', and 'work'. Paley (1988) has reported that when asked, young children suggested that work is whatever the teacher wants you to do, and involves sitting at tables, having your name on something or following directions. In contrast, play is something that involves things you do for yourself, like running and playing superheroes. If we are to promote play both as an approach to learning and as a valuable exercise, we need to be very clear about the messages that are conveyed in our program and in our actions.

As well as encouraging a range of play, open ended experiences such as family corner, construction and playdough can be used to encourage children to participate in a way that is meaningful for them, rather than having to produce a predetermined product. We will learn much more about the child's capabilities by observing the processes they employ, than by setting them up for failure when they cannot exactly reproduce the required product.

The preschool period is characterised by incredible development both socially and emotionally. The preschooler moves from being immersed in their own needs and desires with a strong dependence upon parental care, to greater degrees of independence and mastery of the environment. This is seen in the ability to take others needs into account and in the development of skills required to cooperate with others (Zigler and Finn-Stevenson 1987: p.394).

The preschooler is moving from what Erikson (1963) terms the 'autonomy versus shame and doubt' stage into that of 'initiative versus guilt' stage. We see this in the child who is still very adamant that they want to do it themselves, and who extends upon this to take the initiative in experiences, through planning and working towards goals. The child's desire for independence is highlighted, and the preschool child gains great satisfaction from choosing their own experiences, implementing their own plan of action, and deciding upon what the outcome will be.

Early childhood educators need to encourage this initiative both verbally and through the environment they provide. By 'directing' children to pre-prepared, closed experiences we allow no opportunity for children to utilise and experiment with their own ideas; instead, this implies that the use of initiative within this setting is not appropriate, which can lead to a sense of guilt. Children will use their initiative regardless, and may channel this into activities or experiences that the early childhood educator believes to be inappropriate behaviour. We need to encourage the individual child's use of initiative in meaningful, everyday experiences within the program, such as open-ended experiences, choices at meal times and flexibility in indoor/outdoor experiences. We will then be able to observe the preschool child developing their physical/cognitive/social skills and having a constructive avenue to apply these within their social environment, free from guilt.

Friends become increasingly important to the preschool child, as they practise and develop social skills. Often friendships are based on physical proximity, where children are friends because they live close by, see each other often, or happen to be playing together at the moment. Very often, friends seem only temporary, as the cry of 'You're not my friend anymore' is echoed. Within a short while, the accompanying comment 'You're my friend' is likely to be heard instead.

The concepts of friends and friendships develop over this period to be more adult-like. However, it is not the case that a 5 year old has the same concept of a 'friend' and the obligations related to friendship that an adult or even an older child has. Children will certainly prefer the company of some other children, and may even have an imaginary friend that keeps them company, but the sharing nature of friends and friendship will probably not be present until the school years.

Some children will show a greater ability than others to initiate social interactions, and to join in and take part in social interactions. Some

Figure 11.4: Some children quite readily engage in social interactions; others may need some guidance.

children do not feel comfortable in approaching a group, or trying to gain entry into a game or play situation. There will be instances where the educator can act as a model for participating, or can point out how others join groups (figure 11.4). There will probably also be times when the educator has to actively help a child develop appropriate strategies for group participation and involvement. This may be helping a child to watch and work out what is happening in a play situation before rushing in, or helping them identify a particular role that might be accepted within the play.

The early childhood educator needs to be a keen observer to recognise the individual child's development of friendships and interactions. It is important to provide experiences that will encourage the level of play and social interaction displayed by the individual child. Often the toddler's need for duplicate equipment is recognised, but the preschoolers is not. Children do not change overnight, but need time to practise the art of 'sharing' equipment — we should be providing an appropriate environment where they are not forced to share, but are encouraged to participate in social interactions with other children and adults. Zigler and Finn-Stevenson (1987: p.405) note that:

> Children are also valuable social resources for one another and they learn a number of social skills through their interactions, including how to approach another child and initiate an interaction and how to maintain that interaction.

An important role for the early childhood educator is to encourage children to verbalise their feelings, whether in a situation of conflict or otherwise. If language skills do not allow a verbal solution to a situation, physical force and frustration, on the part of the child, is likely to take over. The early childhood educator who is supervising the environment should make themselves aware of possible conflict situations and, while allowing enough time for the preschooler to practise their conflict resolution skills, be ready to offer assistance where necessary (figure 11.5). This may mean verbalising for the child as in the following: 'please do not take the blue block away from me, I need it for my building'. In this and similar instances, the adult is providing the words the child may be looking for as well as a positive conflict resolution model.

The early childhood educator is an important model of prosocial behaviour, and staff need to be aware of the examples they provide for children. When the inevitable conflicts arise in early childhood services, we should 'practise what we preach', by being active listeners and reflecting thoughts back to the other party.

Preschoolers are capable of both prosocial behaviour, where they direct positive feelings and actions towards others and aggression. These areas are both related to the young child's developing self-control or self-regulation. The infant or toddler is likely to settle a dispute over a toy or object by hanging onto it and not letting go, or by hitting the other child. This is instrumental aggression, which generally declines — though does not disappear — in the preschool period as children find alternative ways to resolve conflicts. While this type of aggression declines, hostile aggression, or that directed towards hurting another, does not. The theme 'he/she hit me first' remains a common one throughout the early school years.

Prosocial behaviour is seen when a child shows empathy, the ability to put themselves in the place of another, or altruism, where a child acts to help someone else. It is not uncommon to see one child hugging another child who is crying, or offering a favourite toy to a child who is upset. Sroufe and Cooper (1988: p.379) report that while preschoolers are capable of both empathy and altruism, we rarely see instances of these. They suggest that

> Just because a child can experience the distress of others does not guarantee that the child will immediately offer comfort or assistance...preschoolers sometimes do not come to the aid of others because they know that adults will often offer help.

Within the preschool period, many children experience fears in some way. It may be a fear of the dark, or a fear of monsters or animals. These fears are real for the children, and need to be taken seriously by adults. Talking about these fears, and helping the child feel secure, are steps that can assist here. With children about to start school, there is often a fear of the unknown. Visits to the school and visits by the kindergarten class to the preschool or centre can help overcome what may be a very strong fear for some children.

Figure 11.5: When conflicts arise, we can encourage children to talk about their feelings rather than to use physical force.

From about the age of 2 years, children use gender-linked terms such as 'girl', 'boy', 'Mummy' and 'Daddy', and tend to show an awareness of gender-linked toy preferences (Berk 1991). By the preschool years, it is not uncommon to hear children apply a set of 'gender rules' such as 'girls can't be police' and 'boys don't wear skirts'. These 'rules' usually reflect an incomplete understanding of the biological differences between male and female, as well as information from their environment, which includes advertisements, books, and people. Early childhood educators have an important role to play in both helping children develop an awareness of their own gender, and in providing an environment where gender stereotypes do not predominate.

As the child is interacting with the world around them, they develop a sense of themselves, or a self-concept, of what they are like. The self-concept changes as the child interacts within their social world. Preschoolers, when asked to describe themselves, tend to use physical references, such as 'I'm 4½', or 'I'm a girl and I've got long hair'. They show a developing awareness of physical attributes.

In addition to this, we now know that preschoolers are developing an understanding of their 'inner self'. This enables them to realise that their ideas, imaginings and dreams are not accessible to everyone else; they are a private or inner part of themselves. Children often demonstrate this understanding when they use words such as 'know', 'remember' and 'forget' in contexts that indicate a mental, or inner function that is not shared by others (Dockett 1987).

Related to the idea of self-concept is that of self-esteem. This part of self-concept covers the judgements that are made about the worth, or value, of the self. Self-esteem can relate to many areas of life, such as academic performance, social ability and physical appearance. Preschoolers are sensitive to the messages conveyed to them and about them by others. A child with a negative self-esteem is less likely than a child with positive self-esteem to actively engage in new and/or challenging experiences. Once again, it is important for educators to be aware of children's developing concepts of themselves, and the values that are placed on this. By designing experiences where all children are capable of success, where there is no one right answer, where individual differences and diversity are respected, we can encourage all children to experience positive feelings and values about themselves and their worth.

COGNITIVE DEVELOPMENT

Traditionally, the cognitive development of preschoolers has been described in terms of what they could not do. Piaget's description of children between the ages of about 2 and 7 years as 'pre-operational', or not really capable of logical thought, has contributed to this view. Much of the more recent research has taken a more positive approach, focusing on what children can and do do, on a regular basis. Indications are that children are not nearly as egocentric as was supposed by Piaget, though this should not be taken to suggest that young children are never egocentric. Similarly, young children are constantly learning about people and interactions, and about the mental processes used in a range of experiences. The 4 year old who tells another child to stop making so much noise, because they are trying to concentrate, or the $3\frac{1}{2}$ year old who remembers your promise from the day before, are both telling us that they are aware of at least some of the mental processes that make up cognition.

These same children would probably still be described as pre-operational in Piagetian terms, and probably would not perform terribly well on standard Piagetian tasks of conservation or perspective-taking. However, there is debate as to the relevance of these tasks to the children concerned, as well as to the possible use of confusing language in the tasks. Piaget's description of cognitive development remains a valuable tool in considering children's cognitive development. If though, we look at a range of other abilities as well as these, we are likely to have a more complete picture of the child's understanding of the world around them.

An area of research interested in how children process information has focused on aspects such as attention, memory and retrieval of information. Anyone who works with preschoolers is aware that they are quite capable of 'paying attention', however, that attention may not always be directed towards the desired area. While preschoolers have been generally described as having a short attention span, it is remarkable how long and how intense their attention can be when they are genuinely interested in something. This suggests that we need to have a flexibility in the organisation of services and settings for preschoolers, so that there is sufficient choice for them to move from one experience to another as their attention shifts, but also that there should be the opportunity for children to follow something through if their interest and attention is maintained. The idea that all children should select an experience or task, and remain at it for ten minutes, or until told they can move to the next one, is totally at odds with our understanding of young children's attentional capabilities.

The adult who promises a special treat and then forgets it does not need to be told that young children have, at times, a very good memory. While preschoolers are developing their memory skills, they do not have the complex understanding of memory and how we remember, that older children have. There are many indications in the behaviour of preschoolers that they have remembered, such as when they enact a particular story or television program, or when they are asked to find a particular toy that has been misplaced. However, it is interesting that there are many occasions where, when asked where the toy is, an almost automatic response is 'I don't know', indicating no real attempt to remember.

Suggestions for the seemingly inconsistent nature of the preschooler's memory include the idea that young children do not have access to a range of strategies for remembering, such as rehearsal. It may well be that the capacity for memory exists, but the range of strategies that young children can use is limited.

The early childhood educator can play an important role in helping children to become aware of the sorts of strategies that are available and that work when trying to remember something. Talking about how we remember, about what sorts of things help to remind us of what to do and when, and even talking about how often we forget, are all things that can increase children's awareness of memory strategies.

It is often in the preschool period that there is a focus on teaching children 'concepts'. These are perceived to be the building blocks of the child's later academic development. If however, we think of a concept merely as a way of grouping things, or categorising and labelling things, then we have a better idea of what is involved in concept learning.

The child's experiences with the world and all the things in it all help to group or categorise things. For example, after seeing, hearing and patting a range of dogs, and hearing them all called dogs, the young child is developing the awareness that 'dog' is a group of things, a concept, and that there are many different types of dogs.

Learning concepts does not have to occur in a formal classroom environment; it may even be that learning concepts is much more effective and meaningful when done in informal but interesting and relevant ways.

Bruner's (1964) idea that young children learn effectively through discovery or guided discovery methods, where the connections and relationships between concepts are worked out by the individual, is particularly relevant to young children. Bruner's approach is for the adult to help children make these connections, rather than to present children with a body of information that is complete. Because the focus is on the child actively sorting things out, environments that encourage problem solving are an important aspect of this approach.

There are many things that young children regard as problems. Often, these are not the issues that adults would consider problems. In designing environments that facilitate problem solving, we need to allow children to focus on things that are problems for them, and that they want to solve. The child who, for example, does not feel any discomfort from shoes being on the wrong feet, does not perceive this as a problem. Asking the child to swap the shoes over will not seem meaningful or important if there is no reason for doing so. In contrast, the following conversation

ROSE: I saw a black Santa Claus and a white Santa Claus.

KENNY: He can't be black. He has to be only white.

ROSE: I saw him at Sears.

WARREN: Santa Claus is white.

WALLY: If you're black, Santa Claus is black, and if you're white, Santa Claus is white. But I think he's white.

TEACHER: But aren't you black, Wally?

WALLY: I know. But I see Santa Claus and he's white.

DEANNA: There's both kinds. Because we went to Sears and saw a white Santa, so the black one must have been sick.

EARL: He's very white. My sister said he's a spirit and spirits are white.

TEACHER: Why can't a spirit be black?

EARL: I'm not black so I don't know.

TANYA: I haven't seen a black Santa Claus but I know he could be there, because everything comes in black or white. (*She looks around.*) Or Japanese or Chinese.

EDDIE: No. I know only one colour he should be. White. I saw him in the store.

TEACHER: But Rose saw a black Santa.

EDDIE: He could have been dressing up like a black Santa.

WALLY: Did he talk, Rose? Maybe he had wires.

ROSE: He said,'Ho, ho, ho!'

WALLY: I think he was real.

TANYA: If he was real that means someone was dressed up like Santa Claus because he lives at the North Pole and he can't come here. Maybe he has other people meet the children while he stays there.

TEACHER: Is the Santa at the North Pole white or black?

TANYA: There's two. The white Santa Claus goes to meet the children and the black one stays at the North Pole.

WALLY: He's magic.

ANDY: Wally's right! He changes colours. That's how it's done.

EDDIE: Now I get it! He's a magician.

TANYA: See, someone must be dressed up to be a certain kind of Santa Claus. If they need a white one, he comes out. If they need a black one, he comes out.

recorded by Vivian Paley (1981: pp.91–93) between a group of young children discussing Santa Claus was a problem relevant and important to them. It was also one that resulted in a solution that suited the children involved, rather than a solution that matched adult expectations.

A striking feature of environments that encourage children's problem solving is that the adults are also actively involved in solving problems, and are willing to talk about the ways in which they try to solve problems. Thinking out loud as we attempt to solve problems as well as discussing with children what we thought of trying, and why it did not work, are ways of focusing attention on what is involved in problem solving. It is remarkable that we are keen for children to develop problem solving skills, but spend little time modelling for children the processes we go through in trying to find solutions.

One of the standard tasks used by Piaget to investigate the preschoolers cognitive ability involved perspective taking. Most often, children could not successfully complete tasks such as the 'three mountains' experiment, where they were asked to find the picture that represented the ways someone else would see the mountains. Yet, within pretend play situations, children are called upon to take different perspectives, and to see things from different points of view with great regularity. They are expected to know what happens in a typical play sequence, such as getting ready to go to work, to adopt appropriate roles, and to know how a certain character typically acts. All this is handled proficiently, and without the child ever being confused about what is pretending and what is for real. It is through observing these sorts of situations that we can develop a realistic picture of the child's abilities to take the perspectives of others.

Play experiences are also opportunities for children to explore, experiment and to express their creativity. The preschool child is often not constrained by expectations as adults and older children are, and when supported, will use their imagination to create a host of novel and unique experiences. This may include putting words together in new ways, building something different, or even developing a new storyline or script in dramatic play (figure 11.6). Creativity is encouraged in many ways, however, one of the most powerful is modelling. As with problem solving and remembering, the adult who is creative and who talks about that creativity, who responds to children's questions and interests openly, and who is prepared to listen to children's ideas and suggestions is likely to encourage the children's creativity.

LANGUAGE DEVELOPMENT

One of the most noticeable differences between toddlers and preschoolers is their use of language. They develop a greater appreciation of what language can be used for. In addition, preschoolers are exploring and refining their understandings of the meanings we make through language. This is reflected in their language structures through the rapid expansion

Figure 11.6: Opportunities for imaginative and dramatic play encourage children to explore, experiment and to express their creativity.

of vocabulary and the gradual move towards the use of predominantly adult like language structures.

Often children within the early childhood setting will speak or be familiar with a community language or dialects other than Standard Australian English in the home, and will be learning to speak Standard Australian English as a second language. For these children it is crucial for their emotional wellbeing and their cognitive development that we value the language(s) or dialect(s) of the home and encourage the maintenance and further development of the first language(s) or dialect(s). Concept development will also be much easier for the preschool child if this takes place and is consolidated in the first language(s) or dialect(s) before adding a second language(s) or dialect(s). As children develop confidence in the use of the English language they will also acquire understandings as to which language it is appropriate to use when speaking to particular people.

For all children, whatever their first language, they will initially use language mainly to get what they want and to regulate the behaviour of themselves and others (Halliday 1975). In the preschool years children generally use language for a greater variety of purposes. In addition to satisfying their own wants and needs — *Don't want it, I'd like some*, they begin to use language more often to find out about the world around them, with questions of 'what's that?' — *Are you a policeman?* (because the adult was wearing a blue shirt) and 'why?' — *Why do clouds move?* being frequently heard. They also use language imaginatively — 'let's pretend' — *You the baby!*. There are numerous other functions that preschoolers

Figure 11.7: Opportunities for talking with each other through-out the day are important.

Figure 11.8: 'allo, yes, yes, yeah! (laughter), 'es, yes, yes, byee!'

use language for, including 'persuasion' — *Caity talk!* and 'awareness of mental states' — *I thinking.*

Preschoolers are increasingly able to take on the role of others and to be able to use language to talk about how others might be feeling. There is also a greater tendency to use language to reason and to predict what might happen next (Tough 1986).

As well as this developing awareness of the functions for which language can be used, the preschooler also begins to understand the need for specific language in certain interactional situations. The child further develops the turntaking aspects of conversation, sometimes showing the use of 'appropriate' language in 'appropriate places', like when playing with a telephone *'allo, yes, yes, yeah! laughter, 'es, yes, yes, byee!'* (figure 11.8).

At the same time that preschoolers are adding to the ways that they use language, they are also rapidly increasing their meaning making through their expanding vocabulary and language structures to fulfil their own functions. As with younger children, preschoolers can usually understand much more than thay can actually say, and providing them with an environment that is rich in language will help in the development of understandings about the world and use of new words and structures. Language, particularly unfamiliar words and structures, should be used in situations where there is something real to talk about that is of interest to the child. At this stage experiences where children are involved in handling objects and exploring their environment are necessary to give children something that is interesting and meaningful to them to talk about, and something to which they can relate their past experiences.

Greater control over the sound system is also developing, so that preschoolers are able to articulate a greater range of sounds than younger children, although it is not uncommon for children to have difficulty at this stage with particular sounds such as 'th', 'r' and 's'. Preschoolers are also developing a greater understanding of the role of stress, rhythm and intonation in helping them to express meaning. Often children will try out different 'voices', particularly in their role play.

Understanding of how words join together to make sentences is also developing, so that preschoolers are able to use increasingly complex language structures to express their meanings about the world in sentences. As children are beginning to be able to use language not only to talk about the immediate situation of the 'here and now', but also to talk about events in the past or to anticipate future events, their sentences become more complex. Again children will practise these skills and try out new findings as they make new meanings. They may use lots of question structures to do this. One instance of this involved a preschooler Toby and his toddler sibling Phoebe who was eating bark as they sat in the garden. Louise, the adult retrieved the bark from the toddler's mouth and Toby asked *'What's that?'*. Louise replied *'Phoebe was eating bark.'* Toby was intent on making sense of this with the retort — *'What, out of the dog?'*

Preschoolers' understanding and use of words and their meanings is developing, including the understanding of plurals and past tense. They often develop their own rules for language as they are trying to make sense of the language system and this may result in over-generalisations, such 'I runned' or 'sheeps'. It may appear at times that children have actually regressed in their language ability, although in fact it is usually that children are trying out their latest rule to see if it works.

Garvey (1984) has outlined ways in which preschoolers, as they develop greater control over the structure of language, are increasingly able to engage in cooperative talk. This involves children developing understandings of the rules of conversations and of being able to follow the intended meaning of the speaker and respond accordingly. Although children will still often engage in monologues and have conversations that appear to be about unrelated topics, they are beginning to be able to focus on the same topic.

As knowledge of communication rules develops, children realise that they need to get the attention of the listener before speaking, take turns at talking, and follow social conventions such as using peoples' names and saying please and thank you. Play experiences provide children with opportunities to practise and further develop these understandings. As children develop greater competence with the functions, meaning making and the structures of language, they will begin to play around with them, such as making up ridiculous names for people and playing around with sounds by rhyming words.

It needs to be remembered that each child will differ in the ways that they use language and that early childhood educators should provide opportunities for children to use language for a variety of purposes. Within the early childhood setting a range of open-ended experiences can be provided throughout the day that encourage children to use language in different ways. Adults can also help children to develop a greater repertoire of language uses by acting as a role model and using language themselves to reason, predict, imagine and project into the feelings of others.

Language experiences within each family may vary and children will bring with them to the early childhood setting their own unique ways of using language, which may include the vocabulary they use, grammatical structures, ways of responding to adult questions and directions and so on. The language that children bring from home should be valued and respected. We can show this respect by actively listening to the message that the child is giving and ensuring that we use language in a way that makes sense to each child. This may mean at times that we need to check with the child that we have understood what they intended to say, as well as making sure that what we say is understood by each child. Rather than correcting children's language we need to 'tune in' to the experiences and language that the child is bringing from home and to develop shared understandings. This can best be done by engaging in conversations with each child that enable them to share their experiences and feelings in an environment of mutual respect and trust.

It is important for the early childhood educator to provide a supportive environment where each child is able to use language to meet their needs and interests and to practise their developing skills through experimenting with language. We need to focus on what children are saying rather than how they are saying it, while at the same time modelling conventional language use. Adults who truly listen to the intended meaning of the child are then able respond to each child with appropriate words and actions whilst at the same time extending the child's language skills.

The role of the early childhood educator then becomes one of following the interests and the meanings expressed by each child and extending on these. This can be done by commenting on the child's actions, extending on information or expanding on what the child is saying. Open-ended rather than closed questions will also enable children to share their experiences and understandings and to use language to develop new understandings. It is important that we are pursuing topics that are of interest to the child, not what we think that the child needs to learn, and that we give children sufficient time to think about and respond to our comments and questions. Through this shared interaction we are assisting the child to make meaning.

We also need to think about who is doing most of the talking. If children are to develop skills and confidence in using language then they need opportunities to use it, both with adults and with other children. Language is used in a social context, and as preschoolers become increasingly social beings, they use language more frequently to communicate with others.

Figure 11.9: Adults need to listen well.

Often we underestimate what children understand about how language works, and as a result we fail to recognise the developments taking place. Not only are children in the early years developing communication skills, they are also developing their understandings of print.

Children's increasing language competence is developing on many fronts as a result of their experiences within their families and their communities. Usually, as a consequence of being part of a print society, many children are aware of and able to recognise print in their community, such as the 'McDonalds' logo, the 'STOP' sign, the 'Dairy Farmers' symbol on the milk carton and so on.

Dramatic play centres featuring writing materials and printed matter play an important role in continuing this print awareness. Props such as telephone books, notepads and pencils, typewriters, menus and magazines may be added to dramatic play areas, depending on children's interests and the focus of their play, and provide opportunities for children to further explore print. Purposeful play with these types of print props enables children to understand more about the functions and real

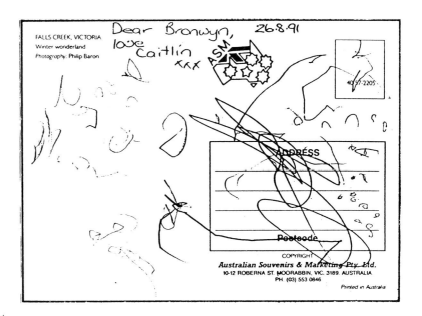

Figure 11.10: Caitlin's postcard shows her developing concept of writing.

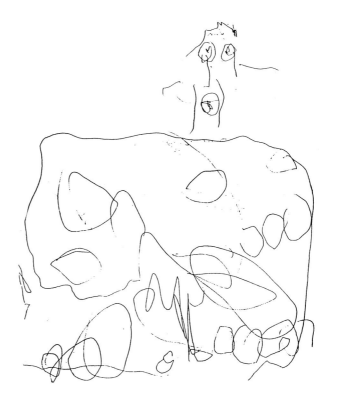

Figure 11.11: Emma's awareness of the difference between writing and drawing is seen in these examples.

purposes of print in action as well as the puzzle of how to 'do' and 'read' their writing.

Surrounding children with print, such as charts, labels, posters and so on that are relevant to children's daily lives, and the frequent reading of these with children, also helps to develop understandings of the role of print. If we present a model to children by regularly engaging in purposeful reading and writing ourselves, such as writing shopping lists or notices and reading notes from parents, we demonstrate to children the role of print in our everyday lives. Occasionally acting as a scribe for children by writing down their messages, whether on a greeting card, a letter to a friend or a sign to be part of the block construction, demonstrates the conventions of print and helps children to understand the connections between the spoken and the written word. Of course, it is far more beneficial for the child to 'have a go' with their own writing, regardless of the degree of approximation to the adult form.

Preschoolers will all be at different stages in their understanding of and their interest in writing, with some doing scribble writing, some making approximations of letters, and others beginning to write words. Repeated, meaningful encounters with print, as well as access to writing materials and an environment that values their beginning attemps at writing, will enable each child to develop confidence in their own writing.

Preschoolers will also be at different stages in the development of their concepts of print and bookhandling skills. Some children will have had many shared book experiences with family members where they have been invited to join in the reading, and other children may have been immersed in a rich oral tradition, where they have listened to and joined in nursery rhymes and stories, sung songs and been part of spontaneous storytellings. Children will therefore all bring their own understandings to the early childhood setting of how books work, the relationship between speech and print and the language of books and stories.

CONCLUSION

The preschool child shows developing independence and confidence in their interactions with the world. It is important for early childhood educators to plan environments that can provide a range of challenges for young children, but that can also facilitate their development of a sense of worth and wellbeing.

Early childhood educators need to ensure that our planning recognises and values individual differences in a variety of ways. We can do this by noting the differences in development, as well as the ways in which children select and seek to use materials. Finally, it is important to believe in the value of the years before formal schooling, and to consider the wealth of growth, development and learning that occurs. This is a dynamic time in a child's life, not merely a time of preparation for 'formal schooling'. Early childhood educators can make a significant contribution in this important phase of the young child's life.

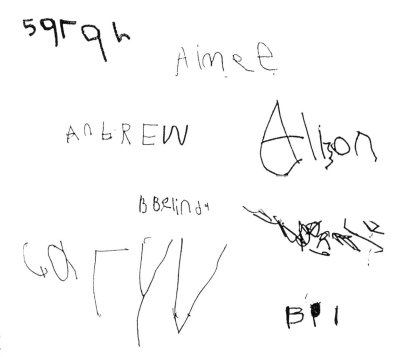

Figure 11.12: Children in the preschool years will show many variations in their name writing.

Figure 11.13: The opportunity to share books is an enjoyable experience for children and adults.

USEFUL RESOURCES

Berk, L.E. (1991). *Child development.* (2nd edition). Allyn & Bacon: Boston.

Faragher, J. (1985). *Children's development (3-5 years).* Collingwood, Vic.: TAFE Publications Unit.

Schickendanz, J.A. (1986). *More than ABC's: The early stages of reading and writing.* Washington, DC: NAEYC.

Sheridan, M. (1985). *Spontaneous play in early childhood: From birth to six years.* NFER-Nelson: Berkshire UK.

Zigler, E.F., and Finn-Stevenson, M. (1987). *Children – development and social issues.* DC Heath and Co.

12

THE FIRST YEAR OF SCHOOL

INTRODUCTION

The child who comes to school often 'looks different' to the preschooler, especially in a school uniform instead of everyday play clothes, and 'acts differently' to the preschooler, especially when going to school and engaging in typical 'school' experiences. However, we need to remember that the child does not suddenly undergo an incredible transformation when they put on a school uniform at the age of $4\frac{1}{2}$ or 5 years. We do know that growth and development is an ongoing process and that future growth and development is influenced by what has gone before.

We also know that children are learning and developing at all times, not just when they are at school, and not just when they are engaged in learning or teaching experiences at school. Children's development continues to be affected by many different things, including the school environment. Within that environment, understandings developed by children are not always the same as those taught by the teacher. In planning learning environments within school settings, we need to take account of each individual child and the experiences they bring with them, as well as all the things that happen during the day. As with other early childhood settings, schools have routine and transition times that should not be overlooked as opportunities for learning experiences as well as a variety of resources on which to call.

The age at which children can start school varies from state to state. In NSW, a child age 4 years and 6 months can commence school in the first term of the year, while in other states this varies, with children not starting school in some cases, until age 6. The fact that children starting school can range in age from 4½ years to 5½ years, or even 6 years, which is the age at which children are legally obliged to start school, should be enough in itself to point out the vast range of individual differences that are likely to be encountered. The age is important, but more important than the age alone are the experiences that children have had and the development to which these experiences have contributed. A child at age 5½ has had a whole year more that the 4½ year old in which to experience the world. When we consider that one year in the life of a 4½ year old is almost a quarter of their life, we should not be surprised that individual differences are considerable. In addition, children have had different experiences influencing their development, thus it is likely on close observation that two 5 year olds have more variations in their development than similarities (figure 12.1). Our role as early childhood educators must be to both become aware of those differences and to ensure that our planning reflects and builds upon those differences.

SOCIAL-EMOTIONAL DEVELOPMENT

The first year of school can be an anxious and stressful time. The young child may feel insecure in a strange and very different environment to that which was experienced before school. There may also be fears of the unknown before school actually begins. To help alleviate and overcome these very real fears, there are many things that can be done to make the school environment more familiar. Familiarisation experiences may include substantial orientation programs for new schoolers and their families, family interviews, staggered enrolments and increasing lengths in the new schooler's day. Liaising with the home and the range of early childhood settings which children attended offers insights into past programs, routines, transitions, and experiences known to the child. Using this information the early childhood educator can plan the day and organise the environment that offers a degree of similarity and hence some sense of security for the new schooler.

Sometimes the anxiety or stress that children feel is expressed in their behaviour, which may be labelled 'difficult' or 'demanding'. It is important to remember that young children's fears and worries are real, and that they shouldn't be lightly dismissed. We need to spend time listening to and talking with children, and to encourage them to talk about their feelings. Discussions should stress that it is all right to feel particular ways, and that there are many things we can do to express these feelings. Some of these are acceptable, others are not. At times like this, it is also vital to focus on positive aspects of a child's behaviour, rather than on the negative.

Depending on past experiences, by the time most children start school, they are capable of being involved in cooperative play. While still preferring solitary or parallel play on some occasions, there is often a preference for playing in a small group. Some of the dramatic play that occurs in such groups is incredibly complex, with very definite roles

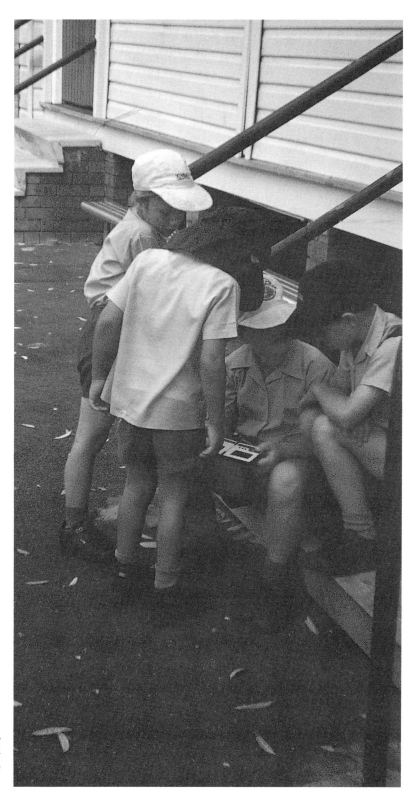

Figure 12.1: There are many obvious, and not-so-obvious, differences among children who start school.

to be played, and definite rules about how those roles are to be enacted. Through experiences such as dramatic play, the young child is adding to their knowledge and understanding by encountering and dealing with people who have different views or perspectives of the world. Within the first year of school, some children will also show a move towards playing games with rules. Indeed, some of the complex dramatic play could be called games with rules. Games with rules, such as skipping to a rhyme or playing soccer, indicate that the young child is able to recall and apply particular guidelines to play, and to adapt their behaviour to these rules.

As early childhood educators, we need to continually stress the power of play as a learning medium, and to provide experiences that encourage children to play. Children are not 'just playing', rather they are engaged in often quite complex learning. The child who enters school should not be expected to abandon 'play' for structured and adult-directed experiences which are perceived as 'real work'. The following quotes reflect some of the important features of play that we need to be aware of in our planning.

> Above all, play motivates. That is why it provides a special climate for learning, whether the learners are children or adults. (Moyles 1989: p.28)

> Play is an experimental mode of confirming or denying the connections we make with out world... It can thus occur at many levels and at each level something is understood and worked through that could not be understood and worked through in any other way. (Hans 1981: p.12)

> ...the teacher's role in children's play is to create an environment that invites children to play (provide play props and encourage play) and to participate in play episodes (as players or directors). (Pelligrini 1986: p.87)

> Adults can provide the appropriate materials and the setting, but only the child can select the best match in which learning is most likely to occur. (Rogers and Sawers 1988: p.viii)

> An activity ceases to be play, and children's interests dwindles, if adults structure or even interfere inappropriately with the play. (Rogers and Sawyers 1988: p.2)

> Play enables children to learn about learning — through curiosity, invention, persistence, and a host of other factors. (Rogers and Sawyers 1988: p.60)

Play is widely referred to in several state school curriculum documents. Clear directions about the role of play in children's learning and the teacher's role in organising the environment to facilitate that learning is a feature of Kindergarten — the first year (NSW Department of Education 1986). Such acknowledgments are evident in the following excerpts.

How does a child learn?
The child learns to communicate, investigate and express through:

■ play
■ exploring the environment
■ sensory experiences
■ informal interaction with others (parents, peers, teachers and community)
■ role play
■ participation in activities that involve first hand experience
■ interaction in a variety of situations for a variety of purposes
■ the reactions and responses of others
■ motivation, stimulation and the opportunity to try new things
■ having the confidence to persevere
(NSW Department of Education 1986: p.8)

The role of the teacher is further explored:
The teacher...

■ selects activities which cater for individuals, and which cater for all areas of a child's development
■ selects experiences which are
   * openended
   * multipurpose
   * safe and hygenic
   * for groups and individuals
   * of varying complexity
■ selects activities which allow children to
   * express
   * investigate
   * communicate

■ sets up spaces/areas for activities based on
   * blocks
   * visuals arts
   * outdoor play
   * books
   * natural materials (eg water, sand, clay)
   * writing
   * domestic and make believe play

■ organises activities which promote and develop language
(NSW Department of Education 1986: p.21)

The benefits of these experiences are explored:
■ The activities are important because play allows:

the child to:	the teacher to:
* interact	* observe
* initiate	* involve

* observe	* interact
* discover	* intervene
* communicate	* express
* express	* communicate
* investigate	* extend
* verbalise	* initiate
	* facilitate
	* question

■ Play provides the opportunity for the physical, social, emotional and intellectual development... (1986: p.22)

Some documents detail research findings and come to certain conclusions about play as in the Victorian document, *Learning through an Integrated Curriculum.*

> Learning that takes place in the work context is thought by many to be more effective or more important than learning that occurs in a play context. However studies of cognitive development indicate that children's development is facilitated by activity of a pleasant or playful nature. (Matthews 1986: p.22)

Since play is such a powerful means of learning and is an integral part of the child's world, the classroom environment can be organised to offer experiences which strongly link to school and department documents. Often the understandings, skills, attitudes and values described in these documents can be achieved by the child through concrete, child initiated experiences. Early childhood educators need to make explicit these connections with the learning outcomes of the children's play (figure 12.2).

There are many school and state documents which specify the nature of the intended learning outcomes which often coincide with the nature of play experiences. For example:

The teacher has a leading role in:
■ planning and selecting learning experiences which:
  * emphasise first hand experience, inquiry and problem solving
  * promote the importance of knowledge and understanding
  * allow specific skills to be practised
  * take account of the needs and interests of learners
  * are geared to the developmental and ability levels of students
  * select appropriate content for achieving thinking, valuing and acting objectives
  * creating an accepting classroom climate in which students have the freedom to explore feelings and thoughts;
  * developing students self esteem so that they are more able to act positively towards others and their own environment.
(NSW Department of Education 1986: p.27)

Further individual Key Learning Area documents (NSW) refer frequently to first hand active experiences, concrete materials, problem solving, small group work, social interaction etc. The following quote illustrates this in relation to mathematics.

> Students already participate in and enjoy mathematics before they are even aware of what it is or that it is called mathematics eg games [figure 12.3], cooking, measuring, counting, estimating, building. (NSW Department of Education 1989)

One of the aims of mathematics education K-12 document for NSW schools is to develop:

Confidence and enjoyment in doing mathematical activities:

- confidence in their ability to do mathematics
- a positive attitude to mathematics as an interesting, enjoyable and challenging subject
- an appreciation of mathematics as a creative activity with aesthetic appeal. (1989:3)

> Through language — through talking, and listening, reading and writing — children learn about themselves, other people and the world. In using language for communicating, investigating and expressing, they make meaning for themselves and share meaning with others. (NSW Department of Education 1989)

Further, the document states that: The potential of the play approach within curriculum is unlimited and warrants closer consideration and implementation in classrooms beyond Kindergarten. Play experiences can be offered in developmental play sessions or within learning centres running as part of the integrated unit or curriculum workshop approach in the later years at school. Chapter 8 explores these issues further.

In their play, and their interactions in general, children in the first year of school display an interest in 'fairness' and 'being fair' as well as more interest in competition. Part of the role of the early childhood educator is to help children resolve conflicts and to develop the ability to interact on a cooperative basis. Curriculum approaches such as the anti-bias approach, can be implemented to ensure that the concepts of fairness and cooperation are extended to all concerned.

Things like classroom seating arrangements can be planned to encourage cooperation as well as opportunities to practice social and conflict resolution skills.

Competition can be seen in games with rules, where one child seeks to outperform another, for example by skipping right through the rhyme without getting 'out'. Competition in this sense is not imposed by any external force or agent, and is likely to be a typical aspect of the development of rule-governed play. It is very different to the competition that

LEARNING EXPERIENCE	RESOURCES	POTENTIAL LEARNING OUTCOMES	CURRICULUM/ KEY LEARNING AREAS
dramatic play – newsagent context	shelving, pens, paper cards, note pads, books, magazines, comics, newspapers (representing a variety of language) cash register, coins, post box.	• social interaction skills • decision making skills • selection skills of preferred reading and writing materials • meaning making skills • valuing reading and writing skills to meet own social purposes • positive attitudes to literacy skills and experiences • concepts of print • understandings of reading and writing processes	*English* – oral, written and 'read' language – social skills – perspective of children *Personal Development and Health and P.E.* – decision making – self esteem – self concept – fine motor development – hand/eye co-ordination *Creative and Practical Arts* – role play *Mathematics* – measuring – space – shapes – qualities *Human Society and its Environment* – people's needs – diversity of people

Figure 12.2: Learning potential of play in curriculum areas.

is often imposed upon children by adults, such as in class tests, as children themselves still have control over the rules that are applied. It is even possible for children to 'change the rules' or to combine the existing rules in a new way. Rogers and Sawyers (1988) suggest that children in the early school years develop rules or an awareness of rules, and then can combine these to make new rules.

In describing games with rules, Piaget noted two criteria: competition and rules that were either mutually agreed upon by the players, or that were formally applied. There has been some debate as to whether games with formally imposed rules can be called play at all, as the children themselves often do not have control over the play situation. In determining whether children are engaged in games, or in play, the determining factor relates to control and who imposes the rules (figure 12.4). Participating in an athletics activity, where rules are imposed, is very different to engaging in a clapping rhyme where rules have been developed and changed by those participating.

The ability to engage in games with rules develops over time and involves aspects of both social and cognitive development. Rogers and Sawyers (1988) note that children:

> must remember and co-ordinate more than one perspective...they must be conscious of the rules, and remember to apply them while employing a sensorimotor (football) or symbolic (charades) skill. Following rules is much harder than playing roles because of the need to co-ordinate cognitive and social demands with sensorimotor skills. (pp.51–52)

Competition is also an element of games with rules. It is often not possible, or even desirable, to eliminate all competition, however, there must be a balance within the classroom that acknowledges that competition does exist, but that also supports and encourages cooperative learning. There will be great differences among children as to their comfort and willingness to engage in competition. These differences can relate to cultural issues, where some cultural groups emphasize competition and others stress cooperation; personality issues, where some children show a level of competitiveness in many areas; and experience, where some children will have had positive experiences after competition, while others will have negative experiences with competition.

Children in the early school years often engage in competition with their friends. This competition can often appear quite fierce. Berk (1991) reports research that concludes that children perceive friendships to be based on equality, and 'seem especially concerned about losing a contest to a friend' (p.463). While there may well be some opportunities for competition within a classroom, it is important that these do not predominate, and that all children have the opportunity to engage in cooperative learning experiences, where all can experience success.

Erikson (1963) reports that children in the early school years are resolving a conflict between their desire to be industrious and to show

Figure 12.3: Play is an integral part of the maths curriculum.

initiative, as opposed to feeling inferior. Early childhood educators can support children at this time by valuing all their efforts and by helping children identify the reason, or purpose behind what they do. This can help children feel that there is a real purpose to what they are doing and that they are both needed and important. A project approach can be really valuable here, as sometimes a cooperative product can add a sense of achievement. However, when considering an end product, it must be stressed that it needs to be something that the child or children can see as worthwhile and can see a reason for completing. A worksheet would not fit this definition of a suitable product, whereas a large model or representation of a bus constructed in response to a child's or small group's interest in learning about buses and how they work, may do.

Children's friends and friendships assume a particular significance during the school years. As children are less likely to be egocentric in outlook and so less likely to expect others to see things in the same way that they do (figure 12.5), there is a developing awareness that other people have different perceptions. Children often focus on physical characteristics, with another's level of development often being equated with their size. Children who are taller or shorter, larger or smaller, are often very conscious of these differences and this can have an effect on their developing self-esteem. These physical differences can also influence our expectations of the child without taking into account all areas of development that is, we may be lulled into expecting 'more' from the 'tall child'.

Figure 12.4: Children may invoke mutually agreed rules in their play.

As already noted, having friends and being part of a group assumes strong significance. Children's concepts of what makes a 'friend' change as they develop, moving to a definition of a friend in the early school years as someone who knows about your dislikes and likes and who can help you when you need it. Later, a friend is someone who does these things, and for whom you would do the same. Even then, however, friendships are not regarded as enduring, with specific arguments or disagreements being sufficient to sever the friendship. Friendships are an important aspect of social development, as they promote cooperative learning as well as providing children with an environment in which they can practise certain behaviours and learn how to interact. In addition, friendships provide young children with a context in which they learn about themselves and their self-image.

The growing importance of peers and friends is indicative of the changing role of the adult in the life of young children. The role of the adult has changed considerably, from the dependence role of the infant and toddler years to the role of supporter. This occurs as children obtain more and more information and feedback about themselves from their peers. Belonging to a group becomes important, as it indicates a level of acceptance. Early childhood educators can support this move to peer involvement in many ways. We can firstly demonstrate what it means to be a friend and friendly to others. We can demonstrate strategies for working with others and for valuing the contribution that others make. We can also plan small group experiences that encourage children to form and to interact with other children in groups. Important here is letting the children choose, at least some of the time, with whom to interact and what to do.

Thirdly, we can step into situations when needed to help children enter or participate in group interactions. To do this, we must be aware of the individual children and their needs; something to achieve through observation and recording. While we know that most children need little encouragement to form and interact in groups, Katz (1988) reminds us that some children are not successful in group interactions. She suggests that there is evidence 'that young children who do not have minimal social competence by the time they are about age 6, give or take a year, are at significant risk in adulthood' (p.204). The child who is unable to join in social interactions with a group, as opposed to the child who chooses not to, needs help from an adult. When the child has regularly experienced rejection and is unable to modify their actions to be accepted into the group, the early childhood educator can respond and intervene, maybe demonstrating to the child some strategies for interaction.

Within the workshop approach, as described in chapter 8 'Making the most of resources' there are many opportunities for the child to interact in small group situations. The development of interaction skills comes from extended and purposeful experiences and growing awareness of interaction strategies within small groups. There is often little time and space available for young children to develop in these ways within whole group or strictly individual experiences.

PHYSICAL AND MOTOR DEVELOPMENT

By the time they enter school, most children have refined and developed considerable control over their physical movements. Actions like jumping, running, kicking and hopping are usually performed with ease. Some skills though, such as skipping, elude some children for quite a while. This is also related to the opportunities that children have to practise skills, and this is perhaps best seen in the example of skipping, which girls tend to master earlier than boys. The most likely explanation for this relates to the encouragement received by girls, more than boys, to practise skipping.

The child's ability to engage in cooperative play and games with rules is important in developing physical skills. Having someone to play soccer or skipping with can encourage practise, which in turn, helps the child become proficient with those particular skills. At the same time, skills of social interaction and of perspective taking are also practised.

While children are becoming more coordinated in their gross motor actions, we should not expect them to be perfect. There is still a lot of development that will occur and this needs to be accounted for in our approaches to planning. Practise remains a critical element in developing skills, as do the elements of time and the space and encouragement to be involved.

As children mature, their body shape and size changes, with proportions

Figure 12.5: Friends can be those who like to do the same things.

becoming more adult like by about age 6. As well, children have developed strength in bones and muscles and will improve in terms of speed, power, coordination, agility and balance. The result is that they will be able to run faster, have greater accuracy in things like throwing and kicking, and cover greater distances, such as in jumping. Children who have a supportive environment will practice these gross motor skills just about anywhere and everywhere (figure 12.6). Once again, play is an important context in which these skills can be practised and refined.

Happenings in the playground before school, at recess, and lunchtime need to be acknowledged as part of the child's learning experiences with the promotion of cooperative play and the availability of appropriate equipment (fixed and moveable) and access to satisfactory spaces (open areas, quiet places) which are attractive and appealing.

One disturbing aspect of growth within the early school years is that children are reported to develop a 'dislike of obesity between the ages of six and nine' (Papalia and Olds 1990: p.399). These same authors describe a six year old girl, Vicky, who 'looks into every mirror she passes, and she often refuses a favourite food because she is afraid of getting fat'. In reality, Vicky is of average weight. It seems that the messages from our society generally, are that 'thin is beautiful'. The damage that this can do to children and adults alike, both physically and psychologically, is of great concern. We need to be very aware of the messages we transmit to children, particularly relating to appearance and the desirability of certain types of appearance.

Childhood obesity is relatively common in countries like Australia

Figure 12.6: School playgrounds provide opportunities for motor development.

and the United States, and is an issue we should be aware of. What we should not do, is to present stereotypes about the size and shape of children and adults. Obesity occurs when the intake of kilojoules is greater than that expended. The causes of childhood obesity are probably numerous, and include genetic make-up as well as the children's environment. The activity-level of children is also related, in that inactive children will have less opportunity to use up energy. Another factor that has been related to childhood obesity is television, with the suggestion that children who watch a lot of television will also eat more snacks, often of high-kilojoule food, as well as engage in less activity (Papalia and Olds 1990).

Children who are obese are more likely to have health problems, and to have negative self-esteem. Early childhood educators — working with parents, and appropriate medical personnel — can be involved in treating childhood obesity. A plan that allows all concerned to be aware of what is happening and how, enables a program to be developed and implemented effectively.

Fine motor skills are also developing in the early school years. The child entering school may well display a preference for being right or left handed. Thankfully, gone are the days when children who were left handed were expected to change and adopt a right handed approach to everything. Early childhood educators should be aware that most environments are designed to make things easier for the right handed, and as such often make things difficult for the left handed. In considering the planning of the environment, the accessibility and ease with which left and right handed children can undertake experiences should be considered. Things like the arrangement of desks or writing spaces can be altered, and specific resources, such as scissors that can be used by both left and right handers, can be purchased.

Children in the first year of school are developing greater control over the fine muscles in their hands and arms. This is most clearly seen in the use of materials for writing and drawing. Early childhood educators have important roles to play in encouraging both writing and drawing. Children are more likely to want to write and to enjoy writing when they see others, especially adults, engaged in writing for different purposes; when there is plenty of opportunity to practise without fear of failure; and when there is a real purpose or reason to write.

Fine motor skills are also involved in the use of manipulative materials, such as construction equipment, and in art and craft experiences. By the first year of school, children's drawings are often an attempt at representation of a particular thing. Drawings at this time may 'look' like something recognisable. Early childhood educators though, should not assume that a drawing or painting is only 'good' if it 'looks like' something. Encouragement from an adult to make a drawing or painting more realistic, or to add certain detail, is more likely to inhibit creativity than to develop it. Children's art and craft work should be an expression of themselves, rather than a copy of something the adult recognises. Early childhood educators can support this by again, acting as models in accepting and creating novel items, and by providing a wide range of materials for experimentation and exploration.

COGNITIVE DEVELOPMENT

The Piagetian approach to cognitive development in the early school years identified children as moving from the stage of 'pre-operations', where children were not involved in mental operations to the next stage of 'concrete operation', where children are capable of thinking logically about concrete things, but are still not able to deal effectively with abstractions.

Within the period of concrete operations, children develop competence in applying logical principles in a range of actual situations. Skills such as classifying, sorting, seriating (putting items such as different lengths of stick into a series), and understanding concepts such as number and time are all things that are associated with this stage of cognitive development.

In addition, Piaget described how children at this stage were able to 'conserve'. He developed many tests of conservation, where children needed to realise that something will remain the same even if it is rearranged. Standard tests of conservation included those where children were presented with two glasses containing equal amounts of liquid. The liquid from one glass was poured into a different shaped container, and the child asked to comment on whether or not one container had more or less, or the same amount of water. Children in the preoperational stage usually responded that the container with the higher water level had more water, whereas children in the concrete operational stage made comments such as 'if you tipped it back into the glass it would still be the same' and 'you haven't taken any away so it must be the same'. These responses were significant, in that they indicated that children at this stage could understand several principles of logic, that is that the identity of the substance remained the same (it was still the same water); that the sequence events could be reversed (the water tipped back into the original glass) and that the child could focus on more than one aspect of the situation at the same time (so that they were able to consider the shape or width of the container as well as the height).

Piaget reported that children were at the stage of pre-operational thought until about age 7. More recent research has indicated two things: one is that children may be much more capable than was once assumed, and the second is that there are large individual differences in the attainment and use of cognitive skills in different areas. It is quite possible then, for a young child to show skills associated with the stage of concrete operations in some areas, and yet to also show skills related to the pre-operational period in other areas.

What is clear in terms of the cognitive development of children in their first year of school is that they are continually expanding and refining their abilities to organise ideas and concepts and to perform mental operations. Often, expectations of children change when they start school, and they are suddenly expected to achieve what are described as 'academic' or 'intellectual' skills. Sometimes these skills are taken out of context and presented as unrelated skills. For example, children can be expected to learn letter names or sounds out of the context of reading. It is no wonder that many of these experiences do not make sense to the children involved.

Though children are developing their ability to use mental operations, they develop these abilities through experiences with concrete, rather than abstract means and items. Accordingly, we would expect a child to be able to count the things in front of them, one by one, much before we would expect the same child to perform the same action without the items. Some children in their first year at school will be able to solve conservation problems, some will not. Some will make decisions based on perceptual cues only, and so prefer the glass that looks like it has more because it is taller, and others will be able to reason that the tall glass is also thinner and so actually has the same amount of water as the shorter, squatter glass. Play is a valuable context in which early childhood educators can both observe the understandings of children, as well as introduce new and different perspectives.

Within the early school years, the ability to take on the role of another is developing. This is particularly important in areas such as social skills and play, as well as in moral development. The ability to take on the role of another involves a move away from egocentric thought, and so is also related to cognitive development. In describing the stages of role-taking observed in young children, Selman (1973 cited in Papalia and

Olds 1990: p.423) has proposed that between the ages of about 6 and 8 years, children develop an awareness that others will see and interpret things in different ways to themselves. This ability to consider alternative interpretations is one of the bases of moral development, where children are trying to establish standards of behaviour that are considered appropriate within a particular society.

Children's memory within this period can often be quite remarkable. At other times, children seem to forget a lot. The meaningfulness of information to be remembered is thought to be at least part of the reason for the great variation observed in children's memory. There are occasions when young children can recall great detail, usually when the information is important or relevant to them, and other times when the recall is patchy.

During the early school years the child's ability to remember increases, probably because the child is more aware of strategies or processes that will help them remember. Children will often discover ways to help themselves remember, such as saying something over and over again, or rehearsing information. This helps the information stay accessible in short term or working memory. Other ways to help keep information in short term memory include categorising, or grouping information in ways that go together; elaborating, or making up a story around the information to be remembered; or using some external aids, such as writing down information, asking someone to remind you or even placing things to be taken home by the door. Often, young children will not automatically use these strategies. They need to see them used by others, or to hear them discussed by others in order to try them out. Early childhood educators can actively encourage children to use these and other strategies by talking about how they remember, or forget, things and about strategies that work for them. Discussions with children about 'how did you remember that', or 'what reminded you to think of that' can also help children become more aware of their own memory and how it works.

As children become more conscious, reflective and deliberate with their own mental processes, we can observe their developing metacognitive skills, that is, skills that involve an awareness of one's own cognition. Young children are often showing some of the skills related to metacognition from quite an early age. Metacognition starts with children's understanding of their own mental world. A range of recent studies has suggested that this awareness is developing from about the age of 2½ years (Dockett 1990; Wellman 1990), when children regularly start to use words such as 'know' and 'remember' in reference to mental actions. Though developing from this early age, the young child's understanding is basic compared to that of older children and adults. By about age 5, children have a more definite idea of what it means to know something or to think something. This developing awareness of cognitive processes enables young children to be more deliberate in their actions and to therefore exert more control over their own learning. The young child who says 'I have to read that part again because I didn't understand it', or who says 'I'm going to write that down so I can remember it' is taking steps to regulate and control their own learning.

LANGUAGE DEVELOPMENT

Children's increasing language competence means that they are able to communicate and express themselves to others more clearly than in earlier years and they are increasingly able to use language to learn. As language develops, the range of language functions and the situations in which language is used are extended on and children are also gaining greater competency in the various forms of oral and written language. The more that children use oral and written language to express their meanings, the more they learn about language functions, making meaning and language structures (words and the way that words fit together to make sentences).

As children's language develops, they learn the purposes, procedures and interaction rules for language events which prevail in their community; they may in fact have learned these in a different language or a different dialect. As previously discussed this language development needs to be accepted and acknowledged in the school setting. Standard Australian English may not be the child's first language or dialect. Whilst this is the dialect that most teachers use, and the one in which the children will develop competency during their years in Primary school, the child's first language or dialect needs to be accepted and promoted, especially in the first years of school.

Since the transition to school means many new experiences, such as large and unfamiliar buildings and playgrounds, many unfamiliar children and adults, and a classroom where many other children congregate, listening to and understanding people using an unfamiliar language or dialect presents children with an additional challenge. Particularly in the early school years, each child needs to be provided with a supportive language environment, where they can use their first language or dialect with other children whilst learning through other experiences to increase competency in Standard Australian English. Early childhood educators need to recognise that this will take time, opportunities and purposes for practice and use as well as experiences with appropriate and relevant demonstrations.

In addition to language and dialect differences, children may come to school with different interaction styles. Malin (1990) in a study of 5 and 6 year old Aboriginal children, at home and school in Adelaide, found that they were socialised to be autonomous and self-sufficient and to be aware of others' needs. This was reflected in the children's behaviour in the classroom where they were keen to observe and more orientated to peers than the teacher. Malin gives the example of 5 year old Naomi in her first year of school, early in Term 1 involved in a teacher and children experience for the first time. She spent most of her time talking to and observing the children around her, ignoring the teacher's directive to hurry up as she helped others by explaining to others by explaining what to do when finished. Naomi was the last to finish her colouring-in but had learnt from her observations that colouring-in meant staying inside the lines and filling in all the white spaces as well as the routine to follow when finished, whereas most of the non Aboriginal children relied on the teacher to tell them what to do. Many of the skills that Naomi brought from home to the classroom such as her acute observation and practical skills and her willingness to help others were not valued by the teacher. Instead Naomi was viewed as a difficult child because of her autonomous behaviour which was interpreted by the teacher as defiant. This example highlights the need for adults to observe closely and to recognise and value the diverse understandings and skills each child brings to the classroom.

Children in their everyday lives generally use language for a range of functions, such as to get what they want, to establish friendships,to create their own imaginative worlds, to negotiate with others, to find out about things, to inform others and to express their personal thoughts and feelings (see Halliday 1975 and Wells 1986 for categories for functions of language). Each child will bring from their home and local community varying skills in the use of these functions and preferred ways of expressing them, based on what has worked effectively in the past. Most children will have developed effective means for getting what they want, one way or another. Some children will have a highly developed use of imaginative language, while others may be skilful negotiators or investigators.

Within the school setting it is important that we promote each child's use of the full range of functions by providing situations that encourage the use of language for a variety of purposes and in different social settings. (See Pinnel in Jaggar and Smith-Burke (1985) for details of one way to examine the potential for learning language functions within the classroom.) Interactions with other children in small group situations is a powerful way of offering children the time, space and freedom to practice new uses of language and to receive feedback from peers.

Throughout the early school years children demonstrate an increasing understanding of language and how it is used. Children are increasingly able to think about language and are often able to use language to talk about and analyse their own talk. This does not mean that children are ready for formal lessons on the structure of language, rather that as early childhood educators we need to be observing children's uses of language, and planning opportunities for children to practise their oral language. Dalton (1984) offers many ways to promote active listening and responding through the development of small group skills.

Often at this stage children will extend their their meaning making through language as they enjoy playing around with language and they discover new ways to use language and new meanings to make. As children become aware that a word can have more than one meaning, for example, they derive great enjoyment from playing around with meanings, words, sentence constructions as well as finding riddles and jokes amusing. In doing so children are showing their increasing sophistication as language learners and language users.

Each child's home and community experiences will differ and they will all bring to school their own meanings and rules regarding language structure including aspects such as past tense, plurals and word order in sentences. As with younger children, it is important that the language or dialect learnt at home is accepted in the classroom, and that each child is able to use and add to the knowledge about language they already have, in a supportive environment. The issue that dialects and languages other than English are different, not deficient, needs to be addressed. 'I done it' is not simply 'incorrect English' but may be the social dialect of the child's community or it could be their still developing language structures. (See Eagleson (1985) for a rich description of dialects and creoles.)

Just as they bring differing usages and knowledge of oral language to school, children will also have varying experiences of written language that they bring with them. Rather than 'teaching' children to read and write, as early childhood educators we need to build on each child's existing understandings. Being part of a society that is surrounded by print, children are developing their awareness and understandings of print every day as they travel in the car or bus, go to the supermarket or watch television, as well as in book sharings.

Book handling skills develop as a result of close and interactive sharings of books with significant others and children starting school will vary in their experiences in this area. Some children will have been immersed in hundreds of hours of book sharings (figure 12.7), whilst other children, while they have much print awareness from environmental print and everyday experiences in the family and community, will have had few experiences with books. Consequently, some children will know the front, back and middle of a book, will be able to tell the story through the pictures, and will believe that the meaning is in 'those black marks' on the page.

Similarly, children's understandings of writing will show a wide range of development. Many children will bring to school their personal theory of the purposes and functions of writing, such as letters to mum, shopping lists, grandpa's birthday card and so on. This awareness has resulted from (as Harste, Woodward and Burke (1984) call it) being 'dragged around' whilst family members have paid the bills, written notes and letters, filled in forms and cleared the letterbox that is, used writing and reading to fulfil important purposes in their lives.

When they first come to school, some children will be composing their meaning through drawing along with a running oral narrative, whilst others will be inventing letters that may look like the written form of the language with which they are most familiar. Some children will be experimenting with writing the letters in their name, whilst at the same time others will be using invented spelling to present their meaning (See figures 12.8 to 12.11).

As a result of their past experiences with reading and writing, children in their first year of school will be developing concepts about print. Some will be starting to work out: 'what is a letter?'; 'what is a word?'; 'why are those spaces there?'; 'where will I start when I read?'; 'where will I go to next?' and so on. Other children will come being able to read independently. The whole range of literacy development that children demonstrate in the first term of school requires that as early childhood educators we need to identify where each child is and plan appropriate and relevant experiences.

For early childhood educators it is essential that we recognise each child's developing understandings and provide opportunities for each individual to progress at their own rate, taking into account their diversity of experiences and learnings. Providing a writing centre, as well as opportunities to play in a variety of learning centres with relevant literacy materials, offers children opportunities to explore and experiment with writing and to understand more about the functions and purposes of print in a meaningful context. Learning centres can be set up as a newsagency, office, supermarket, hairdresser, travel agency, airport and so on, with relevant props including such things as typewriters, clipboards and writing implements, timetables, brochures, magazines, newspapers, books, and tickets.

In all, both oral and written language is best learnt and used in social settings. This provides a challenge to early childhood educators in the school setting. As with younger children, emphasis on a range of relevant and interactive experiences that are interesting and purposeful to the child, is essential to further facilitate this development. In doing so, schoolers may become or continue as competent communicators and avid readers and writers.

CONCLUSION

Children in their first years of school may look different because of their school uniforms, however the ways in which they learn and develop are simply continuations from their preschooler stage. The best school environment for them is one which effectively promotes continued growth and development, taking account of the interests and needs of the individual child whilst providing many opportunities for active learning that have a balance of child and adult initiation. Since the early schooler will spend so many years at school, it is vital that these first years build on previous development and learning as they promote positive attitudes to learning in all areas.

USEFUL RESOURCES

Gibson, L. (1989). *Literacy learning in the early years through children's eyes*. New York. Teachers College Press.

Moyles, J. R. (1989). *Just playing? The role and status of play in early childhood education*. OUP: Milton Keynes.

Papalia, D. E., and Olds, S. W. (1990). *A child's world: Infancy through adolsecence* (5th edition). McGraw-Hill: New York.

Schickendanz, J.A. (1986) *More than the ABCs: The early stages of reading and writing*. Washington, D.C. National Association for the Education of Young Children.

Figure 12.7: Some children start
school with a love of books.

Figure 12.8: Children create meaning in different ways. Zaklina explores writing repeated letter patterns as she writes about the Little Red Hen.

Figure 12.9: Adam draws and talks through the meaning of his composition about his classroom.

Figure 12.10: The meaning of Karl's writing is clear through his use of conventional language structures.

Figure 12.11: Karl is playing with language patterns — 'One big flower, one bird, one plane, one orange, one man — as he uses invented spelling to convey his meaning.

BIBLIOGRAPHY

Agius, L. (1989). Some Aboriginal perspectives on child rearing in the city, *Aboriginal Children in Child Care,* Resource Folio No. 68, Adelaide: Lady Gowrie Child Centre Inc.

Amidon, E.J. and Hunter, E. (1966). *Improving teaching: The analysis of classroom verbal interactions.* New York: Holt, Rinehart and Winston.

Anselmo, S. (1988). *Early childhood development: prenatal through age 8.* Columbus, OH: Merrill.

Azmitia, M. (1988). Peer interaction and problem solving: When are two heads better than one? *Child Development,* 59, 87–96.

Bates, E. (1975). Peer relations and the acquisition of language. In M. Lewis and L. Rosenblum (eds.), *Friendship and peer relations.* New York, John Wiley and Sons.

Beecher, B., Dockett S., and Farmer, S. (1990). Planning and evaluation within the program. In R. Baxter (ed.). *Working smarter...not just harder.* Proceedings of the Australian Early Childhood Association (NSW) Conference, September.

Beecher, B., Dockett, S., and Farmer, S. (1990). Program planning and evaluation. *Sounding Board,* 4(3), 13–15.

Berger, E.H. (1987). *Parents as partners in education* (2nd edition). Columbus, OH: Merrill.

Berk, L.E. (1991). *Child development* (2nd edition). Boston: Allyn and Bacon.

Berman, P.W. (1987). Children caring for babies: Age and sex differences in response to infant signals and to social context. In N. Eisenberg (ed.). *Contemporary topics in developmental psychology.* New York: Wiley.

Berman, P.W. and Goodman, V. (1984). Age and sex differences in children's responses to babies: Effects of adult's caregiving requests and instructions. *Child Development,* 55, 1071–1077.

Berman, P.W., Monda, L.D., and Myerscough, R.P. (1977). Sex differences in young children's responses to an infant: An observation within a day-care setting. *Child Development,* 48, 711–715.

Bjorklund, G. and Burger, C. (1987). Making conferences work for parents, teachers and children. *Young Children* 42(2) 26–31.

Brady, L. (1989). *Curriculum development.* Sydney: Prentice Hall.

Bredekamp, S. (ed.) (1984). *Accreditation criteria and procedures of the National Academy of Early Childhod Programs.* Washington, DC: National Association for the Education of Young Children.

Bredekamp, S. (ed.) (1987). *Developmentally appropriate practice in early childhood programs servicing children from birth through age 8.* Washington, DC: National Association for the Education of Young Children.

Bredekamp, S. (ed.). (1991). *Accreditation criteria and procedures of the National Academy of Early Childhood Programs.* Washington, DC: National Association for the Education of Young Children.

Brennan, D. and O'Donnell, C. (1986). *Caring for Australia's children: Political and industrial issues in child care.* Sydney: Allen and Unwin.

Brody, G.H., Stoneman, Z., and Mackinnon, C.E. (1982). Role asymmetries in interaction among school aged children, their younger siblings and their friends. *Child Development,* 53, 1364–1370.

Brown, A.L. and Reeve, R.A. (1985). Bandwidths of competence: The role of supportive contexts in learning and development. *Technical Report No. 336.* Champaign, Ill. Centre for the Study of Reading.

Brown, P. (1989). *Involving parents in the education of their children.* ERIC Clearinghouse, DOC:EDO-PS-89-3.

Bruner, J. (1964). The course of cognitive growth. *American Psychologist,* 19, 1–15.

Bruner, J. (1980). *Under five in Britain.* Ypsilanti, MI: High Scope.

Chamber, B., and Pettman, J. (1986). *Anti-racism: a handbook for adult educators.* Canberra: Australian Government Publishing Service.

Clarke-Stewart, K.A. (1987). Predicting child development from child care forms and features: The Chicago study. In D.A. Phillips (ed.) *Quality in child care: What does research tell us?* Washington, DC: National Association for the Education of Young Children.

Clyde, M. (1991). Child care: Who needs it? *Viewpoint,* (4) p. 21–28.

Cole, J. (1990). *Filtering people: Understanding and confronting our prejudices.* Philadelphia: New Society Publishers.

Community Child Care (1991). National Review of Child Care. *Broadside,* August.

Connelly, F.M. and Clandinin, D.C. (1988). *Teachers as curriculum planners.* New York: Teachers College Press.

Cox, E. (1983). Child Care is a political issue. Keynote address, National Association of Community Based Child Care Conference.

Cummings, M. and Beagles-Ross, J. (1984). Towards a model of infant daycare: Studies of factors influencing responding to separation in daycare. In R.C. Ainslie (ed.) *Quality Variations in Daycare.* New York: Praeger.

Derman-Sparks, L. (1989). *Anti-bias curriculum.* Washington: NAEYC.

Dimond, E. (1979). From trust to autonomy: Planning day care space for infants and toddlers, in Jones, E. (ed.) *Supporting the growth of infants, toddlers and parents.* Pasadena, CA: Pacific Oaks College.

Dockett, S. (1987). *The role of animism in early cognitive development.* Unpublished M.Ed (Hons) thesis, University of Sydney.

Dockett, S. (1990). Young children's distinction of animate and inanimate. *Australian Journal of Early Childhood.* 15 (4), 41–44.

Duffie, J. (1991). Increasing expectations for early childhood education. *Independent Education.* (21) 1.

Eagleson, R.D. (ed.) (1982). *English and the Aboriginal child.* Canberra: CDC.

Ebbeck, M. (1979). Parent participation in pre-school education. *Australian Journal of Early Childhood.* 4(1), 29–32.

Elkind, D. (1987). Multiage Grouping. *Young Children.* 43, p.2.

Elkind, D. (1988). Parent involvement. *Young Children.* 43(2), 2.

Elkind, D. (1988). *The hurried child.* (revised edition). Reading, MA: Addison-Wesley.

Ellis, S., Rogoff, B., and Cromer, C.C. (1981). Age segregation in children's social interactions. *Developmental Psychology.* 17, 399–407.

Erikson, E. (1963). *Childhood and society.* (2nd edition). New York: Norton.

Farmer, S., Dockett, S. and Beecher, B. (1989). Evaluating and planning for children in the early years. In R. Nott (ed.). *Evaluation and planning for literacy learning. Proceedings of the Tenth Macarthur Reading/Language Symposium.* University of Western Sydney, Macarthur.

Freedman, P. (1981). A Comparison of multi-age and homogenous-age grouping in early childhood centres. In L. Katz (ed.). *Current topics in early childhood education.* (Vol. 4). 193–209. Norwood, N.J.: Ablex.

French, D.C., (1984). Children's knowledge of the social functions of younger, older, and same age peers. *Child Development,* 55, 1429–1433.

French, D.C., Waas, G.A., and Stright, A.L. (1986). Leadership asymmetries in mixed-age children's groups. *Child Development.* 57, 1277–1283.

Galinsky, E. (1988). Parents, teachers and caregivers: sources of tension, sources of support. *Young Children.* 43(3), 4–12.

Galinsky, E. (1990). Why are some parent/teacher partnerships clouded with difficulties? *Young Children.* 45(5), 2–3, 38–39.

Garvey, C. (1984). *Children's talk.* Oxford: Fontana.

Gerber, M. (1979). *A manual for parents and professionals.* RIE: Los Angeles.

Gething, L. and Hatchard, D. (1989). *Lifespan development.* (First Australian edition). Sydney: McGraw-Hill.

Goldman, J.A. Social participation of preschool children in same- versus mixed-age groups. *Child Development* (1981) 52, 644–650.

Gonzalez-Mena, J. and Eyers, D.W. (1989). *Infants, toddlers and caregivers.* Mountain View, CA: Mayfield.

Graziano, W.G., French, D., Brownell, C.A., Hartup, W.W. (1976). Peer interaction in same and mixed-age triads in relation to chronological age and incentive condition. *Child Development*, 47, 707–714.

Greenberg, P. (1989). Parents as partners in young children's development and education: A new American fad? Why does it matter? *Young Children*, 44(4), 61–75.

Greenman, J. (1988). *Caring spaces, learning places: Children's environments that work.* Redmond, WA: Exchange Press.

Greenman, J. (1989). Living in the real world, in *Child Care Information Exchange*, August, 23–25.

Halliday, M.A.K. (1975). *Learning how to mean: exploration in the development of language.* London: Edward Arnold.

Hamilton, M.L., and Stewart, D.M. (1977). Peer models and language acquisition. *Merrill-Palmer Quarterly*, 23, 45–55.

Hans, J.S. (1981). *The play of the world.* Cambridge, MA: University of Massachussets Press.

Harms, T. and Clifford, R. (1980). *The early childdhood environment rating scale.* New York: Teachers College Press.

Harms, T., Cryer, D., and Clifford, R. (1990). *Infant toddler environment rating scale.* New York: Teachers College Press.

Hartup, W.W. (1976). Cross-age versus same-age interaction: Ethological and cross cultural perspectives. In V.L. Allen, (ed.) *Children as teachers: Theory and research in tutoring.* New York: Academic Press.

Hartup, W.W. (1977). Peer Relations: Developmental implications and interaction in same and mixed-age situations. *Young Children.* March, 4–13.

Hartup, W.W. (1989). Social relationships and their developmental significance. *American Psychologist.* Vol. 44, 120–126.

Helms, D.B. and Turner, J.S. (1986). *Exploring child behaviour* (3rd edition). Monterey: Brooks/Cole.

Herrera, J.F. and Wooden, S.L. (1988). Some thoughts about effective parent-school communication. *Young Children.* Sept. 78–80.

Hopson, E.. (1990). *Valuing diversity: Implementing a cross-cultural anti-bias approach in early childhoodd programs.* Sydney: Lady Gowrie Child Centre.

Howes, C. (1987). Quality indicators in infant and toddler child care: The Los Angeles study, in D. Phillips, (ed.). *Quality in child care: what does research tell us?* Washington, DC: National Association for the Education of Young Children.

Howes, C., and Farver, S.A. (1987). Social pretend play in two-year-olds: Effects of age of partner. *Early Childhood Research Quarterley*, 2, 305–314.

Human Rights and Equal Opportunity Commission (1991). *Racist violence: Report of national inquiry into racist violence in Australia,* Canberra: Australian Government Publishing Service.

Hurford, Hon. C. (1987). Child care since 1983 — Priorities and achievements. *Australian Journal of Early Childhood.* 12 (2), 3–8.

Irvine, J. (1986). Play in day care, in Australian Early Childhood Association (eds.) *Handbook for day care.* Watson, ACT: Australian Early Childhood Association.

Jaggar, A. and Smith Burke, T. (1985). *Observing the language learner.* Newark, NJ: International Reading Association.

Johnson, D.W. and Johnson, (1991). *Joining together: group theory and group skills.* London: Prentice Hall.

Johnson, P. (1989). *Constructive evaluation and the improvement of teaching and learning.* Teachers College Record. 90(4), Summer.

Jones, E. (1991). Macarthur Lecture Series. Future directions in curriculum: A United States perspective.

Jorde-Bloom, P. (1988). *A great place to work: Improving conditions for staff in young children's programs.* Washington, DC: NAEYC.

Jupp, J. (ed.) (1989). *The challenge of diversity,* Canberra: Australian Government Publishing Service.

Katz, L. (1988). What should young children be doing? *The Wingspread Journal*, Special Edition.

Katz, L.G., Evangelou, D., and Hartman, J.A. (1989). *The case for mixed age grouping in early childhood education programs.* ERIC Clearinghouse on Elementary and Early Childhood Education: University of Illinois at Champaign-Urbana.

Katz, P.A. The acquisition of racial attitudes in children. In Katz P.A. (ed) *Towards the elimination of racism*, Pergamon Press, NY, 1976.

Lady Gowrie Child Centre (1989). *Rural and remote children's services.* Erskineville, NSW.

Lambert, B. (1988) Socio-cognitive conflict and the development of children's problem-solving strategies. *Australian Journal of Early Childhood.* 13, 9–12.

Lambert, B., Clyde, M., and Reeves, K. (1987). *Planning for individual needs in early childhood services.* Watson, ACT: Australian Early Childhood Association Resource Booklet.

Lougee, M.D., Grueneich, R., and Hartup, W.W. (1977). Social interaction in same-age and mixed-age dyads of preschool children. *Child Development,* 48, 1353–1361.

Maccoby, E.E. (1980). *Social development: psychological growth and the parent-child relationship.* New York: Harcourt Brace Jovanovich.

Malin, M. (1990). Why is life so hard for Aboriginal students in urban classrooms? *The Aboriginal Child at School,* Vol. 18, No. 1.

Matthews, B.J. (1986). *Learning through an integrated curriculum: Approaches and guidelines.* Melbourne: Curriculum Branch Ministry of Education (Schools Division).

McCaughey, W. (1979). Large and small group child care centres, in P. Langford and P. Sebastian (eds.). *Early Childhood Education and Care in Australia,* Sydney: Harcourt Brace Jovanovich, Australia.

McConnochie, K. (1989). *Race and racism in the Australian experience.* Wentworth Falls, NSW: Social Science Press.

Mellor, E. (1990). *Stepping stones: the development of early childhood in Australia.* Sydney: Harcourt Brace Jovanovich.

Melson, G.F. and Fogel, A. (1988). The development of nurturance in young children. *Young Children.* March, 57–65.

Melson, G.F., Fogel, A., and Mistry, J. (1986). A study of nurturant interactions: From the infant's persective. In A. Fogel and G.F. Nelson (eds.), *Origins of nurturance: Developmental, biological and cultural perspectives on caregiving.* Hillsdale, NJ: Erlbaum.

Monighan-Nourot, P. (1990). The legacy of play in American early childhood education. In E. Klugman and S. Smilansky (eds.). *Children's play and learning.* New York: Teachers College Press.

Morrison, G.S. (1978). *Parent involvement in the home, school and community.* Columbus, OH: Merrill.

Moyles, J.R. (1989). *Just playing? The role and status of play in early childhood education.* Milton Keynes: Oxford University Press.

Nedler, S.E. and McAfee, O.D. (1979). *Working with parents.* Belmont, CA: Wadsworth.

Neugebauer, B. (ed.). *Alike and different: Exploring our humanity with young children.* Redmond, Washington: Exchange Press.

Newman, J. (ed.) (1990). *Finding our way.* Portsmouth, NH: Heinemann.

NSW Department of Education (1987). *Writing K-12.* Sydney: NSW Department of Education.

NSW Department of Education (1989). *Mathematics K-6.* Sydney: NSW Department of Education.

NSW Department of Education. (1986). *Kindergarten — the first year.* Sydney: NSW. Department of Education.

NSW Department of Education. *The primary purpose.* Sydney: NSW Department of Education.

NSW Department of Education (nd). *Human rights in education.* Sydney.

O'Brien, C. and Zwiani, J. (1984). *Fine motor development and the preschool child.* Brisbane: Queensland Department of Education.

Paley, V. (1981). *Wally's stories.* Cambridge, MA: Harvard University Press.

Paley, V. (1988). *Bad guys don't have birthdays: Fantasy play at four.* Cambridge, MA: Harvard University Press.

Paley, V. (1990). *The boy who would be a helicopter.* Cambridge, MA: Harvard University Press.

Papalia: D.E. and Olds, S.W. (1990). *A child's world: infancy through adolescence* (5th edition). New York: McGraw-Hill.

Pelligrini, A.D. (1984). Children's play and language: infancy through early childhood. In Y.D. Yawkey and A.D. Pellegrini (eds.), *Child's play and play therapy.* Lancaster, PA: Technomic.

Perrett, R. (1988). *Girls and boys* Watson, ACT: Australian Early Childhood Association Resource Booklet No. 3.

Pettman, R. (1986). *Teaching for human rights* Canberra: Australian Government Publishing Service.

Phillips, C.B. (1988). Nurturing diversity for today's children and tomorrow's leaders. *Young Children*, January, 42–47.

Phillips, D. (1987). *Quality child care: What does research tell us?* Washington D.C. National Association for the Education of Young Children.

Powell, D.R. (1989). *Families and early childhood programs*. Washington D.C. National Association for the Education of Young Children.

Prescott, E. (1979). The physical environment — A powerful regulator of experience. *Child Care Information Exchange*, April.

Ramsey, P. (1987). *Teaching and learning in a diverse world: Multicultural education for young children*. New York: Teachers College Press.

Reid, J., Forrestal, P., and Cook, J. (1989). *Small group learning in the classroom*, Scarborough, WA: Chalkface Press. Primary English Teaching Association.

Reuter, J. and Yunik, G. (1973). Social interaction in nursery schools. *Developmental Psychology*, 9, 319–325.

Rogers, C.J. and Sawyers, J.K. (1988). *Play in the lives of children*. Washington, DC: National Association for the Education of Young Children.

Roopnarine, J.L. (1987). The social individual model: Mixed-age socialisation. In J.L. Roopnarine and J.E. Johnson (eds.) *Approaches to Early Childhood Education*. Columbus, OH: Merrill.

Ryan, P. (1989). *Staff turnover in long day care*. Sydney: NSW Community Child Care Co-op.

Saracho, O. and Spodek, B. (1986) *Understanding the multicultural experience in early childhood*, Washington, DC: National Association for the Education of Young Children.

Schrag, L., Nelson, E., and Siminowsky, T. (1985). Helping employees cope with change in *The Best of Exchange* reprint no. 3 1987 USA Exchange Press Inc.

Schurch, P. (1988). Comfort zones — taking the edge off long day care. *Child Care Matters*, Sydney: Lady Gowrie Child Centre.

Schurch, P. and Hobson, E. (1989). Exploring diversity: reflections ten years on. Watson, ACT: Australian Early Childhood Association.

Shatz, M., and Gelman, R. (1973). The development of communication skills: Modification in the speech of young children as a function of listener. *Monographs of the Society for Research in Child Development*, 38, (5, serial No.152).

Slavin, R.E. (1987). Developmental and motivational perspectives on cooperative learning: A reconciliation. *Child Development*. 58, 1161–1167.

Smith, P. and Connelly, K. (1981). *The Behavioural ecology of preschool*. Cambridge: Cambridge University Press.

Spearritt, P. (1979). Child care and kindergartens in Australia 1890–1975, In P. Langford and P. Sebastian (eds.). *Early childhood education and care in Australia*. Sydney: Harcourt Brace Jovanovich.

Sroufe, L.A. and Cooper, R.G. (1988). *Child development: Its nature and course*. New York: Alfred Knopf.

Stillman, P. and Goswami, D. (eds.) 1987. *Reclaiming the classroom: Teacher research as an agency for change*. Upper Montclair, NJ: Boynton/Cook.

Stone, J.G. (1987). *Teacher-parent relationships*. Washington, DC: National Association for the Education of Young Children.

Stonehouse, A. (ed.) (1988a). *Trusting toddlers*. Watson, ACT: Australian Early Childhood Association.

Stonehouse, A. (1988b). Nice ladies who love children: The status of the early childhood professional in society. *Proceedings 18th National Conference*, Australian Early Childhood Association.

Stonehouse, A. (1989). *Parents and caregivers in partnership for children*. Sydney: Community Child Care.

Stonehouse, A. (1991). *Opening the doors: Child care in multicultural society*. Watson, ACT: Australian Early Childhood Association.

Storer, D. (ed.) (1985). *Ethnic family values in Australia*. Sydney: Prentice-Hall.

Suransky, V. (1982). *The erosion of childhood*. Chicago: University of Chicago Press.

The Macquarie Dictionary (1982). Sydney: Macquarie Library.

Tough, J. (1987). *Talking and Learning*. London: Ward Lock Educational.

Tudge, J. and Caruso, D. (1988). Cooperative problem-solving in the classroom: Enhancing young children's cognitive development. *Young Children,* November, 46–52.

Unsworth, L. (1985). Grouping for personalised classroom learning. In W. McVitty (ed.) *Getting it together*. Sydney: PETA.

Vygotsky, L.S. (1978). *Mind in Society: The development of higher psychological processes*. M. Cole, V. John-Steiner, S. Scribner, and E. Souberma (eds.). Cambridge, MA: Harvard University Press.

Wellman, H. (1990). *The child's theory of mind*. Cambridge, MA: MIT Press.

Wells, G. (1986). *The meaning makers: Children learning language and using language to learn*. Portsmouth, New Hampshire: Heinemann.

Williams, L.R. and De Gaetano, Y.D. (1985). *Alerta: A multicultural, bilingual approach to teaching young children*. Menlo Park, CA: Addison-Welsey.

Zigler, E.E. and Finn-Stevenson, M. (1987). *Children: Development and social issues*. Lexington, MA: DC Heath and Co.

INDEX

285

3 4 5 6 7 8 9 0 1
C D E F G H I J

TO THE OWNER OF THIS BOOK

We are interested in your reaction to *Programming and Planning in Early Childhood Settings*

1. What was your reason for using this book?

    _____ university course _____ continuing education course
    _____ college course _____ personal interest
    _____ TAFE course _____ other (specify)

2. In which school are you enrolled? _____

3. Approximately how much of the book did you use?
    _____ 1/4 _____ 1/2 _____ 3/4 _____ all

4. What is the best aspect of the book?

5. Have you any suggestions for improvement?

6. Would more diagrams / illustrations help?

7. Is there any topic that should be added?

Fold here

- —

(Tape shut)

- -

No postage stamp required
if posted in Australia

▌▌▌

REPLY PAID 5
Managing Editor, College Division
Harcourt Brace & Company, Australia
Locked Bag 16
MARRICKVILLE NSW 2204